A TRAILS BOOKS GUIDE

GREAT MINNESOTA WEEKEND ADVENTURES

BETH GAUPER

TRAILS BOOKS
Black Earth, Wisconsin

Library of Congress Catalog Card Number: 2001087629
ISBN: 0-915024-96-9

Editor: Stan Stoga
Photos: Beth Gauper
Design: Sarah White
Production: Heather Larson
Cover design: John Huston
Cover photo: Richard Hamilton Smith

Printed in the United States of America.

06 05 04 03 02 01   6 5 4 3 2 1

Chapter 41 and portions of chapters 20 and 22 appeared in a slightly different form in the *Saint Paul Pioneer Press.* They are reprinted by permission of the publisher.

Trails Books, a division of Trails Media Group, Inc.
P.O. Box 317 • Black Earth, WI 53515
(800) 236-8088 • e-mail: info@wistrails.com
www.wistrails.com

To Madeleine and Peter,
my Adventure Girl and Explorer Boy

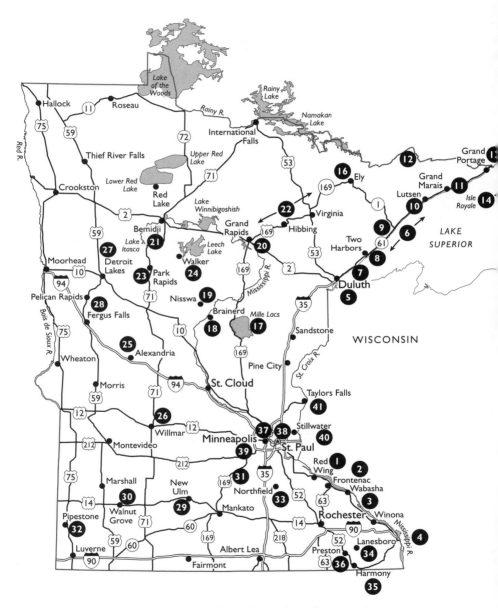

There is no symbol for chapter 15, "Lake Resorts," which covers a large area.

Contents

V. PIONEER PRAIRIE

VI. BLUFF COUNTRY

VII. TWIN CITIES AND ENVIRONS

List of Sidebars

Introduction

Lucky me—I get to explore Minnesota for a living.

As regional travel writer for the *Saint Paul Pioneer Press*, it's my job to explore the state, pointing weekend travelers toward its most interesting and beautiful spots. I've found them everywhere—on the North Shore, settled by Scandinavians; the Iron Range, forged by Finns and Slavs; and the Minnesota River Valley, beloved by the Dakota but claimed by Germans.

The stories of Minnesotans past and present have filled my Sunday columns. Yet it is the land itself that mesmerizes those who visit. When I daydream about the places I've seen, I think of a pastoral glade on a trout stream near Lanesboro. I hear the roaring torrents that empty into Lake Superior and see thunderbolts splitting the sky above Blue Mounds. I smell the tang of moist cedar bark and pine needles along a ravine in Duluth and feel the exhilarating coolness of a lake near Walker as I run out of a sauna under a brilliant canopy of stars.

Minnesota is the stuff of daydreams, no question. But don't be an armchair traveler—get out and see the state. This book will point you in all the right directions, and you'll benefit from everything I've learned since I hit the road in 1993, trying to ferret out the most interesting historic sites, scenic trails, finest restaurants, and inviting inns. I've made quite a few discoveries over the years, and I'm passing them on to you in the hope you'll enjoy them as much as I have.

Each of the destinations in *Great Minnesota Weekend Adventures* is one I'd happily visit again, and each offers the weekend traveler a variety of things to see and do. In the sections called "Trip Tips," I've provided very specific information about tours, festivals, museums, recreation, and nightlife, as well as the best places to stay and to dine. And I've included prices—these may change, but those listed here should give readers a good idea of what they can expect. I've also included more than 30 sidebars that provide additional glimpses into the state—its astonishing array of giant mascots, for example, or the shipwrecks of the North Shore.

When planning a trip, always call ahead to verify crucial details—the dates of a festival, for example, or a tour you don't want to miss. I've included the addresses of many Web sites, which are wonderful resources for travelers; some of the information they contain, however, may not be the latest.

And do plan ahead. As baby boomers have emptied their nests and begun to retire, travel has become more competitive and destinations more crowded. If you want to stay on the North Shore during fall color, for example, make a reservation a year in advance.

But once you've made reservations, be spontaneous. Venture off the beaten paths—I never go anywhere without my *Minnesota Atlas & Gazetteer*, published by DeLorme. And be sure to talk to the locals. You'll be surprised by what you hear—very possibly, not anything you'll read in a guidebook.

Though I've tried to be complete, there's still plenty for you to discover on your own. I'd be happy to hear about it or any other comment you might have about this guidebook, so feel free to contact me in care of Trails Books, P.O. Box 317, 1131 Mills Street, Black Earth, WI 53515.

Meanwhile, happy travels.

Acknowledgments

This book could not have been written without the support of the editors of the *Saint Paul Pioneer Press*, whose faith and financial backing have enabled me to travel without being beholden to anyone in the tourism industry, to forge my own paths, and to write about exactly what I found. Thank you.

Mississippi River Towns

1. Red Wing: History around Every Corner

Ever since anyone can remember, people have gravitated to a sharp elbow in the Mississippi River, framed by a boxy mound French explorers called Mount La Grange, or barn mountain.

The Dakota lived here first, in a village of bark-covered houses. They raised corn, hunted deer, and pulled sturgeon from the river. But then Europeans arrived, starting with a 1680 expedition that included Father Louis Hennepin. The party was captured by the Dakota while camped on Lake Pepin, Hennepin later wrote in his *Descriptions de la Louisiane,* and some Indians "wept the whole night, to induce the others to consent to kill us." Hennepin called Pepin "Lake of Tears."

The French explorers were followed by U.S. government explorers, including Lt. Zebulon Pike in 1806, and then by settlers. In 1853, after the ratification of treaties that appropriated their land, the Dakota returned from their winter hunt to find their houses burned to the ground.

The new town named itself after a local chief who used a dance fan made of a swan's wing, tinted with red ocher. With its choice location, the town was an instant success, and by 1873, it was the largest primary wheat market in the world. When railroads lessened its importance as a transportation center, Red Wing turned to other ventures—among them leather tanning and, from abundant local clay deposits, pottery.

Today, Red Wing is known worldwide for the blue-speckled crocks and jugs of Red Wing Stoneware, founded in 1877. The plant closed in 1967, but the grandson of the last president continued Red Wing Pottery Sales, which carries 500 patterns of dinnerware. Potter John Falconer bought the rights to the name Red Wing Stoneware and began making new versions of the familiar crocks. In early July, the Red Wing Collector's Society Convention brings thousands of collectors to the town; the public is invited to the show and sale. Red Wing Shoes also has spread the town's fame. Founded in 1905, it still uses leather from a local tannery founded in 1873, and its boots and shoes are sold in eighty countries.

But the tourists come to Red Wing because it's so adorable, with its brick storefronts, its flowering planters hung from lampposts, its rows of stately Victorian houses in three historic districts. The views are fabulous, from Bay Point Park on the river, next to a village of houseboats that rise and fall on old-fashioned gin poles, to the top of Barn Bluff, where, wrote explorer Jonathan Carver, he saw "the most beautiful prospect that imagination can form."

Most visitors start on Main Street, where the St. James Hotel has been catering to travelers since 1875. It was restored in 1977, and its 60 rooms, each decorated differently, are now so popular reservations can be hard to get. From its riverside rooms, guests have a view of the whole spectrum of life in Red Wing—barges pushing their way up the Mississippi, freight and passenger trains rumbling past the slate-roofed depot, tourists strolling through Levee Park.

The St. James shopping court is lined with shops, as is the next-door Riverfront Centre, but they're only a starting point for shoppers. Red Wing has become known for antiques stores, which vary from the polished Memory Maker and Antiques of Red Wing on Main Street to the three-level, mazelike Emporium on Third Street and funky Al's on Old West Main Street.

In Pottery Place, a big brick factory that's been turned into a retail and outlet center, the tidy, well-lighted Pottery Place Antiques, and Old Main Street Antiques are likely spots for finding glass, stoneware, and furniture. But anything can be found in these shops—stuffed elk heads, stereoscope scenes, vintage hats, even bits of Red Wing history—perhaps a toy drum signed by Hazen Wakute, the last chief of the Red Wings, in the 1930s or 1940s.

There's more history atop the bluff behind town, at the Goodhue County Historical Museum. Along with exhibits of Red Wing art pottery, Red Wing shoes, and Dakota culture—there's a tepee in the foyer and a bark house in a village re-creation—is a display on Frances Densmore, born in Red Wing in 1867. Trained as a musician, she became an ethnologist for the Smithsonian, transcribing and recording thousands of Dakota, Ojibwe, and even Seminole songs. "I heard an Indian drum when I was very, very young," she wrote. "Others heard the same drum and the sound was soon forgotten, but I have followed it all these years."

A tugboat chugs past Red Wing's Levee Park, a block off Main Street.

When the museum and the shops close, there is still one place everyone should visit—the ornate Sheldon Theatre, which was the first municipally owned auditorium in the nation when it opened in 1904. Its jewel-box interior, with graceful Romanesque arches, murals, and carved figures, was renovated in 1988. Today, with the help of many hard-working volunteers, the Sheldon brings in regional, national, and international performers. When no one is on stage, it shows silent films, accompanied by organ.

With its many charms, Red Wing is a day-tripper's darling.

Trip Tips

Getting There by Train. Amtrak leaves St. Paul at 8 A.M. for the hour-long trip to Red Wing and departs Red Wing at 8:46 P.M. Exact times may fluctuate; (651) 644-6012, (800) 872-7245, www.amtrak.com.

Accommodations. Red Wing is a very popular weekend destination. For holiday, festival, and fall-color weekends, reserve rooms there and along the entire Mississippi River Valley a year in advance. For other weekends in summer and fall, reserve six months in advance.

The St. James Hotel has 61 attractive rooms, each decorated differently, $89–$215. Be sure to ask about packages, especially midweek and in the off-season; (800) 252-1875, www.st-james-hotel.com.

Mississippi Panoramas

The stretch of the Mississippi River Valley extending south of Red Wing and into Iowa is the prettiest along the entire river. Lined by bluffs, from 343-foot Barn Bluff in Red Wing to 575-foot Garvin Heights in Winona, it's a magnet for those who like a bird's-eye view. And since the river is an avian highway, the birds will be right at hand, including warblers and pelicans in spring and bald eagles in early and late winter. Here are a few spots from which to enjoy the views.

Barn Bluff, Red Wing. East Fifth Street leads straight to the foot of the bluff. The main path follows the shady north side of the bluff to an overlook and a grassy slope that faces town. A path atop the bluff leads to the southern overlook, where it dead-ends; those who want to return on the sunny south face have to return to the overlook before heading down.

Frontenac State Park. Turn east off U.S. 61 and drive up to the state park. An overlook can be reached by car, but the steep, bluffside trails also offer views—in the spring, of wildflowers and migrating songbirds, as well as the river.

Garvin Heights, Winona. Turn west off Highway 61 onto Garvin Heights Road. From the Garvin Heights overlooks, there are 20-mile views up and down the river. About 10 miles south of Winona, turn up Highway 3.

Apple Blossom Drive. This is the start of a 17-mile scenic drive that follows a ridge lined with orchards. But just north of I-90, turn into Great River Bluffs State Park. Here, 6.5 miles of hiking trails lead to nine overlooks. Continue across I-90 to Highway 12, through the village of Nodine, to Highway 1. In May, orchards here are engulfed in clouds of pink and white blossoms. Far below, the blue Mississippi flashes in and out of sight.

Just across the river, Wisconsin has three excellent views.

Granddad Bluff, La Crosse. Drive through town on Main Street and up to Granddad Bluff, 590 feet above the town. The sweeping views include the islands and channels created by the Black and La Crosse rivers as they flow into the Mississippi.

Head north on Wisconsin 35, through Onalaska to the village of Trempealeau.

Brady's Bluff, Perrot State Park. From Trempealeau, follow the river north into Perrot State Park. It's a slightly strenuous climb to the top of 520-foot Brady's Bluff, but the view is magnificent. The towers and domes of Winona gleam 15 miles to the north, and just below is little Trempealeau Mountain, which is ringed by the river and was named by French explorers La Montagne Qui Trempe a l'Eau, or, "the mountain that soaks in the water." Continue north on Wisconsin 35.

Buena Vista Park, Alma. At the southern edge of Alma, drive 2 miles up the bluff to Buena Vista Park, 500 feet above town. From the pretty overlook, there's a view of Lock and Dam 4 and the wide river plain, broken by the channels and islands of the wildlife refuge.

From the top of Barn Bluff, hikers can see the Mississippi begin to widen into Lake Pepin.

Five B&Bs are within walking distance of downtown. Rates are significantly cheaper midweek. Golden Lantern Inn is a 1932 Tudor Revival with five bedrooms, four with double whirlpool and/or fireplace, and acres of lovely wood, $95–$189. A patio has a stone fireplace and six-person hot tub. Timothy and Rhonda McKim, (888) 288-3315, www.goldenlantern.com.

Moondance Inn, an 1874 stone house, has five attractive rooms, all with double whirlpool, $110–$175. Chris Brown Mahoney and Mike Waulk, (651) 388-8145, www.moondanceinn.com. Candlelight Inn, an 1877 Victorian with five attractive bedrooms, all with fireplace and three with whirlpool, $99–$169. Lynette and Zig Gudrais, (800) 254-9194, www.candlelightinn-redwing.com.

Red Wing Blackbird, an 1880 Queen Anne, has two rooms, one with double whirlpool, $90–$135. Lois and Paul Christenson, (651) 388-2292, www.pressenter.com/~blakbird. The 1857 Lawther Octagon House B&B, a 35-room Victorian, has five guest rooms with whirlpools, $140–$225. Penny Stapleton, (651) 388-8483 or (800) 388-0434, www.octagon-house.com.

There are several motels near Pottery Place, including Best Western Quiet House, (651) 388-1577; Super 8, (651) 388-0491; Rodeway Inn, (651) 388-1502; and AmericInn, (651) 385-9060.

Dining. The attractive Staghead, in a narrow, high-ceilinged storefront on Bush Street, is known for its grilled meats, fish, risottos, and microbrews. Open Monday–Saturday, (651) 388-6581.

Across the bridge in Wisconsin, in a plain building near the Red Wing airport, the Lavender Rose serves a sophisticated menu, made with fresh ingredients. Reservations are a good idea, (715) 792-2464.

Bev's Café, next to the Staghead, is a homey gem; try the angel food cake. Liberty's, on Third Street, serves American, Mexican, and Italian dishes, (651) 388-8877. In the St. James, the Port of Red Wing serves good food in the lower level, (800) 252-1875, and the more casual Veranda overlooks the Mississippi and has a deck.

Nice places for coffee or lunch include Lily's, down the street from the Sheldon on Third Street, which also sells flowers and gifts, (651) 388-8797, and Tale of Two Sisters Tea Room, 204 W. Seventh Street, (651) 388-2250.

Events. Concerts in the Park, in downtown's Central Park, Wednesday evenings in July. River City Days, first full weekend of August. Fall Festival of Arts, second weekend in October.

Sheldon Theatre. Check for performances. Tours are given at 1 P.M. Saturdays, plus Thursdays and Fridays in summer, including an 18-minute movie on Red Wing history, $2.50; (800) 899-5759, www.sheldontheatre.com.

Nightlife. The St. James Hotel has three night spots—elegant Jimmy's on the fifth floor, the cozy Port of Red Wing, and the rather dank Mississippi Room.

Bicycling. There are two ways to reach the scenic, 19.5-mile Cannon Valley Trail to Cannon Falls. One trailhead is off Bench Street near Pottery Place, and one is 1.5 mile north, off Highway 61.

Scenic Drive. There's a nice view of the city from Memorial Park, atop Sorin's Bluff. It's reached by taking East Seventh Street south from downtown.

Golf. The 36-hole Mississippi National is just south of Red Wing; (651) 388-1874. The 18 holes of Mount Frontenac, 6 miles south, sit on 500-foot bluffs and have a great view of the valley. It's a good value, too; (800) 488-5826.

Downhill Skiing. Welch Village, 10 miles west of Red Wing, is a pretty spot with a vertical drop of 350 feet. Lift tickets are $25–$35, $18–$26 for youths 6–15; (651) 222-7079 or (800) 270-1838, www.welchvillage.com.

Canoeing and Tubing. Welch Mill on the Cannon River rents tubes and canoes and provides a shuttle; (800) 657-6760, (651) 388-9857.

Pottery. Tours of Red Wing Stoneware, 4 miles north of downtown off Highway 61, are given at 10 A.M. and 1 P.M. weekdays in summer, 1 P.M. in fall and spring; (800) 352-4877. Visitors to Red Wing Pottery on Old West Main Street can watch production of new salt-glazed pieces; (800) 228-0174, www.redwingpottery.com.

Goodhue County Historical Society Museum. On the bluff in back of town, it has a great view and also interesting exhibits. It's at 1166 Oak Street (turn up West Avenue, right onto Seventh Street, follow signs); (651) 388-6024.

Casino. Treasure Island Resort and Casino, run by the Prairie Island band of Dakota, is 12 miles north of Red Wing; (800) 222-7077, www.treasureisland casino.com.

More Information. (800) 498-3444, www.prettyredwing.com. or www.red wing.org.

2. Frontenac: Oasis of Old-Fashioned Gentility

Perhaps nowhere in Minnesota are the 1850s preserved as perfectly as they are in Old Frontenac.

That was when entrepreneurs were swarming up the Mississippi, eager to make money. But in 1854, Israel and Lewis Garrard, scions of an aristocratic Cincinnati family, came to hunt. They got no further than Lake Pepin, where the river widens. Struck by the beauty of a point on its western banks, they stopped, bought land from an Indian trader, and lived as country gentlemen while the frontier grew up around them.

When the Civil War started, Israel went back to Ohio and fought for the Union. When he returned to Lake Pepin following the war, he was a general and had a renewed appreciation for tranquility. When development came too close to the quiet point, he rebuffed it: In the 1870s, the Chicago, Milwaukee & St. Paul wanted to go through the riverside settlement—to anyone else, an economic windfall—but Israel made the railroad lay its tracks two miles inland.

Thanks to him, Old Frontenac still is the most peaceful spot on either side of this scenic stretch of river, the only settlement besides Wabasha that is not bisected by a highway or rail line. And yet few of the tourists who whiz by on Highway 61, past the nondescript town of Frontenac Station, even know it's there. Which is just the way the old general would have wanted it.

If visitors turn off 61 and drive the two miles to the river, they'll see a village that is remarkably unchanged since his days. On a terrace overlooking the river, on parklike grounds, stand Southern-style white-frame manors with long verandas. Behind them, along narrow gravel lanes, are smaller houses, many once occupied by the German immigrant workers that Israel Garrard brought from Cincinnati, whose town site his grandfather once owned.

The general's hunting lodge, built in 1855 and named after St. Hubert, the patron saint of hunting, became the hub of a genteel resort. Below, on the oak-shaded point, he turned an 1859 grain warehouse into the Lake Side

The buildings of Chateau Frontenac have kept the look of the village's original homes.

Hotel, opened in 1865. It drew well-heeled vacationers from New Orleans, Memphis, and St. Louis and made Frontenac the site of Minnesota's first resort, a stop on what frontier artist George Catlin promoted as "The Fashionable Tour." In 1881, the *American Travellers Journal* called Frontenac "the Newport of the Northwest."

The society traffic faded when railroads supplanted steamboats in the 1880s, but the hotel operated as the Frontenac Inn from 1907 until 1939, when the Methodist Church bought it and adjoining cottages and used them as a retreat until 1987.

After that, the point was quiet. It's still quiet, but ordinary visitors once again can partake of Frontenac's tranquility. Local cabin owners Linda and Bill Flies bought the church retreat on the point and turned a 1941 dorm into a classy B&B, part of a planned Chateau Frontenac complex that will include a renovated hotel and cottages, all white with green shutters, like the manors on the terrace above.

Israel Garrard's house also is a B&B. Lovingly maintained by local resident Priscilla Flynn, it still contains much of Garrard's furniture and library. The French Gallery–style house, with a two-level veranda across its front, is the anchor of "the Front Row," which includes Dacotah Cottage, built by Lewis in 1858; Winona Cottage, built in 1889 for Israel's son George, with a stone wall added in 1905; and the 1854 Locust Lodge, built for Evert Westervelt, Israel's original partner.

Waterskiing originated off the Lake City waterfront in 1922; today, the area primarily draws sailors and sightseers.

Israel and his family were the only Garrards to stay in Frontenac for good. Three other brothers came and went: Lewis, who was the town doctor for many years; Kenner, a much-decorated Army officer; and Jeptha, a lawyer who lived at the hotel for a time in the 1890s while he tested a flying machine. Jeptha's experiments, in which he sent his airship and a parachute jumper on a track down the steep face of Point No Point and over Lake Pepin, provided entertainment for summer visitors, who called the hired pilot "The Victim."

There's not much to do in Frontenac, besides strolling and watching traffic pass the point: barges, trains rumbling at the foot of the Wisconsin bluffs, yachts from Lake City's marina. In summer, three passing Queens—the *Delta, American,* and *Mississippi*—evoke the steamboat era. Frontenac State Park adjoins the town; it's known for its overlooks, displays of spring wildflowers and bird-watching, especially during the warbler migration in May. But the world at large comes only up to Frontenac's fringes. And that's the way Israel Garrard always wanted it.

Trip Tips

Accommodations. The Chateau Frontenac B&B has three large, attractive rooms, all with gas fireplaces, two with double whirlpools and one with a double steam shower, $125, and roomy common areas; (651) 345-2641.

The St. Hubert House B&B has five rooms, $110–$159, two of which can be made into suites, $199–$209. Many of the antiques in the rooms belonged to the Garrards; (651) 345-2668, www.sthuberthouse.com.

Dining. The Chickadee Cottage Tea Room and Restaurant, along the river in Lake City, is a popular spot for coffee, brunch, or lunch.

Frontenac State Park. The park has 15 miles of hiking trails and an overlook with picnic tables; (651) 345-3401, www.dnr.state.mn.us/parks.

Golfing and Skiing. Atop a 500-foot bluff, Mount Frontenac has an 18-hole golf course and a ski hill, with great views of the river valley; (800) 488-5826.

3. Wabasha: Eagles and Other Exotic Creatures

Bald eagles are hardly the poster bird for the American way. They're famously lazy, would rather steal than make an honest living, hate to share, and have appetites not unlike that of a vulture.

Benjamin Franklin considered the eagle completely unsuitable as a national symbol. He proposed the turkey instead. But who wants to watch a turkey waddle? The bald eagle, on the other hand, is the pop star of the avian world. Just watch it wheel and dip on wings as wide as Michael Jordan is tall. See it dive into a river and snatch a fish spotted from a mile away. Look into its haughty pale-yellow eyes. There's no question: Bald eagles are cool.

From Wabasha's Eagle Watch Observatory, volunteers help visitors spot bald eagles on the wing and "loafing" in cottonwoods along the river.

That's a sentiment echoed by flocks of binocular-toting tourists who go to see them in Wabasha, where many eagles stop on their way south in November and December and on their return north, from mid-February through March. Not only is the quiet river town right on the avian freeway to the south, it's just downriver from the mouth of the Chippewa River, whose fast-flowing waters keep a fishing hole open year-round for the eagles. They are most active on warm days, and mornings and early evenings are the best times to see them diving for food. They often perch in trees midday; look for black blobs in cottonwoods along the river.

In the 1980s, as bald eagles began to bounce back from near-extinction, the town noticed more and more of the birds wintering nearby. Wabasha built an Eagle Watch Observatory deck on the river and staffed it with volunteers. Wabasha also started an annual Soar with Eagles festival in March, at the height of the spring migration.

As more and more tourists came, the observatory's volunteers began to raise money for a National Eagle Center on the river. Its temporary home is a storefront on Main Street; it's also the home of Harriet and Angel, two female eagles who were injured and cannot be returned to the wild. Now people come from all over the world to learn about eagles and to watch them in and around Wabasha.

Tourists also come by the busload to see the fantastical hand-carved carousel in Kellogg, six miles south of Wabasha. This carousel, whose creatures slowly emerged from blocks of basswood over nine years, is the centerpiece of Donn Kreofsky's LARK Toys shopping complex. Kreofsky, who in 1983 began creating and selling old-fashioned wooden toys in response to the plastic goods that fill most toy stores, designed all 26 beasts. There's a dragon ridden by a wizard holding a crystal-tipped wand. There's a pop-eyed goldfish and a giraffe with orangutans dangling from its neck. A river otter wears a string of freshwater-clam shells, its punched-out holes representing the button industry that flourished on Lake Pepin.

When Gov. Jesse Ventura visited, he rode the carousel's Celestial Chariot and commented, "This is art, this is real art."

The same could be said of the wares in Kreofsky's Boomer Heaven shop, packed with high-quality tin and cast-iron toys that bring in regular customers from all over the Midwest. The shop's supply of classic wind-up toys—robots, speedboats, spaceships—will take anyone over age 45 straight back to the good old days of childhood.

Thousands of antique toys are on display behind glass, but reproductions are sold at LARK's Moosetrack Museum Shop, and new toys, books, and gifts are offered at End of the Tale Books, Carousel Christmas, and Magic Troll Toys, where a barefoot troll named Kral lives in the rafters. A Vietnamese potbellied pig named Gip lives in the hall, and there's a miniature golf course outside.

And Wabasha has yet another claim to fame. It was the setting for the 1993 hit movie *Grumpy Old Men* and its sequel, *Grumpier Old Men,* though both films were shot elsewhere in Minnesota. Slippery's restaurant, the main characters' favorite bar in the movie, now is a virtual *Grumpy* shrine, with two video monitors, movie posters, and news clippings about the real Slippery and the 40-pound catfish who lived briefly in his minnow tank.

Locals say the movies' crusty, steeped-in-habit townsfolk—the screenwriter's grandfather, who lived in Wabasha, inspired the movies—accurately reflect those in the town, which doesn't like to change much. Wabasha is the only town north of Winona that's not separated from the river by a highway or rail line, and its wide main street still looks much as it did decades ago, lined with old brick storefronts and a Gambles store.

The Anderson House, in business since 1856, is a favorite stop for tourists who want a taste of the old days.

There are no billboards and no neon-lit franchises. The Anderson House still is operating, as it has since 1856, making it Minnesota's oldest continuously operating hotel. As a living museum, it's a favorite with bus tours of senior citizens, who come to take what the hotel advertises as "a true step back into yesterday." Rooms have patterned wallpaper, dark antiques, and hissing radiators; guests with chilly feet can request a hot brick, delivered in a quilt envelope, for their bed. Guests with a cold can ask for a mustard plaster, delivered with instructions.

The Anderson House is most famous for lending out cats from its Cat Room, lined with kitty bunks. The dozen or so cats change, but the names don't; there is always an Aloysius, a Morris, a Pepper, and a Tiger available for cuddling—though reservations are advised.

Downstairs, Grandma Anderson's Dutch Kitchens is a temple of comfort food—chicken and dumplings, turkey and dressing, ham potpie, even liver. Once, an Italian trattoria opened at the other end of the hotel, but pesto and tiramisu turned out to be no match for sour cream raisin pie and Grandma's chicken noodle soup.

Sedate old Wabasha likes things the way they are. Started as a fur post, it was one of the first settlements in the state, named for a prestigious line of Dakota chiefs. And even though foreign languages can now be heard on its streets, and the occasional art gallery, deli, and coffeehouse has given new flavor to downtown, it can be counted on to remain a solid outpost of small-town Minnesota.

Trip Tips

Accommodations. Eagles on the River B&B, on the river just south of downtown, has picture windows for eagle-spotting. The lower level is devoted to guests and includes a game room, fireplace, and VCR with movie library, including the *Grumpy Old Men* movies. Two rooms, one with a king bed and mirrored double whirlpool, go for $119 and $159. Duane and Sandra Lexvold, (800) 684-6813, www.eaglesontheriver.com.

Bridgewaters B&B, on Bridge Avenue just off Main Street, has six attractive rooms, $79–$145. Two have double whirlpools, one has a fireplace, two share a bath. Bill and Carole Moore, (651) 565-4208, www.bridgewaters bandb.com.

At the homey Anderson House, each room is different. Rates vary from $53 for a room with shared bath to $149 for the Bridal Suite, which has a double whirlpool; (800) 862-9702, www.theandersonhouse.com.

Dining. Three Sisters Bakery & Deli, next to the Eagle Center, is a pleasant place for lunch. Grandma's Kitchen at the Anderson House is famous for old-fashioned food and lots of it. At Slippery's, on the riverfront at the north edge of downtown, the burgers are huge and delicious. The Eagle's Nest Coffeehouse, on Second Street West, behind the Anderson House, serves sandwiches, soup, and ice cream. On Thursdays, much of the town gathers at the American Legion for Taco Night.

Events. Grumpy Old Men Festival, last Saturday of February. Soar With Eagles, usually the second weekend of March. Outdoor concerts under the bridge, Friday evenings in July and August. Riverboat Days, last weekend of

July. Kellogg Watermelon Festival, weekend after Labor Day. The *American, Delta,* and *Mississippi Queen*s make stops during the season.

Eagle-Watching. The Eagle Watch Observatory deck is open 1–3 P.M. Saturdays and Sundays from November through March. North of town, the village of Reads Landing and three pull-offs on Highway 61 are good places to look.

National Eagle Center. The center is open every day but Mondays; weekend hours may be shorter, so check for exact times. Call (651) 565-4989 or check www.eaglecenter.org.

LARK Toys. It's open daily except in winter, when it closes on some weekdays. Call (507) 767-3387 or check www.larktoys.com.

Nightlife. The Eagle's Nest Coffeehouse often has folk music on Saturdays, (651) 565-2077. Slippery's sometimes books bands on Saturdays, (651) 565-4748.

Downhill Skiing. Coffee Mill is a small slope just outside town, (651) 565-2777.

Hiking. Kruger Recreation Area, a lovely part of the Richard J. Dorer Memorial Hardwood Forest in the bluffs above town, has a 2-mile hiking and ski trail that leads to an overlook with a spectacular view of the twisting Zumbro River. There's also a 5-mile hiking/snowshoeing trail, a .75-mile paved nature trail for people in wheelchairs, and campsites surrounded by red pines. To get there, drive up the bluffs along County Highway 60 and turn off on County Highway 81.

More Information. (800) 565-4158, www.wabashamn.org.

4. The Wisconsin Side: Arty Villages and Awesome Vistas

When city folk think about going for a drive, Lake Pepin is the spot that often pops to mind. This 26-mile-long, 2-mile-wide stretch of the Mississippi was created by the Chippewa River, which dumps sediment at its mouth near Wabasha and creates a natural dam. The resulting lake is lined with picture-postcard views that have been admired from the start; nineteenth-century poet William Cullen Bryant wrote that Lake Pepin "ought to be visited by every poet and painter in the land."

In the spring, tawny limestone outcroppings in the bluffs gleam in the sun. In the summer, flotillas of white sails bob on the luminous blue waters. In fall, the wooded bluffs burst into scarlet, russet, and gold.

The Wisconsin side of the Mississippi River, where the highway is squeezed between bluffs and river, is serene as well as scenic. Life moves slowly here, and traffic is light on Wisconsin 35, except on nice weekends in summer and fall, when day-trippers cruise down to visit its villages.

In the 1980s, artists and small-scale entrepreneurs began discovering these sleeping beauties and built studios and businesses along the river and atop the bluffs. The fading burg of Stockholm became known as a mellow place to shop for antiques, artworks, and Amish goods. Pepin, already famous as the 1867 birthplace of Laura Ingalls Wilder, drew throngs who wanted to eat at the Harbor View Café.

Farther down the river, antiques shops and a fine restaurant have opened in Alma, to complement the magnificent bluff-top view that already had been drawing tourists for a century. In Fountain City, a boulder crashed into a house, creating another tourist attraction for that town. Hidden-away Trempealeau has become a destination for reggae fans, vegetarians, and bicyclists.

The most interesting stretch starts in Maiden Rock, where the bikers who also like to cruise down the river gather at Ole's Bar. The Happy Days ice-

Between Maiden Rock and Pepin, Wisconsin Highway 35 provides scenic views of Lake Pepin.

cream shop across the street is a trip in itself; it's awash in smiley faces and talking toys, and there's a fun house in the back.

Atop the bluffs, with a sweeping view of the valley below, Rush River Produce grows acres and acres of you-pick blueberries and raspberries, which begin to ripen in July. Down in Stockholm, shoppers crisscross the single street, from the flower-lined patio of Bogus Creek Café and Bakery to the Crocus Oak and Amish Country shops and around the corner to Out of the Blue and Joan of Art galleries.

Pepin is the first stop on the Laura Ingalls Wilder circuit, which draws legions of *Little House* fans. The little house is a reconstructed log cabin on Laura's birth site, seven miles up the bluff amid farm fields. In town, the Laura Ingalls Wilder Museum displays pioneer items like those described in her books.

Across from the marina, on a shady corner, hungry diners wait for hours to get a table at the Harbor View Café, their loyalty inspired by such well-prepared dishes as halibut, pork loin, and seafood stew. Diners who'd like a pre-dinner drive through gorgeous coulee country can follow the Chippewa River up to Arkansaw, where the funkier Easy Creek Café serves excellent cuisine with a view of a garage.

Farther down the river, Alma has the river's best view. "Such scenes have the power to quiet the restless pulse of care," notes a 1924 memorial plaque at

Buena Vista Park, where a stone-paved ledge provides a sweeping view of the channels and sloughs that mark the beginning of the Upper Mississippi River National Wildlife and Fish Refuge.

There's an unusual confluence of oddities in Fountain City, another village squeezed at the foot of the bluffs. A collection of colorful concrete folk art sits along Wisconsin 35 at Prairie Moon Museum and Garden, 8 miles north, and in town, a 55-ton boulder has created an attraction called Rock in the House. On the bluffs above town, Elmer's Auto & Toy Museum holds an incredible collection of pedal cars, tin toys, and vintage vehicles.

Just down the river, Trempealeau National Wildlife Refuge is a magnet for bird-watchers and also the northern trailhead for the 24-mile Great River State Trail, one of the most scenic in the region. The trail passes Perrot State Park, where a climb up Brady's Bluff yields another great panorama. Then it heads into the tucked-away town of Trempealeau and through bottomlands to Onalaska, where I-90 returns travelers to Minnesota.

It's a fascinating stretch, full of beauty and intriguing stops. Even though Minnesotans can't claim it as their own, it's just next door.

Trip Tips

When to Go. Along Lake Pepin, the season generally starts with the opening of Pepin's Harbor View Café in late March and ends in late October, though some shops and cafes stay open all year. In spring and fall, Thursdays–Sundays is the best time to catch the most businesses open; in summer, some places are closed Tuesdays and Wednesdays.

Unless you love motorcycles, you may want to avoid the Spring and Fall Flood Runs, the third Saturdays of April and September, which draw many thousands of bikers.

Accommodations. In Maiden Rock, the Harrisburg Inn has four attractive rooms with sunset views of the lake, $90–$135, (715) 448-4500, www.harrisburginn.com. In Pepin, Lake Pepin Inn on the highway is a good value, offering very pleasant motel rooms for $50–$65, (715) 442-5400, and A Summer Place B&B has three rooms with double whirlpools, $115–$135, (715) 442-2132. In Alma, the Gallery House B&B has three attractive rooms overlooking the river, $85–$105, (608) 685-4975, www.wbba.org.

Set into the bluff above Fountain City, the five Hawk's View Cottages have two stories, full kitchens, decks, fireplaces, double whirlpools, and panoramic views of the river valley; one is wheelchair-accessible. Rates are $100–$150 weeknights, $130–$180 weekends, including a bottle of wine and breakfast fixings; (651) 293-0803 or (608) 687-4231, www.hawksview.net.

In Trempealeau, the Trempealeau Hotel's Doc West suites have whirlpools and gas stoves, and the Pines Cottage has a kitchenette, whirlpool, and deck,

$100–$120, (608) 534-6898, www.greatriver.com/hotel.htm. The Riverview Motel has nice rooms right on the river, $50–$90; (608) 534-7784.

Warning: Rooms with a river view at these lodging places often come with the rumbling of trains throughout the night.

Dining. The Star Café in Stockholm is open Friday-Sunday for lunch and dinner. Open seasonally; (715) 442-2023. (Entrees here and at the next two restaurants below are in the $15–$25 range.)

The Harbor View in Pepin is open for lunch and dinner Fridays-Sundays March-November. It's also open Thursdays May–October and Mondays in summer. Since the restaurant doesn't take reservations, it's wise to arrive on Saturdays by 4:45 P.M., when names are taken; (715) 442-3893.

Easy Creek Café in Arkansaw is open for lunch and dinner Tuesday–Saturday year-round; (715) 285-5736.

In Alma, Currents serves fine cuisine behind an ordinary storefront. Open seasonally; (608) 685-4880.

In Fountain City, the 1894 Monarch Tavern and Preservation Hall is a friendly place with a great beer garden facing the river; (608) 687-4231.

In Trempealeau, the Trempealeau Hotel is famous for its walnut burgers, served in a screened porch with a view of the river, (608) 534-6898.

Events. Summerfest in Maiden Rock, third Saturday in June. Stockholm Art Fair, third Saturday in July. Laura Ingalls Wilder Festival in Pepin, third weekend in September. Coulee Country Art and Culture Tour, first weekend of October. Tundra Swan Watch in Alma, November.

Attractions. In Fountain City, Elmer's Auto & Toy Museum is open on some summer and fall weekends. Admission is $5, $3 for children; (608) 687-7221. Rock in the House is open daily. Admission is $1; (608) 687-6106.

Nightlife. Easy Creek has acoustic music Wednesdays–Thursdays and bands Fridays–Saturdays. In summer, the Lake Pepin Players stage tried-and-true comedies at their Allen-Hovde Theatre in Pepin; (800) 823-3577. And in Trempealeau, the Trempealeau Hotel has outdoor blues and reggae festivals in May and schedules concerts through September.

More Information. Mississippi Valley Partners, (888) 999-2619, www.Mississippi-river.org. In Stockholm, Amish Country, (800) 247-7657. In Pepin, (715) 442-3011, www.pepinwisconsin.com.

Duluth and the North Shore

5. Duluth: Excitement at the Foot of the Lake

Anyone who loves a Cinderella story has to love Duluth. Built into steep hillsides around the foot of Lake Superior—a century ago, it was called "the San Francisco of the North"—this beautiful city is used to hard work.

Its natural assets made millions for the men smart enough to exploit them. In 1817, John Jacob Astor opened a fur-trading post at the mouth of the St. Louis River. John D. Rockefeller snapped up shipping and mining interests in the 1880s and 1890s. In 1901, J. P. Morgan seized control of Oliver Iron Mining, and Duluth became a U.S. Steel town.

In 1907, Duluth surpassed New York as the nation's No. 1 port, and in the 1910s, it claimed more millionaires per capita than any other U.S. city. But most of the millionaires took their money east, leaving only mansions to testify to bygone opulence. Those deteriorated, along with much of Duluth's heavy industry, and by the 1970s, the town had sunk into shabbiness. The lakefront was littered with debris. Warehouses blocked views of the lake and lighthouses, and people had to run a gauntlet of seedy bars to watch boats coming into the harbor through the Aerial Lift Bridge.

For tourists, Duluth was just a pit stop on the drive up to the North Shore. But that all changed in the early 1990s, when the rejuvenation of Duluth's lakefront magically transformed this workaday town into the belle of the lake.

Today, Duluth's Canal Park has a party atmosphere. Day-trippers stream in to ride horse-drawn carriages, feed the gulls, and stroll among old brick warehouses, which now contain galleries, shops, restaurants, and coffee-houses. In summer and on fall weekends, rooms at its five hotels, as well as those at the 10 B&Bs and other hotels around town—are hard to come by.

Duluth still is a working town, and Duluth-Superior Harbor still is the largest and busiest on the Great Lakes. Except now, industry is part of the tourist show. When a boat appears on the horizon—a sleek corporate laker, coming to take Montana coal to the steel mills of Detroit, or a oceangoing salty, to take grain to Poland or India—tourists come running. As bells ring and the steel deck of the 1930 Aerial Lift Bridge rises, they watch the boat squeeze through the narrow canal and listen as an announcer from inside the Lake Superior Maritime Visitors Center tells how big the boat is, where it's from, and what it's come to load.

The size of these boats is part of their appeal. One 1,000-foot ore boat can take away 600 rail cars of coal. From the side of the ship canal, just a few yards away, these boats look immense. The grain elevators and ore terminals inside the harbor, at which they load, are even bigger; tourists can get a close-up view from the decks of the Vista Fleet launches, which give narrated tours of the harbor and also go under the Aerial Lift Bridge to give passengers a view of the city, planted solidly on its hillside terraces.

The Duluth entry to the harbor, unlike the Superior, Wisconsin, entry, is not natural: Duluthians dug it out by shovel in 1871, just ahead of a federal

When a big freighter approaches Duluth's Aerial Lift Bridge, a bell clangs and the tourists come running.

Duluth's B&Bs

With its vast resources—white-pine forests, rich veins of iron ore, a harbor—Duluth couldn't fail to make money for the men who came to tap its riches, and it didn't. Oliver Iron Mining enriched William Olcott, its president, and Joseph Bell Cotton, the lawyer who helped Rockefeller seize control of the mine.

Charles Duncan was a lumber baron who brought modern utilities to the town. A. G. Thomson was a grain broker, and George Barnum a grain shipper who brought steamships into the harbor. Harry Dudley was a mining engineer who had silver mines in South America and married Chester Congdon's oldest daughter.

And then there were those who provided services as the city swelled in the 1880s and 1890s: A. Charles Weiss, publisher of the Duluth Herald; Mathew Burrows, who owned the biggest clothing store in town; Ellery Holliday, who sold real estate; and Mortimer Stanford, a legislator.

Some left their names on nearby towns—Cotton, Barnum, Thomson—and left homes that, having been built in the days before the stock market, represented a goodly portion of their riches. Today, they're B&Bs, sitting on hillsides just a block or two off Superior Street, on one-way streets that often end in wild, tree-lined ravines. In early May, these and other historic homes are open during the Duluth YesterDays festival. Ticket proceeds go toward restoration. In summer and for fall and festival weekends, reserve as early as possible.

The Mansion. This 1930 stone Tudor, two doors down from Glensheen and the former home of Harry Dudley and Marjorie Congdon, was the first B&B in Duluth when it opened in 1983. Part castle, part cathedral, it has gorgeous common rooms, including a wood-paneled library with a big stone hearth, and 525 feet of Lake Superior shoreline. Ten attractive rooms, some with views, and a carriage-house apartment with one to three bedrooms, $115–$245. Sue and Warren Monson, (218) 724-0739, www.mansion.Duluth.com.

A. G. Thomson House. This stately 1909 Dutch Colonial was the starter home for grain broker A. G. Thomson and has a handsome living room with burgundy walls and an Asian motif; wine is served in a very pleasant sunroom. Four very attractive main-house rooms and two carriage-house rooms, some with whirlpools, fireplaces, and/or view, $139–$199. Bill and Becky Brakken, (877) 807-8077, www.visitduluth.com/thomsonhouse.

Cotton Mansion Inn. This 1908 yellow-brick Italian Renaissance, with 16,000 square feet, is the largest home in Duluth after Glensheen. Six very attractive rooms, most with whirlpool and fireplace, $120–$245. Ken and Kimberly Aparicio, (800) 228-1997, www.cottonmansion.com.

Mathew S. Burrows 1890 Inn. This Victorian has a stunning carved mantel designed by a young Louis Sullivan, a church-style dining room, and a kitchen stocked for guests. Five attractive rooms, $85–$175. The Lakeview Suite has a

(Continued)

23

(Continued)

pretty sunporch facing the lake, and the Ballroom Suite sleeps five. Alan and Kathy Fink, (800) 789-1890, www.visitduluth.com/1890inn.

Manor on the Creek. This 1907 yellow-brick manor was the home of timber baron Charles Duncan and is lined with windows overlooking picturesque Oregon Creek and its ravine. The 15,000-square-foot house has Italian Renaissance, French Empire, and Gothic common rooms. Eight attractive rooms, some with whirlpools, fireplaces, and/or CD players, $99–$199. The Oregon Creek Suite has a screened-in porch. Dinners served on request. Chris and Tom Kell, (800) 428-3189, www.visitduluth.com/manor.

Ellery House. This 1890 Queen Anne is friendly and informal. Four attractive rooms, some with fireplace or view, $69–$125. Daisy's Suite has a sunporch and wood-burning fireplace. Jim and Joan Halquist, (218) 724-7639, www. visitduluth.com/elleryhouse.

Olcott House. This stately 1904 Southern Colonial, across from the Cotton Mansion, once was the UMD's Olcott School of Music. Seven attractive rooms, all with fireplaces, $125–$165, and carriage house, $165–$185. Grandma's Suite has a three-season porch, and the Lake Superior Suite has a bay window overlooking the lake. Barb and Don Trueman, (800) 715-1339, www. visitduluth.com/olcotthouse.

Firelight Inn on Oregon Creek. This 1910 brick mansion, formerly known as the Barnum House, has lovely woodwork in its common rooms, especially around the cunning Arts and Crafts fireplace nook. Six attractive rooms, some with fireplace or whirlpool, $135–$235. Jim and Joy Fischer, (888) 724-0273, www.duluth.com/firelightinn.

A. Charles Weiss Inn. This classic 1895 Victorian is outfitted with period antiques. Five attractive rooms, one with whirlpool, $90–$140. Peg and Dave Lee, (800) 525-5243, www. duluth.com/acweissinn.

Stanford Inn. This 1886 brick house was the first gay-owned B&B in Minnesota when it opened in 1988 and welcomes all people. One room with private bath and three smaller, attractive rooms that share two baths, $75–$115. There's a sauna. Kevin Fairbanks, (218) 724-3044, www.visit duluth.com/stanford.

injunction sought by their neighbors in Superior. Today, the entry and harbor still need to be dredged regularly, but they handle 85 percent of the shipping traffic.

The Maritime Center and Vista Fleet dock are just two of the attractions squeezed onto Canal Park, a sliver of land separated from downtown Duluth by Interstate 35. The Maritime Center should be everyone's first stop; video screens give the estimated arrivals and departures of the boats, and U.S.

Army Corps of Engineers employees answer boat watchers' questions. The most common one is, "Why is that boat just hanging around on the lake?" Answer: There are already one or more boats loading at the terminal it needs to go to, and it saves docking fees by waiting on Lake Superior.

As romantic as it may be to imagine life traversing the Great Lakes, the Maritime Center shows another side. In a re-created cabin from an 1870s schooner, a papier-mâché sailor complains of "a regular dog's life." Around the corner, a miniature of the *Edmund Fitzgerald* lies broken in the sand on the floor of a glass case. Its demise during a 1975 storm still is debated—no call for help was received, so it likely hurtled to the bottom within seconds—and the discussion reaches high pitch at the annual Gales of November program in Duluth, at which experts talk about shipwrecks on the lake. The public is invited.

Those who want to get an idea of what life was like on the 729-foot *Fitzgerald* can walk over the Minnesota Slip Drawbridge from Lake Avenue and tour the regal red *William A. Irvin,* a 610-foot ore carrier that was built in 1938. It was the Great Lakes flagship of U.S. Steel, until the 1,000-foot boats pushed it into retirement; a tour of the tugboat *Lake Superior,* docked next to it, is included in the tour price. At Halloween, actors from the University of Minnesota–Duluth theater department put the *Irvin's* cold steel decks and echoing corridors to good use, turning it into "The Ship of Ghouls."

Next to the *Irvin,* the Omnimax Theatre shows 3D science and nature films. The Duluth Entertainment Convention Center, or DECC, is next door; it brings in nationally known performers and also is ground zero for the fifteen thousand people who pour into Duluth every June to run in Grandma's Marathon, the Garry Bjorkland Half Marathon, and the William Irvin 5K.

Around the corner on Harbor Drive, the wooden castles and walkways of Playfront are always open for children who need to let off steam. Next door, free concerts are held under the canopy at Bayfront Festival Park, home of the immensely popular Bayfront Blues Festival in August.

The newest attraction is right at the edge of the harbor. The Great Lakes Aquarium, the only exclusively freshwater aquarium in the nation, displays 70 species of lake life, including birds, snakes, turtles, frogs, and river otters, in five replicated habitats from around Lake Superior. There's Isle Royale, the island off Grand Portage; the Baptism River, which flows into the river through Tettegouche State Park, north of Silver Bay; the St. Louis River, as it flows into Lake Superior; Pictured Rocks National Lakeshore, on Michigan's Upper Peninsula; and Otter Cove in Ontario's Pukaskwa National Park, featuring two river otters playing in a waterfall and on a slide.

But visitors do more than look. They can take a virtual-reality submarine ride to the lake floor to see deepwater sculpin and shipwrecks. They can guide an ore boat through the ship canal and listen to Ojibwe legends. If they dare, they can handle—briefly—a sea lamprey, an eel-like parasite that virtually destroyed the commercial fishing industry in the 1960s. Attaching its suction-cup mouth to the sides of whitefish and lake trout, the lamprey scrapes a hole in its victim's skin and eats the blood and tissue.

Across Harbor Drive is the 1892 brownstone Depot, which houses the Lake Superior Museum of Transportation, the Duluth Children's Museum, the St. Louis County Historical Society, and Duluth Art Institute, and is the headquarters for the city's ballet, playhouse, orchestra, and chorale.

Passengers of the North Shore Scenic Railroad board here for excursions to the Lester River, on the city's eastern flank; to the Sucker River, halfway up Scenic Old 61; or all the way to Two Harbors, crossing six rivers along the way.

There's another transportation hub in western Duluth. At Grand Avenue and 71st Avenue West, across from the Lake Superior Zoo, three trailheads converge: the Willard Munger State Trail, the 72-mile paved bicycle trail from Hinckley whose last 14.5 miles from Carlton probably are the state's most scenic; the 5-mile Western Waterfront walking trail, which follows the St. Louis River estuary; and the Lake Superior & Mississippi Railroad, which takes passengers for a 12-mile round-trip up the St. Louis.

Spirit Mountain ski hill rises behind the estuary, giving skiers panoramic views in winter. In summer, motorists can catch views from the 24-mile Skyline Parkway, which winds along the ridge above the city, past the top of Spirit Mountain, the photogenic Enger Tower, the secluded little Chester Bowl park and the bird-watching mecca of Hawk Ridge before reaching the Lester River, at the city's eastern edge.

The river marks the unofficial end of the city and start of the North Shore. At the turn of the century, the park was countryside, and Duluthians came on streetcars to picnic, dance in the pavilion, and compete in sack races and blueberry-pie-eating contests. Today, Lester Park still exudes an old-time beauty, with low stone walls lining gravel paths that follow two branches of the river, under towering cedars and pines. On the western branch, there's a beautiful waterfall, its crown crossed by a stone footbridge.

To the east, the 27-hole Lester Park Golf Course sits on land donated by a mining tycoon, Thomas Cole of Oliver Iron Mining. Oliver Mining also was the financial springboard for Chester Congdon, who, in 1915, bought and donated 11 miles of shoreline from the Lester River to Stony Point, near the Knife River, with the stipulation that it would always remain parkland. Chester Congdon's restrictions still stand, ensuring that nothing comes between highway travelers and their view of Lake Superior.

Congdon's mansion, Glensheen, is two miles toward town, off London Road. The 39-room Jacobean gabled brick castle now is owned by the University of Minnesota, which gives tours year-round of the house and its stunning grounds. Built between 1905 and 1908, it's the largest home in Duluth;

Glensheen is a magnificent reminder of Duluth's glory days.

visitors can pretend they're dinner guests of the Congdons at gourmet dinners catered in Glensheen's ornate dining room.

Once, only the wealthy of Duluth had views of the big lake. Now everyone does, since the completion of the Lakewalk in 1994. Starting as a boardwalk outside the Maritime Center, lined with bronze sculptures, it winds 3.8 miles around the lake, past the renovated 1881 Fitger's Brewery. One of the pioneers in Duluth's renaissance, Fitger's is full of shops, restaurants, and a hotel. From Fitger's, the walk heads up a rock-lined hill to the Rose Garden and Leif Erikson Park, a bowl of green with a band pavilion flanked by stone towers with shingled cone tops.

Walkers and in-line skaters are just part of the bustle around the Canal Park end of the Lakewalk. Horse-drawn carriages clop by, and the Port Town Trolley trundles from stop to stop. On the rare occasions when the air is warm enough, teenagers use the battered ruins of Duluth's first, short-lived pier as a diving board into the 40-degree water.

On Canal Park Drive, shoppers stroll from shop to shop—the Sivertson Gallery, the Duluth Pack Store, Northern Lights Books—and stop for cappuccino and a piece of cheesecake at the Blue Note Café. Facing the Lift Bridge, the DeWitt-Seitz Marketplace, a former warehouse, holds two floors of shops, including the popular Hepzibah's Sweet Shoppe and the Art Dock,

Duluth Walks

Thanks to Duluth's creeks, ravines, and waterfronts, a hiker can be just off the beaten path, yet seem far from the city.

Duluth, gateway to the hiking paradise of the North Shore, has its own lovely trails. Here, a stone's throw from busy city streets, hikers can inhale the fragrant tang of cedar bark and loam just as surely as if they were deep in the woods.

Three trails are particularly worth walking. Congdon Park Trail, starting off Superior Street at 32nd Avenue East, follows Tischer Creek 1.5 mile up the hillside. Waterfalls course over sharp basalt boulders into a bed heaped with granite. Norway pines line the red clay path.

Mining and timber baron Chester Congdon gave this land to the city in 1908 and developed the pathways and stone steps himself, along with the wooden bridges that once spanned the creek. His mansion, Glensheen, is at the creek's mouth, and the trail bisects a neighborhood of hilly one-way streets and mansions that is as much fun to explore as the trail.

The 4-mile Park Point Trail, at the end of the 7-mile spit of sand that created Duluth-Superior Harbor, has some of everything: the ruins of a lighthouse, a working lighthouse, quiet coves, and a breakwall with views across the lake of far-off Duluth. To get to it, drive over the Aerial Lift Bridge and to the airport at the end of the road. Park and start out on the wide gravel track that leads hikers into a quiet world, broken only by the sawing of crickets and the occasional grunt of cranes in Superior Harbor.

From a hushed thicket of pine, the trail emerges into sand dunes—carpeted with poison ivy, so watch out—and passes the remains of an 1855 lighthouse and an abandoned boat factory with stepped gables. From here, hikers can watch ore boats load up at the Burlington Northern Terminal, which was the last stop for the *Edmund Fitzgerald* in 1975. At the end of the trail, a lighthouse winks at the entry, and a breakwall curves around a polished-pebble beach.

There's another trail on a waterfront that's less known. The 5-mile Western Waterfront Trail, across from the Lake Superior Zoo at Grand Avenue and 72nd Avenue West, follows the St. Louis River estuary. The shady trail skirts the foot of Spirit Mountain Ski Area, with views of river and cattail marshes that are prime waterfowl habitat.

Other trails include the 1.3-mile Kingsbury Creek Trail, which winds along Kingsbury Creek above the zoo. In the heart of the city, the 2.5-mile Chester Park Trail follows an isolated ravine. The 3.25-mile Mission Creek Trail follows part of the old Skyline Boulevard. Three-quarter-mile Lester Park and 1.5-mile Lincoln Park trails are easy hikes for families. For maps, contact the Department of Parks and Recreation, 12 E. Fourth St., Duluth, MN 55805, (218) 723-3337.

a showcase for north-woods artists. In the basement, Amazing Grace Café & Bakery puts together hefty sandwiches, with rich brownies, bars, and tortes on the side.

In the middle of it all, Grandma's Restaurant still draws throngs. The first outpost of the new Canal Park when it opened in 1976, it brought more visibility to Duluth when it sponsored the first Grandma's Marathon in 1977. The marathon, considered one of the nation's best and most scenic, draws runners and spectators from all over the world.

Back in 1977, a crowd of people in Canal Park was a once-a-year event. Now, it's life as usual.

Trip Tips

Accommodations. Rates are highest in summer. In the off-season, ask for weekday specials.

In Canal Park, three attractive newer hotels face the lake. The Inn on Lake Superior has patios and balconies, (888) 668-4352. The Comfort Suites, (218) 727-1378 and (800) 228-5150, and Hampton Inn, (218) 720-3000 and (800) HAMPTON, also are comfortable.

The motel-style Canal Park Inn, (800) 777-8560, is older, colder—rooms are reached via open-air hallways—and also faces the lake. A block away on Lake Avenue, the well-appointed rooms at the Hawthorn Suites, a renovated warehouse, have full kitchens, and a hot breakfast buffet is included, (800) 527-1133, www.hawthornsuitesduluth.com. All have pools.

At Fitger's Inn in the Fitger's Brewery Complex, many rooms have lake views and exposed brick walls, (888) FITGERS, www.fitgers.com.

Downtown, the newer Holiday Inn, (800) 477-7089 or (218) 722-1202, can be a good value during the peak season. The older Radisson, (218) 727-8981 and (800) 333-3333, often offers inexpensive weekday specials and is known for its revolving rooftop restaurant.

Bicyclists, walkers, train aficionados, or even skiers and snowmobilers may want to stay at the modest but comfortable Willard Munger Inn in western Duluth, which is next to the trails and rents bicycles and snowmobiles; (800) 982-2453, www.mungerinn.com.

Dining. In Canal Park, the Lake Avenue Café in DeWitt-Seitz Marketplace is sophisticated but friendly, (218) 722-2355. Bellisio's is more romantic, with the atmosphere of a Tuscan villa, and offers flights of wine from its large list, (218) 727-4921. Grandma's has a convivial atmosphere and is a good place to take children, (218) 722-4724. Little Angie's Cantina attracts a young, party-loving crowd.

At Fitger's, Bennett's is well-appointed and traditional, (218) 722-2829. Next door, the Pickwick, a Duluth institution since 1914, is a local favorite that's known for its barbecued ribs and its view of the lake, (218) 727-8901.

Across Superior Street, Sir Benedict's Tavern on the Lake is a good place to have a beer and a sandwich and watch the world go by. For a snack, stop by the Portland Malt Shoppe, a tiny brick building built in 1921 as a gas station.

Boat Watching. The Maritime Center, free admission, gives daily programs and pier history walks in summer; (218) 727-2497, www.lsmma.com. For boat arrival times, call the hot line, (218) 722-6489. The Web site www.duluthshippingnews.com has wonderful photos and loads of information. Interlake shipping ends for the season when the Soo Locks in Sault Ste. Marie close on January 15, and resumes March 21.

Great Lakes Aquarium. Open daily. Admission is $10.95 for adults, $5.95 for children 4–17, $1 less in winter; (218) 740-3474, www.glaquarium.org.

Duluth in Winter

Duluth, which early on called itself "the air-conditioned city" to attract tourists from the sweltering South, can be positively polar in the winter. The same lake winds that cool brows in summer can chill bones in winter. If you don't keep moving, you might wind up as stiff as the bronze sculptures that line the lakefront.

Luckily, Duluth gives visitors many reasons to move. Spirit Mountain has long alpine ski runs, a vertical drop of 700 feet, and sweeping views of the St. Louis River estuary and Duluth-Superior Harbor. On weekdays, lift tickets are free to those who stay at certain hotels and ask for the Ski Free Midweek special; it's a great deal.

Spirit Mountain also has 22 kilometers of cross-country trails, in the forests behind the ski hill, and charges for daily passes. And the Duluth Parks Department maintains 46 kilometers of trails, including the 14 of Magney-Snively, past Spirit Mountain off Skyline Parkway, and the 18 in Lester Park at the other end of the city, including a 3.5-kilometer inner loop that's lit every night.

In January and February, Duluthians warm their blood competing in the Winter Sports Festival: speedskating, ski-jumping, skiing, snow-sculpting, curling, and playing hockey and broomball. In early February, mushers come from all over the nation to compete in the John Beargrease Sled Dog Marathon, which commemorates the iron-willed Ojibwe man who delivered mail up and down the North Shore between 1887 and 1900. The start is always exciting: dogs leap against their harnesses, starting guns crack, spectators pound mittened hands and shout the countdowns with the announcer.

Train Excursions. The North Shore Scenic Railroad offers daily excursions from Memorial Day weekend through mid-October. The 90-minute run to the Lester River and back leaves daily at 12:30 and 3 P.M. and at 10 A.M. on weekends; $9 adults, $5 for children 3–13. The 2.5-hour Pizza Train goes to the Sucker River, halfway to Two Harbors, at 6:30 P.M. Wednesdays–Fridays; $16 adults, $11 children, including pizza. The 27-mile, six-hour run to and from Two Harbors leaves at 10:30 A.M. Fridays and Saturdays, arrives in Two Harbors between noon and 12:30 P.M. and leaves for Duluth at 2:30 P.M. $17 adults, $8 children ages 3–13; (800) 423-1273, www.cpinternet.com/~lsrm.

The Lake Superior & Mississippi Railroad, run by train-buff volunteers, travels along the St. Louis River for 90-minute tours, leaving at 11 A.M. and 2 P.M. on weekends from early June to early October. It departs from the Western Waterfront Trail parking lot at Grand Avenue and 71st Avenue West, across from the Lake Superior Zoo. Adults, $7; children under 12, $5; (218) 624-7549.

The Chester Bowl is the scene of many events. Hidden in a forest in the middle of the city, it has a ski hill with lifts and Big Chester, a 115-foot-high wooden jump that still is supported by its 1926 steel scaffolding.

Nightlife is at its best in winter, with the ballet, orchestra, and theaters at the peak of their seasons and nationally known acts regularly scheduled at DECC. After a night out, get rid of the winter chill by easing into a hot tub or stretching in front of a fireplace; Duluth's B&Bs and inns will be happy to oblige.

Trip Tips

Downhill Skiing. If you want to ski at Spirit Mountain midweek, ask for a list of hotels that honor its Ski Free Midweek program. The inns closest to the slopes are the treehouse-like, luxury Mountain Villas at the top of Spirit Mountain, (800) 642-6377, Ext. 543; the Country Inn and Suites, (800) 456-4000 or (218) 628-0668; and Spirit Mountain TraveLodge, (800) 777-8530. Spirit Mountain, (800) 642-6377, www.spiritmt.com.

Cross-Country Trails. For maps, contact the Department of Parks, (218) 723-3337. A Great Minnesota Ski Pass is required. Cost is $3 daily, $10 annual, and $25 for three years. They can be purchased at sports shops or where hunting and fishing licenses are sold, such as K-mart, Wal-Mart, and SuperAmerica and Holiday stations. By phone, purchase at (888) 646-6367; processing fee is $3.50.

John Beargrease Sled Dog Marathon. The race starts and ends in Duluth and is held in early February; (218) 722-7631, www.beargrease.com.

Harbor Cruises. Narrated Vista Fleet cruises (about two hours), $9.75, $5 children 3–11, are given several times a day from mid-May to mid-October. Lunch, dinner, and moonlight cruises also are offered, as well as Mother's Day brunch and other theme cruises; (218) 722-6218, www.visit duluth.com/vista.

Glensheen. Tours are given year-round, with hours limited to 11 A.M. to 2 P.M. weekends November through April, $8.75–$4. Multicourse dinners, $40 including tour, are given regularly, along with such seasonal events as Mother's Day brunches and holiday brunches in December. On Wednesdays in July, concerts are given on the lawn, and the annual Festival of Fine Arts and Crafts is held the third Saturday of August; (888) 454-4536, www.d.umn.edu/glen/.

The Depot. The Depot houses the Duluth Children's Museum, Lake Superior Museum of Transportation (including old locomotives), Duluth Art Institute, and St. Louis County Historical Society. Open daily; admission is $8, $5 for children; (218) 727-8025, www.duluthdepot.com.

Hawk Ridge. Hawk Ridge, rated one of the Top 10 hawk-watching spots in the nation, is off Skyline Parkway in East Duluth. To reach it from East Superior Street or London Road, travel north on 43rd Avenue, turn left on Glenwood Street and right on Skyline Parkway; www.hawkridge.org.

Events. Duluth YesterDays, last weekend in April or first weekend in May. Grandma's Marathon, third Saturday of June, (218) 727-0947, www. grandmasmarathon.com. Park Point Art Fair, fourth weekend in June. The Bayfront Blues Festival, on the second weekend in August. The NorthShore Annual InLine Marathon, the nation's largest and a stop on the World Cup in-line skating tour, follows the Grandma's course on the second Saturday of September. Hawk Ridge Weekend, second Saturday of September. Ship of Ghouls, the two weeks before Halloween. Black Magic Duluth National Snocross, Thanksgiving weekend. Winterfest, December 31 through the first weekend of February, when the John Beargrease Sled Dog Marathon begins.

Summer concerts are held at Bayfront Park Friday evenings from late May through August; family entertainment at Playfront at noon Saturdays.

Nightlife. Duluth has lots going on, especially in the winter. The Minnesota Ballet, Duluth-Superior Symphony Orchestra, Duluth Playhouse, and Renegade Comedy Theatre have a full schedule of performances, augmented by recitals and concerts at the University of Minnesota–Duluth, the College of St. Scholastica, and the Sacred Heart Music Center, in a deconsecrated neo-Gothic cathedral four blocks from downtown. For a complete, up-to-date list of events, call the city or check www.visitduluth.com, which also lists college hockey and basketball games.

DECC brings in national touring shows and nationally known performers; call (218) 722-2000, www.decc.org.

At Fitger's, Bennett's puts on a dinner theater four times a year; (218) 722-2829.

On Canal Park, Amazing Grace Bakery & Café, in the lower level of the DeWitt-Seitz Marketplace, often brings in performers on weeknights; (218) 723-0075, www.amazinggracebakery.com.

Casino. The Fond-du-Luth Casino, in a Superior Street storefront, is operated by the Lake Superior Band of Chippewa; (800) 873-0280.

More Information. (800) 438-5884, www.visitduluth.com, www.duluth.com.

6. The North Shore: Hallowed Ground for Minnesotans

Ten thousand years ago, the melting of Minnesota's last glacier transformed a placid beach into a rugged coast.

It's a 150-mile stretch of wild beauty, lined by piles of jagged black basalt, cobblestone beaches, and the mouths of dozens of rivers, tumbling down from the old beaches of Glacial Lake Duluth. Seven state parks follow their winding gorges, marked by rapids and waterfalls, and the Superior Hiking Trail crosses them on its way from Two Harbors to the Canadian border.

This is Minnesota's breathing space, to which we return like spawning salmon, year after year, or whenever we need to fill our lungs with brisk Lake Superior air. We can't swim in the water—it's about 40 degrees, even in summer—but we can look at the views and walk through the forests, and we do.

The romance of crashing waves and wooded solitude makes the North Shore a favorite honeymoon and anniversary destination, but its popularity is universal—every year, the readers of *Lake Superior* magazine vote it the No. 1 attraction on the lake.

Only a few decades ago, most visitors stayed in mom-and-pop resorts, usually a string of small cabins perched on the rocky shore. The traditional spots since have been joined by fancier inns, villas, and townhouses, as well as a top-flight golf course. But the North Shore still is primarily for people who just want to spend time outdoors.

The first stretch, on Scenic Highway 61 between Duluth and Two Harbors, retains the feel of the old shore and has many old-fashioned resorts. In spring, fishermen flock to the French, Sucker, and Knife rivers for smelt, salmon, and trout.

The near North Shore is very scenic. There, Highway 61 passes through two tunnels cut through rock and over the waterfalls of Gooseberry State Park, Minnesota's most-visited state park. Split Rock Lighthouse, just up the road, is the most-photographed spot on the shore and probably the state.

The stretch between Schroeder and Lutsen attracts a well-heeled crowd to the cushy resorts and condos around Lutsen Mountains. Many of the shore's most popular hiking trails are here, along the Temperance, Onion, and Poplar rivers, as well as Eagle Mountain, the state's highest point.

Grand Marais was founded by fur traders, loggers, and fishermen and still is the favorite spot of die-hard outdoorsmen and women, especially cross-country skiers. It's also the beginning of the Gunflint Trail and one of the gateways to the Boundary Waters Canoe Area Wilderness (BWCAW). Hiking around here, especially around the Devil Track, Kadunce, and Brule rivers, is the most dramatic on the shore.

Few venture beyond Grand Marais, but those who do will be rewarded. Two centuries ago, Grand Portage was a fur-trading metropolis, and Grand Portage National Monument re-creates its colorful past in and around a reconstructed stockade. Next door, ferries leave for Isle

The furious waters of the Temperance River swirl down a twisting gorge to Lake Superior.

Royale National Park, one of the nation's best backpacking destinations. Six miles north, in Grand Portage State Park, the 120-foot High Falls of the Pigeon River cascade over a sheer basalt face. This is the unpassable chasm that forced the Ojibwe to make an eight-and-a-half mile grand detour, a route the voyageurs later adopted to reach the fur-rich interior.

The British-owned North West Company post moved across the border in 1803, and that era is re-created at Fort William, where costumed interpreters work their magic in and around the 42 buildings of the continent's largest reconstructed post. It's just one of the attractions of Thunder Bay, the largest city on Lake Superior and the most ethnically diverse.

Trip Tips

Accommodations. There are many resorts, hotels, and B&Bs. In addition, Superior Properties out of Lutsen rents privately owned houses and cabins all along the North Shore, inland, and on the Gunflint Trail; (800) 950-4361, www.northofnorth.com.

Make reservations a year in advance for the peak color season—the last two weekends of September—as well as early October and the third weekend of October, when Minnesota schoolchildren have a four-day break. Also reserve early for summer, weekdays as well as weekends.

Planning a Trip. A blue brochure, "North Shore Drive of Lake Superior," issued annually since 1937, is indispensable, especially because it lists all

Hiking along the North Shore

In the summer and fall, hikers by the thousands take to the eight state parks of the North Shore and the Superior Hiking Trail, the 235-mile path that follows a ridgeline above Lake Superior from Two Harbors to the Canadian border. It's been called one of the nation's most beautiful trails, for it traverses an area of spectacular beauty. Cutting along the flank of the Sawtooth Mountains, at some points more than 1,000 feet above Lake Superior, it crosses dozens of creeks and rivers, cascading down from the former beaches of Glacial Lake Duluth.

Each season gives the North Shore a new look, from the wildflowers of spring to the glowing colors of fall. In winter, the trails can be traversed on snowshoe, though they're often packed enough for walking. These are some of the most popular hikes:

Gooseberry Falls State Park. Few miss this picturesque park, which straddles the highway. Eighteen miles of trails wind through the park, most likely named for the seventeenth century explorer Sieur des Groseilliers, whose name means "gooseberry" in French. But most people will want to spend their time clambering around on the lumpy floes of ancient lava that hold up Upper and Lower Falls, and down to the river's mouth on Lake Superior.

Split Rock River Loop. The trail starts 4 miles north of Gooseberry, at the mouth of the Split Rock River; there's a parking area. It's 5 miles up the west side of the red-rock gorge and back down the other side.

Split Rock Lighthouse State Park. Tour the 1909 lighthouse and history center, then follow easy trails along the lake for a good view of the lighthouse atop its 130-foot cliff.

Tettegouche State Park. From the office, a trail follows the Baptism River and merges with the Superior Hiking Trail. At High Falls, it crosses a suspen-

landmarks by milepost—from the Vista Fleet dock in Duluth at 0.0 to the Canadian border at 151.5. It's free at all tourism bureaus.

Every spring, *Lake Superior* magazine, based in Duluth, publishes an indispensable travel guide, $6.95. It's available at newsstands or can be ordered at (888) 244-5253, www.lakesuperior.com.

When to Go. Peak season along the North Shore is summer, when people from all over the nation come to bask in the cool breezes of Lake Superior. Bring a jacket and pants even in the dog days, as nights can be cold, even around the traditional shore bonfire.

Fall weekends, when throngs come up to see the hardwood forest burst into color, are even busier.

---

sion bridge, heads back, and crosses again at Two Steps Falls. And don't miss the half-mile trail to Shovel Point, where basalt headlands form a coastline that looks more like northern California than Minnesota. The view, which includes Palisade Head to the south, is incomparable.

Temperance River State Park. Trails at this park, named because the river has no bar at its mouth, follow the tortuous course of the Temperance River, seething and twisting like a flume ride from hell. Pebbles in the swirling water have scraped potholes in the riverbed and in the sides of the gorge.

Carlton Peak. This massive pile of volcanic rock, whose 924-foot summit commands a spectacular view up and down the shore, is 3 miles north of Temperance via the Superior Hiking Trail. The other way to reach it is by driving 3 miles up the Sawbill Trail to the parking lot at Britton Peak; from there, it's 3 miles round-trip.

Oberg Mountain. This 2-mile hike probably is the most popular on the shore, especially in fall, when overlooks provide views of the mountain's maple forest. Take Forest Road 336, or Onion River Road, 2 miles to a parking area. Cross the road to the trail; after a short distance, turn onto the 1.8-mile Oberg loop, which winds around the summit. From the other side of the parking area, the Superior Hiking Trail leads to Leveaux Mountain. It's 1 mile to a spur trail that goes to the summit.

Cascade River State Park. The trails that hug both sides of this river are popular with everyone, especially children. If they're surefooted, they can jump from boulder to boulder and watch the river crash down to the lake. Don't miss the Upper Cascade, where the trail is lined with old cedars and feathery ferns and hikers can sit on the shore watching the river tumble over a series of small falls.

Devil Track River. On the rim of this deep, narrow canyon is a 2.4-mile stretch of the Superior Hiking Trail, with views of the red cliffs and waterfalls

(Continued)

(Continued)
below. To get there, drive 5 miles north of Grand Marais to County Highway 58 and turn; there's a parking area on the left.

Kadunce River. From a wayside 10 miles north of Grand Marais, a trail follows the rust-tinted waters of the Kadunce through its narrow gorge. It's a spectacular and intimate little hike, 1.5-mile round-trip, and the cobblestone beach opposite the wayside is one of the shore's prettiest.

Judge C. R. Magney State Park. Trails in this park, named after the populist who proclaimed, "Our state parks are everyman's country estate," follow the Brule River past three waterfalls: the Lower, the Upper, and Devil's Kettle. At Devil's Kettle, the river splits, half cascading 50 feet into a pool and the other disappearing into a pothole; no one know where it ends up. It's 2.5 miles round-trip.

Grand Portage State Park. The Pigeon River, which marks the international border, was the bane of voyageurs. Its lower 20 miles, a series of cataracts and chasms, are unnavigable, so the paddlers had to make an 8.5-mile uphill portage to its upper waters. Today, visitors can follow a half-mile, handicapped-accessible trail to the state's tallest waterfall, gorgeous High Falls, cascading 120 feet over a sheer basalt wall. The Middle Falls Trail goes farther, over ridge tops, about 3 miles.

Trip Tips

What to Know. Allow an hour for each 1.5 to 3 miles. Bring water and snacks and be prepared for sudden weather changes.

Lodge-to-Lodge Hiking. Fifteen lodges allow hikers to hike the trail in sections. The package, which starts at $277 per person for three nights, includes lodging, breakfast, trail lunch, and shuttle to the trailhead. Call (800) 322-8327, www.boreal.org/adventures.

Superior Hiking Trail Association. This nonprofit trail association maintains the route, sells maps, and sponsors naturalist-guided hikes year-round. Call (218) 834-2700, www.shta.org, or stop by the headquarters in Two Harbors at 731 Highway 61 (Seventh Avenue). The group's *Guide to the Superior Hiking Trail* (Ridgeline Press, $15.95) is very useful.

Superior Shuttle. Pick-ups and drop-offs start at $8 and run Fridays–Sundays from mid-May to mid-October; (218) 834-5511, www.shta.org.

More Information. Lutsen-Tofte Tourism Association, (888) 616-6784, www.61north.com.

Late October and early November is an excellent time to hike; muddy trails harden, falling leaves open up new vistas, the bugs are gone, and hotel rates drop by half. Just remember to wear blaze-orange if you're not hiking in a state park—deer season starts in November.

In winter, the North Shore is a sports paradise, with hundreds of miles of trails for downhill skiing, cross-country skiing, snowshoeing, and snowmobiling. When there's not enough snow—unfortunately, not an uncommon occurrence—trails and frozen rivers are fine places to hike. Temperatures along the shore actually are 10 or more degrees warmer than they are inland, thanks to heat held by the lake, but biting winds often erase the advantage.

The ski season at Lutsen Mountains extends into mid-April. But away from the Lutsen area, prices at many hotels drop to half-price in March. However, spring weather is unpredictable at best, and trails are sloppy. The best bet in spring is May, when wildflowers start to appear in the forests. And in June, the roadsides are lined by pink and purple lupine.

7. Scenic 61: Rustic Remnant of the Old Shore

Thanks to a four-lane expressway on Highway 61, tourists can zoom up to Two Harbors from Duluth in 15 minutes flat. The question is, why would anyone want to? There's much more to see along the 19-mile stretch of Scenic 61, a part of the North Shore that has changed little in the last few decades. It's not the fanciest part, but it may be the most genuine.

The 11 miles of shoreline from the Lester River to Stony Point are undeveloped, thanks to Chester Congdon, who donated it to Duluth with the stipulation that nothing would ever come between highway travelers and their view of Lake Superior. Except for angling and boat-watching, not much goes on there, which is how Congdon wanted it. His heirs consider his wishes a sacred trust—in 2000, a great-granddaughter successfully fought the city's plan to build a boat launch with breakwall, ramps, docks, parking, restrooms, picnic area, and pedestrian tunnel.

Fishermen haunt the mouths of the Lester, French, and Sucker rivers at dawn, angling for trout and salmon. In May they wait, along with hundreds of ducks, for the smelt to run up the Lester and Knife. In fall, they wait for Chinook salmon, which congregate at the rivers' mouths before their spawning run.

Those who don't want to catch fish can watch them at the DNR's hatchery on the French River, where thousands of steelhead, rainbow, and Kamloops trout yearlings wiggle inside long raceways, making the water boil as they slap the wire of demand feeders and gulp the pellets that rain down.

Grown-up fish are served a mile farther up the road at the New Scenic Café, which serves a mean pistachio-crusted walleye as well as such entrees as chipotle chicken and Thai green curry. It's not much to look at, but it could be the best restaurant on the North Shore, and its pies can stand up to any in the state.

Three miles east, take Stony Point Drive to Stony Point, a grassy meadow lined with pebble beach. On warm days, it's popular with boat watchers, picnickers, and fishermen, and on windy days, it's a good place to watch the surf.

Stony Point, along a loop just past the Sucker River, is popular with picnickers and lake watchers.

Nearby is the kind of roadside attraction that will be instantly familiar to anyone who took long car trips in the 1960s. Off the highway, in a spruce and balsam forest, Tom's Logging Camp shows what life was like in the logging camps that once dotted the shore. Visitors can wander among a blacksmith shop, bunkhouse, and cook shanty and see a goofy Paul Bunyan. But children will most appreciate the petting deer and pygmy goats, as well as the Old Northwest Company Trading Post, an old-fashioned repository of souvenirs.

The only stretch of the Superior Hiking Trail between Duluth and Two Harbors is 2 miles farther, just short of the Knife River. From a parking lot, a 3.6-mile trail winds up through meadows and groves of pines to meet the cascading Knife River at Second Falls.

Knife River is one of the oldest North Shore towns. It was the site of a logging operation and a commercial-fishing port; it's now the site of the North Shore's largest marina. At least two shipwrecks lie offshore—the log-rafting tug *Niagara,* which sunk in 1904, and the freighter *Onoko,* which sunk in 1915.

Smoked fish is still sold from wooden storefronts along the highway. Russ Kendall's is best-known: His family has been in the business ever since his father's fish truck broke down in Knife River on a 1924 delivery run to Grand Portage. The townspeople bought the fish, the father built a fish stand, and now Kendall dispenses his own smoked slabs of trout, whitefish, and salmon.

At Emily's Knife River Inn, the aroma of allspice fills the 1929 general store on Fridays, when the deli serves all-you-can-eat Scandinavian soul food: boiled onions and potatoes, boiled whitefish with white sauce, meatballs, coleslaw, homemade oatmeal bread. Emily's also rents rooms, throwing in a breakfast that includes its homemade caramel rolls, and packs box lunches for hikers.

Three miles north of Knife River, a Norwegian stabbur appears by the side of the road. In the Middle Ages, stabburs were used as warehouses and built top-heavy to keep out rodents; this one, complete with acanthus carving, was built by local silversmith Brad Nelson as a Scandinavian imports shop.

There's a string of small, old-fashioned resorts on the last stretch of Scenic 61, which ends on the outskirts of Two Harbors. On the third Saturday of June, 9,000 runners gather here for the beginning of Grandma's Marathon. On that day, Scenic 61 is a party, lined with bands and cheering spectators. But to those with a little extra time to spend, it's a lot of fun any time.

Trip Tips

Accommodations. Dodge's Log Lodges, on the lake just south of Knife River, has six cabins, five with fireplaces, $74–$124. The newer ones are very attractive; two-night minimum; (218) 525-4088, www.dodgeslog.com.

Emily's Knife River Inn rents a pleasant three-bedroom suite above the store, $60, $80, or $100 depending on number of bedrooms used, with a two-night minimum on weekends. A continental breakfast is included; (218) 834-5922.

Island View Resort in Knife River would be a good place to take young children. It's across the road from the lake and it has a beautiful view and a large lawn. Eleven small cabins, $47–$97; (218) 834-5886, www.ej-fransen.com/islandviewresort.htm.

Dining. Emily's in Knife River is a good place to pick up a box lunch for hikes, and it has a fish boil and full dinners on Fridays, $11, half-price for children.

The New Scenic Café has imaginative, healthy food and a children's menu. Open daily for breakfast, lunch, and dinner; (218) 525-6274, www.scenic cafe.com.

Tom's Logging Camp. It's open from May through late October. For a free family pass, register at its Web site, www.tomsloggingcamp.com. Admission is $3 adults, $2 children 6–15; (218) 525-4120.

More Information. Duluth Visitors Bureau, (800) 438-5884, www.visitdu luth.com.

8. Two Harbors: Beacon on the Lake

The story of Two Harbors can be summed up in three words: Trains, boats, and automobiles.

The trains roll down from the Iron Range on the Duluth, Missabe and Iron Range line, as they have since the first load of high-grade iron ore left Tower for Two Harbors in 1884. In Agate Bay, 1,000-foot boats glide in to take the ore—today, in the form of taconite pellets—to the steel mills in the East. The automobiles zoom up Highway 61, the scenic highway on which a constant stream of tourists heads for the North Shore. Too often, their sights set northward, they fail to stop at the historic harbor.

There's plenty of Two Harbors up on the highway—muffin shops, cafés, franchise hotels, bait shops, even the headquarters of the Superior Hiking Trail Association. But the most interesting part of Two Harbors is along the waterfront. Tourists can see it via smaller trains and boats—the North Shore Scenic Railroad, which comes up from Duluth twice a week, and the *Grampa Woo*, a 115-foot yacht whose captain sails up to the foot of the towering ore docks and gives passengers a few dusty red pellets to roll around in their palms.

The most striking building on the lakefront is the 1891 lighthouse, particularly when the late-afternoon sun sets its red-brick tower aflame. It's a working lighthouse, the last one on the North Shore, with a beam electronically controlled from Duluth. But hundreds of lighthouse keepers take care of the details, raising and lowering the flag, checking the light, weeding the garden, filling the birdfeeder.

The keepers are paying guests at the Lighthouse B&B, conceived by the Lake County Historical Society as a way to pay for the restoration of the crumbling beacon. Most of the guest keepers take their job very seriously, entering completed duties in a leatherbound journal, as real keepers did a century ago. When they're finished, they can walk the grounds, watch for ghosts and retire to spare but tasteful rooms furnished with quilts, wrought-iron beds, and steamer trunks.

The lighthouse is part of a museum complex that includes a gift shop, fog-signal building, and the pilot house of the *Frontenac,* pushed onto a Silver Bay reef by a 1979 squall and eventually scrapped. Included in the *Frontenac's* exhibits is the bill of lading for the *Edmund Fitzgerald's* last load, picked up at the Burlington Northern docks in Superior on November 9, 1975.

For sailors in trouble, the steam-powered *Edna G.* was the St. Bernard of the North Shore. The 93-foot tug rescued 13 men off the *Niagara* in 1904 and 24 off the *Edenborn* in 1905. She pulled boats off reefs and broke through ice, often damaging herself. One of the few wrecks in which she wasn't involved was right in Agate Bay, when an 1896 gale drove the wooden schooner *Samuel P. Ely* into the breakwall. A fisherman's sailboat rescued the 11-man crew, and the *Ely's* wreck was incorporated into a new breakwall, atop which visitors can walk today. Today, the little green tug, retired in 1981 after 85 years of service, can be toured at its mooring across from the ore docks, along an area sailors once called Whiskey Row.

The sturdy tugboat *Edna G.,* in service from 1896 to 1981, is now a museum.

Just up from the harbor, the 1910 depot welcomes arrivals of the North Shore Scenic Railroad from Duluth. That little train, however, is dwarfed by the massive black locomotives that stand outside the depot—the 1883 Three Spot and the Mallet 221, which weighs more than one million pounds and is one of the largest locomotives in existence.

Inside the depot, the Lake County Historical Society Museum includes exhibits on the town's logging and mining history and photographic glimpses of a colorful past: legendary musher John Beargrease with his wife and four kids; a local judge as a baby in an Ojibwe cradleboard; a moose team pulling a sleigh; hopeful miners during the Lake Vermilion gold rush of 1865–68.

Two Harbors also houses the 3M Museum, which occupies the building in which the billion-dollar Twin Cities–based company was founded in 1902. The founders—an attorney, doctor, meat cutter, and two railroad executives from Two Harbors—were after corundum, a hard mineral in high demand as an abrasive, but instead mined anorthosite, a lower-grade mineral worth little except on sandpaper. So they made sandpaper, and eventually other abrasives and adhesives, and the company grew into a blue-chip behemoth.

Two Harbors also has places to stretch the legs. Burlington Bay, just around the corner from Agate Bay, is a good place to look for Lake Superior agates, the Minnesota state gemstone, as is Flood Bay, 1 mile north.

In town, 1 mile up County Highway 2 from 61, the Two Harbors Municipal Trail provides 8 kilometers of well-groomed skiing, 3 kilometers of it lighted. And the grand Superior Hiking Trail, which *Backpacker* magazine calls "one of the 10 prime trails that leave all others in the dust"—starts just north of town.

Trip Tips

Accommodations. The Lighthouse B&B has three rooms, $110–$125, that share one bathroom. The Boathouse room, on the grounds adjoining the visitors center, has its own bathroom, $99, but lacks the charm of the other bedrooms. The inn is run by volunteers from the historical society; (888) 832-5606, www.lighthousebb.org.

Superior Shores, 1 mile north of town, is a large complex of attractive hotel rooms, studios, suites, and townhouses, with two outdoor pools, one indoor pool, two saunas, a whirlpool, tennis courts, and restaurant with patio, $49 for a midweek hotel room in the shoulder season to $429 for a three-bedroom manor with loft on a summer weekend. The townhouses are on the lake; the other units aren't, but most have views; (800) 242-1988, www.superiorshores.com.

Halcyon Harbor is a small resort 6 miles north of town, with four large cabins and a studio, all with fireplaces, $85–$150. The 1930s Cliff House is particularly choice; it hangs over the lake and has entertained such guests as Sinclair Lewis and Milton Berle. A swinging staircase carries guests to a curving, pebbled beach 30 feet below at the foot of the cliff, a wonderful spot; (218) 834-2030, www.halcyoncabins.com.

Grand Superior Lodge, 11 miles north of town, is a new full-service resort on the lake, within view of the highway. It has a restaurant, pool, and gear rental in the main lodge and accommodations in rooms, $55–$95; suites,

$85–$155; one- to four-bedroom homes, $115–$929; and studio to two-bedroom cabins, $99–$249. Most units have fireplaces and/or whirlpools; (800) 627-9565, www.grandsuperior.com.

Dining. The Kamloops at Superior Shores is a pleasant place to eat. Its deck overlooks a commons with a fish-boil area and a little bridge that carries guests over wetlands to a long beach.

Betty's Pies, 1 mile farther east, is a longtime favorite that also serves breakfast, lunch, and dinner; (218) 834-3367.

In town, along Highway 61, Miller's Café, Judy's Café, and Blackwoods Grill offer a traditional menu; the Vanilla Bean Bakery and Café serves lighter fare.

Events. Band concerts in Thomas Owens Park, summer Thursdays at 7:30 P.M. Summer Solstice, the Saturday of Grandma's Marathon (generally, third Saturday in June). Heritage Days, first weekend after Fourth of July. Two Harbors Folk Festival, second or third weekend in July. Two Harbors Kayak Festival, first weekend of August. Railroad Days, third weekend in August.

Museums. The Lake County Historical Society offers tours and sells tickets at the Depot, $9 admission to all four of the museums it runs: The *Edna G.* tugboat, lighthouse, 3M, and Lake County Historical Museum; (218) 834-4898.

Superior Hiking Trail. The Superior Hiking Trail Association's office and store in a Victorian house at 731 Highway 61 (Seventh Avenue) is open year-round; (218) 834-2700, www.shta.org. The main trail starts 5 miles north of town, along County Highway 301 (reached from Highway 3, off 61).

North Shore Scenic Railroad. The 27-mile run to and from Two Harbors leaves Duluth at 10:30 A.M. Fridays and Saturdays, arrives in Two Harbors between noon and 12:30 P.M. and departs for Duluth at 2:30 P.M., from Memorial Day weekend through mid-October. $18 adults, $8 children ages 3–13; (800) 423-1273, www.cpinternet.com/~lsrm.

Cruises. Tickets for the *Grampa Woo* are available at the Depot. Two-hour daily cruises $20, $10 children 3–12, take passengers past Encampment Island, Palisade Head, and Split Rock and around the wrecks of the *Madeira, Hesper,* and *Ely;* itineraries vary. Dinner cruises, scuba-dive trips, and overnights to Thunder Bay also are offered; (334) 421-4211, www.grampawoo.com.

Skiing. The 8 kilometers of the Two Harbors Municipal Trail includes a very nice 3-kilometer loop that's lighted daily, 5–11 P.M. Donations help the local ski club maintain it. It's less than a mile from Highway 61, off County Highway 2.

Golf. The 18-hole Lakeview National includes scenic overlooks and challenging elevation changes; (218) 834-2664. The facility also boasts a winter curling facility.

More Information. Two Harbors Chamber of Commerce, (800) 777-7384, www.twoharbors.com.

9. The Near Shore: Nature's Spectacle on Display

In one 19-mile stretch of the North Shore, Nature presents a one-two-three punch of incomparable beauty.

For starters, just a half-hour north of Duluth, Gooseberry Falls State Park presents an eye-popping spectacle of waterfalls, lumpy beds of ancient lava, and twisted cedar clinging to rock outcroppings.

Six miles farther, Split Rock Lighthouse sits picturesquely on its cliff, a tourist attraction since 1924, when people could get to it on the newly completed Highway 61. Few tourists on the North Shore fail to traipse the park's lakeside trails, at least far enough to get a good photo of the pale-yellow lighthouse.

And 12 miles past Split Rock, the trails of Tettegouche State Park showcase rugged headlands and a series of wild waterfalls, coursing creamy gold down the faces of black basalt heaved from the center of the Earth a billion years ago. It's an embarrassment of natural riches.

Many visitors to the North Shore whiz right by this stretch on their way to Lutsen or Grand Marais. But those who don't have much time or don't want to spend it driving would be smart to stay right here, near some of the North Shore's best trails and best accommodations.

Gooseberry is the most-visited state park in Minnesota, no doubt because its falls are only yards from the highway and because day visitors pay no fee to park and walk to the river, along a trail accessible to wheelchairs. There's a handsome visitor center of wood and rock, with a gift shop, exhibits, and a room for naturalist programs. In the winter, the falls seethe rather than roar, but they are even more beautiful under translucent curtains of icicles. A 20-kilometer web of cross-country ski trails covers the park; often, skiers will spot the tracks of the wolves who also use the trails.

Four miles up the road, the 5-mile Split Rock River Loop is one of the most popular stretches of the Superior Hiking Trail, following and then crossing the red-rock river gorge. The 1909 lighthouse is 2.5 miles farther, perched atop its 130-foot cliff. Built in response to the epic 1905 storm that wrecked six ships within a dozen miles of the Split Rock River, it was decommissioned in 1969.

Today, the beacon is lit on various holidays and anniversaries and always on November 10, the anniversary of the sinking of the *Edmund Fitzgerald*. On that day, the names of the 29 lost crewmen are read, naturalists lead a lantern hike along the shore, and an interpreter discusses the *Fitzgerald*, which went down off the coast of Michigan's Upper Peninsula, not far from the Soo Locks.

From May 15 to October 15, the lighthouse, fog-signal building, and keeper's quarters are open for tours. The History Center, which includes displays on commercial fishing and tourism and a 22-minute film on the lighthouse, is open all year, along with the 8 miles of hiking and cross-country ski trails in the park.

Beaver Bay, the oldest continuously occupied white settlement along the shore, appears 4 miles up the highway. This was the home of the legendary John Beargrease, who carried mail along the shore from 1887 to 1900, via dog sled in winter. He's buried in the little Ojibwe cemetery on a hill just off County Highway 4; during the annual John Beargrease Sled Dog Marathon, the teams stop to pay tribute.

Beaver Bay has cafés and some interesting shops, the best of which is the Beaver Bay Agate Shop and Museum, a good place to pick up tips on agate-

Even in winter, North Shore visitors never miss a chance to clamber around Gooseberry's spectacular falls.

picking spots and to see odd rocks—a dragonfly calcified in orange sandstone, velvet emerald malachite that looks like it came from another planet.

Silver Bay is 3 miles away, home of a giant taconite-processing plant and the roly-poly mascot Rocky Taconite. The 19 kilometers of the Northwoods Ski Touring Trail, 3 miles up County Highway 5 from Highway 61, follow the Beaver River and climb up to overlooks.

Tettegouche State Park is just 4.5 miles farther. Its 70-foot High Falls on the Baptism River is the highest in Minnesota, not counting the 120-foot High Falls of the Pigeon River, whose cascade along the Minnesota border is shared with Ontario. The 17 miles of hiking and cross-country ski trails wind through the park to four lakes, including Mic Mac, where the park rents four restored 1910 cabins. The most popular trails lead to Shovel Point, a dramatically rocky palisade on the lake, and upstream to Two Step Falls and, across a suspension bridge, High Falls.

And just up Highway 1 near Finland, the campus of Wolf Ridge Environmental Learning Center includes a river, two gentle mountains, and two lakes, on which guests can paddle voyageur canoes. The center also has a treetops ropes course and a rock-climbing wall, and provides outdoors sports according to season—skiing, mushing, snowshoeing, and hiking.

On the near North Shore, there's a trail for everyone.

Trip Tips

Accommodations. Gooseberry Trailside Suites adjoins Gooseberry Falls State Park and has a spur trail leading to the park's trails; it's a great base for skiers. It has four attractive two-bedroom suites, each with woodburning fireplace, VCR, CD player, deck, and full kitchen, $85 weekdays, $110 weekends for two adults, $105–$130 for families. A big sauna and a ski-waxing room are located outside. Scott Udenberg; (800) 715-1110, http://members.aol.com/gooseberrytrails/.

Across the highway, j gregers inn has less modern but nicely decorated rooms, suites, and a cabin, some with kitchens and gas fireplaces, $55–$95. The former Gowdy's Inn now is owned and operated by Bryce and Judy Gregerson; (888) 226-4614, www.jgregersinn.com.

Cove Point Lodge, just outside Beaver Bay, is an attractive newer lodge on the lakeshore, in a secluded cove protected by an island-like point onto which guests can walk. It's well-positioned for hikers and cross-country skiers, being within 10 miles of Gooseberry, Split Rock, and Tettegouche state parks. There are 45 rooms and suites in the lodge, $70–$139, $85–$325, some with Jacuzzis and/or fireplaces. Five cottages have kitchens, two bedrooms, two baths, and a Jacuzzi overlooking the lake, $195–$325; (800) 598-3221, www.covepointlodge.com.

Tettegouche State Park rents four rustic log cabins on Mic Mac Lake, in a complex that includes a log lodge and modern shower building. The cabins, built in 1910 as a private retreat, have been renovated and include kitchenettes, a wood stove, and a canoe but no running water. They're a 1.5-mile walk from the nearest road, and occupants are responsible for cleaning the cabins. Rates are $60–$90 for one or two people; each additional person is $10. Reserve from the Connection, (800) 246-2267. The park's number is (218) 226-6365.

The Stone Hearth Inn in Little Marais is one of the nicest B&Bs on the North Shore. There's a big stone hearth in the guests' living room, decorated with mounted fish and snowshoes, and a big dining room overlooks a long porch and the lake, lapping away at the end of the lawn. Seven attractive rooms and a suite, four with whirlpools and fireplaces, in the inn, boathouse, and carriage house, $88–$147. Charlie and Susan Michels, (218) 226-3020, www.stonehearthinn.com.

Fenstad's Resort in Little Marais has 17 traditional cabins, $75–$115, 9 with fireplaces, plus a sauna and a playground; (218) 226-4724.

Camping. Sites at all three state parks are very popular; call the Connection, (800) 246-2267, for reservations. For the best shot at first-come, first-served sites in summer, arrive on a Monday or Tuesday. Split Rock's sites are cart-in or kayak or backpack only; Tettegouche also has a cart-in, kayak, walk-in, and drive-up campground without electricity.

Dining. The log Rustic Inn, 3 miles west of Gooseberry, serves homey breakfasts, lunches, and dinners. In Beaver Bay, the dining room at Cove Point specializes in walleye, and Northern Lights serves good fish and chips.

Events. Gooseberry Falls State Park offers frequent naturalist programs and candlelight skiing or snowshoeing; (218) 834-3855. The Superior Hiking Trail Association offers frequent hikes, on foot or snowshoe; (218) 834-2700, www.shta.org.

Split Rock Lighthouse. Admission is $6, $3 for children 6–15. With the exception of November 10, only the visitors center is open in winter, and then for limited hours on weekends; (218) 226-6377, www.mnhs.org.

Wolf Ridge Environmental Learning Center. In addition to its programs for schoolchildren and summer camps, it offers weekend and weeklong family vacations; (800) 523-2733, www.wolf-ridge.org.

North Shore Shipwrecks

There are few forces of nature more vicious than a sudden storm on Lake Superior.

The North Shore is littered with proof. The sidewheeler *Lotta Bernard,* caught in the teeth of a nor'easter, was one of the first wrecks; she was pummeled into pieces off Gooseberry Falls on October 29, 1874. On the same day in 1896, a gale drove the schooner-barge *Ely* into the Two Harbors breakwater, where she broke up and now lies 25 feet under, part of the new breakwall. Off Knife River, the log-rafting tug *Niagara* lies near the reef on which it grounded in 1904. Its occupants were rescued by the tug *Edna G.* before the ship disintegrated in the pounding surf.

But it was the storm of 1905 that everyone talks about. In late November, as dozens of ships set sail in the calm after a violent storm, an even worse storm hit, with driving snow and winds of more than 60 mph. The *Mataafa,* trying to return to port, was slammed into Duluth's concrete pier by a giant wave and tossed aground offshore. Ten thousand Duluthians kept vigil by the light of bonfires as rescuers worked, not soon enough to save four crewmen later found frozen to the masts to which they had lashed themselves.

The steamer *Edenborn* was hurled into the mouth of Split Rock River and broken in two, and the *Lafayette* was pulverized against a cliff near Encampment Island. The steel barge *Madeira* was battered against the base of Gold Rock, within sight of the cliff that now holds Split Rock Lighthouse. Nine of the 10 seamen were saved when one of the crew grabbed the rock, hauled himself up and threw out a line for the others. Today, the *Madeira,* which lies in only 40 to 100 feet of water, is a favorite dive spot for scuba divers.

The storms of 1905 resulted in the construction of the picturesque lighthouse, which operated from 1910 to 1969 and still is one of Minnesota's most popular tourist attractions. Its beacon is illuminated every year on November 10, 1975, to commemorate the *Edmund Fitzgerald,* which passed Split Rock on its way to doom near the Soo Locks.

Two wrecks around Isle Royale are destinations for advanced divers. The freighter *Kamloops,* which sank in 1927 in an early December snow squall but was not found until 1977, lies tipped in 170 to 250 feet of water. All 20 aboard died, and the engine room contains the preserved remains of at least one seaman. A year later, the steamer *America,* which carried mail, passengers, and goods along the North Shore, sunk in less than 100 feet of water after hitting a rock pinnacle just off Washington Harbor. The 30-man crew and 15 passengers were saved.

For more information about North Shore shipwrecks, read Julius F. Wolff Jr.'s *Lake Superior Shipwrecks* or take a look at the Minnesota Historical Society site www.mnhs.org/places/nationalregister/shipwrecks/index.html.

Ski and Snowshoe Rental. j gregers inn, 1 mile north of Gooseberry Falls, rents waxless skis, $12 a day, and snowshoes, $12–$14; (888) 226-4614.

Cruises. Captain Dana Kollars's 115-foot *Grampa Woo III* is based in Beaver Bay and offers cruises up the shoreline past Encampment Island, Split Rock Lighthouse, and Palisade Head. Dinner cruises and overnights to Thunder Bay also are offered; (334) 421-4211, www.grampawoo.com.

The 1909 Split Rock Lighthouse is one of the most photographed spots in Minnesota.

10. Lutsen: Traditional Heart of the North Shore

Back in the 1880s, moose hunters were the first tourists in Lutsen.

In 1885, Charles Axel Nelson was a Swedish immigrant who had homesteaded a rugged but picturesque spot around the mouth of the Poplar River. His house became a lodge for sport hunters, then other visitors, who came by boat since there was no road.

Nelson's house became the North Shore's first resort. In 1948, his son developed the surrounding hills into a ski resort, and in 1952 a lodge was built, right at the edge of a pebble beach. For many people, this cozy pine lodge, with its picture windows, polished leather chairs, and fieldstone fireplace, is synonymous with North Shore.

The Nelsons, who produced an Olympic alpine medalist, Cindy Nelson, sold their property in the 1980s. Today, different owners run the lodge, centerpiece of Lutsen Resort and Sea Villas, and Lutsen Mountains, the Midwest's largest ski resort with a 1,088-foot vertical drop and 72 runs on four mountains.

Rising from the edge of Lake Superior, the runs provide skiers with spectacular views of the lake, whorls of vapor curling from its famously frigid surface. The lake's winds cut through warm clothes, but the same winds also bring the lake-effect snow and temperatures that allow Lutsen Mountains to stay open into mid-April.

The skiing is among the best and most scenic in the Midwest, and in 1994, the resort began an aggressive campaign to compete with ski resorts in the Rockies. The rustic became a thing of the past. Condo units went up at the foot of the chairlift, with fireplaces and whirlpools in which guests could sit and watch the sun set. Papa Charlie's Restaurant and Nightclub was built, a convivial space where rock groups perform on weekends—the North Shore's first regularly scheduled nightlife. There are also sleigh rides, snowshoeing, and cross-country skiing.

In summer, life on Lutsen Mountains is nearly as busy. The little red gondola that ferries skiers up Moose Mountain lifts sightseers and mountain

At Lutsen, skiers choose from runs on four mountains.

bikers, who carom down nearly 50 miles of trails over the four mountains in the mountain-bike park. The Alpine Slide sends riders down a twisting concrete chute in little sleds, and a horse-drawn trolley from the stables takes guests to a waterfall on the Poplar River. Next door, the 18-hole Superior National Golf Course is a destination for golfers, especially those who like a round with a view. In front of Lutsen lodge, the pebble beach becomes a hub for kayakers, many taking a class for beginners.

This is all fun stuff, but not everyone needs the bells and whistles of modern resort life. From the beginning, visitors have gotten around the old-fashioned way, on two legs. Traditional visitors still consider hiking the highest form of recreation, especially on the trails to Oberg and Leveaux Mountains, which, in early fall, provide overlooks onto maple forest that provides the first and brightest color on the North Shore.

Fall also is a good time to hike the 6.5-mile section of the Superior Hiking Trail from Lutsen Mountains to the Caribou Trail, or County Highway 4, along the Poplar River and Lake Agnes and up to White Sky Rock. Ten miles north, the trails of Cascade River State Park, following the river gorge, are an all-time favorite. The colors also can be viewed by car. A drive along the Sawbill and Caribou Trails and the forest roads that wind through state forest will provide a view of maples and aspen bursting into color.

There's something for everyone in Lutsen. But be warned: There isn't really a town of Lutsen. Technically, it's the hardware store, small grocery, and other stores around the post office. Tofte, seven miles south, is more of a town. It's a former fishing village now dominated by the popular resort Bluefin Bay, whose modern luxury units wrap around the bay, just off the highway. Locals call Bluefin "the resort that ate Tofte," but view it more kindly since the opening of the Coho Café, whose breads and gourmet pizzas are favorites of locals and tourists alike.

The area's history is preserved just down the road at the North Shore Commercial Fishing Museum, a replica of the twin fish house built by the Norwegian brothers who were the first settlers of Tofte. Filled with vintage photos and equipment, it evokes an era that ended in the 1950s with the invasion of the lamprey eel.

Trip Tips

Accommodations. If skiing, always ask about packages; call Lutsen-Tofte tourism, (888) 616-6784 or the ski area at (218) 663-7281, www.lutsen.com. Summer and winter weekend rates are highest; they're lowest during "quiet time," from late October to just before Christmas and from April to Memorial Day weekend.

Two resorts and a hotel are within walking distance of the chairlifts. Eagle Ridge is closest and luxurious; all rooms have fireplaces, and some have whirlpools; there's an indoor-outdoor pool, hot tub, and sauna; (800) 360-7666, www.lutsen.com/eagleridge.

The large Caribou Highlands Lodge just down the road, formerly the Village Inn, has nice lodge rooms, condos, and townhomes, plus indoor and

Father Baraga's Cross

Only tough guys lasted for long around Lake Superior, and Father Frederic Baraga was one of them. The Slovenian priest arrived in 1831 and spent a long and frenetic life canoeing and snowshoeing between Ojibwe settlements in Sault Ste. Marie, Michigan; Madeline Island in Wisconsin; and Grand Portage near the Minnesota-Ontario border.

One day in 1846, Father Baraga, learning of a possible epidemic among the Ojibwe in Grand Portage, set out from Madeline Island in a small boat with an Ojibwe guide. A terrible storm arose, but they were blown over a sandbar and into the quiet mouth of the Cross River, where the town of Schroeder is today. In thanksgiving, they erected a small wooden cross at the site, later replaced by a granite one.

Today, the Snowshoe Priest, who compiled an Ojibwe dictionary in his spare time, is buried in the 1890 Romanesque cathedral of Marquette, Michigan, where efforts are under way to canonize him.

outdoor pools, a cafe, and supervised activities for children 4 and up. Call
(800) 642-6036, www.caribouhighlands.com.

Mountain Inn is tucked into the forest just down the road. The decor is
blandly attractive, and amenities are squeezed in: microwaves and fridges in
some rooms, small hot tub, small sauna, small lobby in which to eat the com-
plimentary breakfast; (800) 686-4669, www.mtn-inn.com.

Along the shore, Lutsen Resort and Villas has four kinds of lodging. Lodge
rooms are old-fashioned, but guests are just steps from the pool complex or a
drink in the lobby. The 1970s-era Sea Villas, 3 miles south of the lodge, are
privately owned condos, and décor is the luck of the draw. But the setting is
lovely, and they have their own pool complex and playground. The newer
two-bedroom log cabins are very attractive, with wood-burning stoves and
handmade furniture. They're up the hill from the lodge, at the top of a steep
drop-off to Lake Superior. The new Poplar River condominiums, just north
of the main lodge, have fireplaces and double whirlpools. Call (800) 258-
8736, www.lutsenresort.com.

Lindgren's B&B, at the entrance to Lutsen Mountains, is a big, 1926 log
home right on the lake. Rooms have an old-fashioned cabin look, and the liv-
ing-room walls are covered with the skins of moose, wolf, and bear, many of
which proprietor Shirley Lindgren shot herself. Four attractive rooms, one
with a fireplace, one with a whirlpool, $85–$135, and an outdoor sauna;
(218) 663-7450, www.northshorebb.com.

Ten miles north of Lutsen, Cascade Lodge has a historic main lodge, with
inexpensive rooms and cabins and a restaurant overlooking the lake; it's a favorite with hikers and cross-country skiers; (800) 322-9543 or (218) 387-
1112, www.cascadelodgemn.com.

Four miles south, Cobblestone Cabins is a vintage resort that's a longtime
favorite with traditional visitors; (218) 663-7957.

In Tofte, the AmericInn is right on Highway 61 and doesn't have a view. It
does have a vaulted pool room and a large and attractive lobby, with a wood-
burning stone fireplace and many chairs and sofas where guests eat a large
continental breakfast; (218) 663-7899, www.americinn.com.

Bluefin Bay, on the other side of the highway next to Lake Superior, has
many kinds of units, from standard to luxury suites with whirlpool and fireplace. Bluefin Bay's biggest assets are lake views from its rooms and from a
large outdoor hot tub that is shielded from wind by a glass wall, an outdoor
pool, and a sauna. There's also an indoor pool complex; (800) 258-3346,
www.bluefinbay.com.

For a special treat, stay at the sparkling white "lighthouse" cabin at Sugar
Beach Resort, on the southern edge of Tofte. The house, which has a stone
hearth, big paned windows, and a bedroom and sunroom inside the tower,
rents for $300 nightly and sleeps six. The resort also rents more traditional
cabins; (218) 663-7595.

Dining. The Coho Café in Tofte is known for its freshly baked breads and imaginative pizzas. It also serves pastas, salads, sandwiches, and such dishes as ratatouille, salmon Florentine, and chicken saltimbocca. For take-out, call (218) 663-8032.

Papa Charlie's Restaurant and Nightclub, at the bottom of Lutsen Mountains, is a convivial place for dinner, and there's regular entertainment in peak season; (218) 663-7800, www.lutsen.com.

The dining room at Lutsen Lodge has a view of Lake Superior, as does the dining room of Cascade Lodge.

Downhill Skiing. Lift tickets are $44, but packages make them much cheaper. They're also cheaper if bought early in the season on Lutsen Mountains' Web site. In March and April, weather is warmer, snow is heaviest, days are longer, and rates are cheapest. Midweek also is cheaper. The ski area is open daily from mid-November until mid-April; (218) 663-7281, www.lutsen.com.

Cross-Country Skiing. The North Shore Ski Trail, from Tofte to Bally Creek, north of the Cascade River, has 196 kilometers of tracked and groomed trails. Pick up the three trail maps, $1 each, at resorts and outfitters, many of which provide shuttles to trailheads and to the tops of downhill spurs, such as the 5-kilometer Tofte Trail from the Britton Peak trailhead to Bluefin Bay.

Summer and Fall at Lutsen Mountains. It's tough to go down the Alpine Slide just once, $5; you may want to spend $15 for the five-ride pass. Rides on the red gondolas of the Mountain Tram are $9.50, $5 for children 7–12. A trail and lift pass for the mountain-bike park is $20. An unlimited-access day pass for all three is $23. At Homestead Stables, trail rides are offered in warmer months for $30, ages 9 and up. Pony rides for children 2–8 are $7, and horse-drawn trolley rides are $12. For reservations, call (218) 663-7281, ext. 505.

North Shore Commercial Fishing Museum. Open daily. Admission is $3, $5 for families; (218) 663-7804.

Superior National Golf Course. For tee times, call (218) 663-7195, www.superiornational.com.

More Information. Lutsen-Tofte, (888) 616-6784, www.61north.com.

11. Grand Marais: Artists' Outpost in the Wilderness

Secretly—or not so secretly—every outdoorsman in Minnesota wants to live in Grand Marais.

The aroma of espresso now wafts through this wind-buffeted outpost at the tip of the North Shore, and the whitefish served in the local café may come with chutney, not tartar sauce. But Grand Marais, founded by rugged trappers, loggers, and fishermen, still is in the middle of the wilderness.

Prospectors once hoped to find silver and gold here, as they did farther up the lake in Ontario, or copper, as they did across the lake in the Upper Peninsula. But Grand Marais's greatest treasure turned out to be its glorious setting, which, early on, threw artists and outdoorsmen in with the roughnecks.

Its practical resources—the sheltering harbor, the hardwood forests, the streams full of beaver—also created lovely tableaux for artists. Built down a hillside and around a natural harbor, Grand Marais looks good in watercolors and pastels. The Sawtooth Mountains rise behind the village, and in front of it, a breakwall connects the rocky outcropping of Artist's Point to a small white lighthouse.

Swedish immigrant Anna Johnson was first to create and sell art, at the log trading post she operated with her husband after their marriage in 1907. Trained at Augustana College in Rockford, Illinois, she painted, drew, and worked in stained glass, leather, and ceramics. Some of her many oils now hang in a log replica of her store, the Johnson Heritage Post Gallery.

Other artists came, settling their easels in front of the picturesque fish houses and clapboard churches. One of those artists, a professor from the Minneapolis College of Art and Design, founded the Grand Marais Art Colony in 1947. Its classes drew serious artists from the Twin Cities, but also fed the creativity of the locals, many of whom had been taught by Anna Johnson in the schools.

The Art Colony still flourishes in Grand Marais, offering summer workshops in the visual arts, writing, and dance. Many artists have set up studios or galleries. The best known is the Sivertson Gallery, which displays the detailed watercolors of Howard Sivertson, who grew up on Isle Royale and has become the pictorial chronicler of North Shore history; the bold, colorful animal paintings of his daughter, Liz Sivertson; and the North Woods–themed woodcuts of local artist Betsy Bowen, among others.

Grand Marais also appreciates its performing arts and folk arts. The performing arts have a home in the $3.5 million Arrowhead Center for the Arts. The center, finished in 1998, is the home of the Art Colony and the North Shore Music Association as well as the Grand Marais Playhouse, founded in 1970.

The North House Folk School, inspired by the traditional folk schools of Scandinavia, holds workshops of every kind throughout the year. Local and visiting artisans teach students how to make snowshoes, knives, fur hats, Norwegian sweaters, toboggans, blanket coats, Cree mukluks, and birch bark baskets.

But boats are closest to founder Mark Hansen's heart, and the whir of saws often can be heard as students build lapstrake dories, birch bark canoes, and Inuit kayaks. Moored outside, a green, twin-masted schooner named the *Hjordis* serves as another classroom, where students learn nautical skills.

Busy as Grand Marais is on a summer day, the place to be still is in the forests around it. Hiking here is among the headiest of the North Shore, on

In Judge C. R. Magney State Park, half of the Brule River disappears into the Devil's Kettle.

trails that follow roaring rivers through gorges cut over eons as the rivers rushed toward Lake Superior. Many of the best hikes now are spurs or stretches of the Superior Hiking Trail, such as a 2.5-mile stretch above the red-rock gorge of the Devil Track River, off County Highway 58, east of town 3 miles; the climb along the rust-tinted waters of the Kadunce River, 5 miles farther; and, another 5 miles farther in Judge C. R. Magney State Park, the hike up the Brule River, where a jutting rock splits the boiling river in two. One branch drops 50 feet into a pool. The other plunges into a pothole—the Devil's Kettle—and disappears; to where, no one knows.

For a view, or bragging rights, climb to the top of the highest point in Minnesota—Eagle Mountain, whose summit is 2,301 feet above sea level. The 7-mile round-trip hike isn't particularly steep, but the trail is choked with tree roots and rocks, so the going can be tough. From a vista near the summit, hikers are rewarded with a sweeping view of Eagle Lake, Shrike Lake, Zoo Lake, and the north branch of the Cascade River, as well as waves of treetops reaching into the horizon. Rock cairns point the way up exposed granite to a plaque at the true summit, which is surrounded by brush.

Back in town, hikers can soak their tired feet in the municipal hot tub or relax over a smoothie, latte, or lager from the shops in the renovated brick Fireweed Commons, the town's first "mall."

Despite its rugged past, Grand Marais today is more refined than rough— but no one seems to mind.

Trip Tips

Accommodations. There are many bed and breakfasts around Grand Marais; check the Web site ww.northshorebb.com.

Just east of town, the Old Shore Beach has a sauna, deck, its own pebble beach, and four attractive rooms, $95–$115. Paulette Anholm, (888) 387-9707. Three miles up the Pincushion Trail, guests can ski out the door of the Pincushion Mountain B&B, which has its own 25-kilometer trail system, a sauna, and four attractive rooms with bath, $88–$108. Scott and Mary Beattie, (800) 542-1226.

On a wooded ridge 5 miles west of Grand Marais, the pine-paneled Dream Catcher has a wood-burning fireplace, sauna, lake views, and a separate living room for guests of three attractive bedrooms, $93–$102. Jack and Sue McDonnell, (800) 682-3119. Four miles east of town, on the lake, the Superior Overlook has a guest area with sauna, wood-burning stove and kitchenette, and two rooms, one with whirlpool, $95–$130. Jack and Viola Kerber, (800) 858-7622. Nearby, also on the lake, Skara Brae has a fireplace and three rooms, two with private entrances, $100–$125. Pat Friedt, (888) 325-5300. Eight miles east of town, near the Superior Hiking Trail, the Jägerhaus has three German-style rooms, each with a private bath, $85–$115. Margareta and David Hilton, (877) 387-1476, www.jagerhaus.com.

In town, the MacArthur House has a fireplace, large whirlpool, and six rooms, one with double whirlpool, $75–$150. Max and Sherri Bichel, (800) 792-1840. The Snuggle Inn has four rooms with private baths, $85–$95. Tim Nauta and Greg Spanton, (218) 387-2847. Bally's has four rooms, $70–$75, and is run by Karen Bally, whose parents fished on Isle Royale, and Bill Bally, whose family ran the town blacksmith shop; (888) 383-1817. The Parsonage Guest House and Art Studio has two rooms, $65–$75. W. C. and Daria Blanton, (218) 387-9106 or (651) 779-9482.

On the downtown lakefront, the homey East Bay Hotel has old-fashioned sleeping rooms without bath, $26–$32, and with bath, $38.50–$82. In the addition, which has a hot tub, rooms are $52.50–$169. The largest suites, which have two bedrooms with king beds, gas fireplace, single whirlpool, and kitchenette, are a good deal in the off-season, $99. Pets are allowed, $15 each per stay; (800) 414-2807, www.eastbayhotel.com.

Also on the downtown lakefront, the Best Western Superior Inn & Suites has a large hot tub and rooms with fridges and lake views, some with whirlpools or fireplaces, (800) 842-8439, www.bestwestern.com/superiorinn. Aspen Lodge (formerly EconoLodge) has an indoor pool, whirlpool, and sauna and includes a continental breakfast, (800) 247-6020.

Naniboujou Lodge, 14 miles north, is a striking lakeshore lodge built in 1929 as an exclusive private club. From mid-May to late October, its attractive rooms, some with fireplace, are $70–$90. The dining room is painted with bright, geometric Cree designs and has a 200-ton stone fireplace with a sunburst motif. Two-night winter weekends, including five meals, are $299–$359 for two; (218) 387-2688, www.naniboujou.com.

Camping. The Grand Marais Recreation Area, (888) 998-0959, has lakeshore campsites on the edge of downtown, $15.40–$26.40, and is next to the municipal pool and North House Folk School.

Dining. The cheery Gunflint Tavern downtown prepares fresh, imaginative modern fare and has a nice selection of beer. The Angry Trout Café, open in summer and fall, is known for its well-prepared fish and is very popular; expect a wait on peak weekends. The magnificent dining hall of Naniboujou Lodge, 14 miles north, is a favorite spot, especially for the Sunday brunch buffet; no liquor is served, and reservations are required. At the East Bay Hotel, the dining room overlooks the lake and is known for its green-chili stew, Scandinavian fish cakes, and pancakes, as well as traditional fare.

Downtown, families will eat well at Sven and Ole's, Leng's Fountain Grill, the Blue Water Café, and, nearby, My Sister's Place.

Events. Winter Trail Days, early February during the John Beargrease Sled Dog Marathon. Arts Fair, first or second weekend in July. Fisherman's Picnic, the North Shore's biggest festival, first full weekend in August.

Ancient volcanic rock gives the Lake Superior shoreline a dramatic look visitors love.

Nightlife. The Gunflint Tavern offers live music on many weekend nights, (218) 387-1563. The Grand Marais Playhouse, www.grandmaraisplay house.com, stages plays in the Arrowhead Center for the Arts, www.northshorearts.org, where the North Shore Music Association schedules occasional concerts; the center's phone is (218) 387-1284. The North House Folk School hosts occasional dances and events.

North House Folk School. For a class schedule, call (888) 387-9762, www.northhouse.org.

Art Classes. For Art Colony schedules, call (800) 385-9585, www.boreal.org/arts.

Swimming. The indoor municipal pool, with whirlpool and sauna, is in the Grand Marais Recreation Area on the harbor. Admission is $2.75.

Hiking. The Eagle Mountain trailhead can be reached from Grand Marais by taking County Highway 7 to Forest Road 48, then Forest Road 158 to its junction with 153. It's a little simpler to take the Caribou Trail, also called County Highway 4, from Lutsen to Forest Road 153; from there, it's about 4 miles east to the trailhead. Fill out a registration form and put it in the box before hiking. Allow three to four hours for the hike itself.

Skiing. Pincushion Mountain has 25 kilometers of trails tracked and groomed for striding and skating, with a public warming house and a 1.8-kilometer trail that's lighted most nights. A Great Minnesota Ski Pass is required. Six miles up the Gunflint Trail, the 3.5-kilometer George Washington Memorial Pines Trail is an easy trail that winds through a pretty stand of red pines.

Sailing. Two-hour sails on the *Hjordis* leave from the dock of the North House Folk School, depending on the weather, $35; (218) 370-0675, (218) 387-9762 or (888) 387-9762.

Kayaking. From its waterfront shop, Cascade Kayaks offers guided half-day kayak tours of the shoreline, $39. No experience necessary; minimum age is 14; custom tours are also available (800) 720-2809, www.cascadekayaks.com.

More Information. (800) 897-7669, www.grandmaraismn.com.

12. Gunflint Trail: Adventure at the End of the Road

In the 1920s, when the first resorts appeared along this remote 63-mile high-way that dead-ends near the Canadian border, guests had to have a certain sense of adventure.

The Gunflint Trail was blazed by the Ojibwe, then used by fur traders, trappers, and loggers. It was still a zigzagging roller-coaster through the woods when vacationers began to come. The first visitors in spring often had to patch the single phone line, which moose tended to snag and drag. Gasoline lanterns in their cabins often became plugged, and bears sometimes made appearances near cabins.

Still, guests had it easy. After they left, resort owners faced a long winter of splitting wood for fuel, getting around by dog sled, harvesting ice, and trapping for food and clothing.

But things have changed on Minnesota's last frontier. Today, the snow that presented so many challenges to early resort owners is prized by modern ones. It's the most reliable snow in Minnesota, usually falling in copious amounts from November to April, and it makes the Gunflint Trail a playground for skiers, snowshoers, and mushers.

Now, skiers head out the door to nearly 200 kilometers of trails, superbly maintained by state-of-the-art Pisten Bully groomers. On the frozen lakes of the Boundary Waters, novice mushers try their skill behind teams of eager huskies, for fun, not necessity. Some of them stay on the trail in yurts, peaked-roof canvas huts with wood stoves, but that's about as rustic as it gets these days on the Gunflint Trail.

The biggest resort is Gunflint Lodge, whose founder, Justine Kerfoot, became a North Woods legend through her evocative writings about the early days, when resort owners got by only with help from their trapper and Ojibwe neighbors. Those days, when "luxury" meant a strip of carpet around the outhouse hole, are gone. Today, there's a weather-reporting station on top of the lodge, updated on the Internet every 30 minutes. The contemporary townhouse "cabins" have hot tubs and saunas. Guests still dine on fish, but it's more likely to be rainbow trout farci with chive beurre blanc than shore lunch.

At Bearskin Lodge, guests can dine on four-course prix fixe dinners as a fire crackles nearby, then take a few spins around a 1.5-kilometer loop lined by twinkle lights and have an après-ski soak in the Hot Tub Hus.

And yet there are still traditional resorts around the Gunflint Trail. The Golden Eagle has a rustic 1945 lodge with walls lined with old logging-camp tools and a trail lit by kerosene lamps. Up the road, Clearwater Lodge, built in 1926 of whole logs, has a North Woods atmosphere that's nearly intoxicating; it's on the National Register of Historic Places. Nearby, the Trail Center's convivial Black Bear Bar and Restaurant is one of the few places where skiers happily rub elbows with snowmobilers, and locals with tourists. It was built in the 1930s, as part of a logging camp.

More important, little has changed on the Gunflint Trail's lakes and in its forests. Moccasin flowers still grow in the spring. Loons trill, and moose graze with their calves in marshy meadows. The leaves turn, and beaver gather piles of aspen branches. Winter comes, and hoar frosts make the forest glitter.

There are plenty of magical moments to go around. When a skier first glides through fresh powder along a ridgeline, high above the deep, narrow lobes of a glacier-cut lake, or a canoeist rounds a bend to see a moose grazing in the cattails, he'll realize why the first residents came—and stayed.

Trip Tips

Winter Accommodations. Staying on the Gunflint Trail isn't cheap, though winter stays include access to superb skiing, and summer stays include superb canoeing as well as the usual beach and sports amenities. The trail association has a vacancy search page on its Web site, www.gunflint-trail.com.

On the Central Gunflint Trail, Bearskin Lodge has very nice traditional cabins and lodge suites. There's a large Hot Tub Hus, and a lodge in which delicious four-course dinners are served; (800) 338-4170, www.bearskin.com.

Golden Eagle has a mixture of older and new cabins, some with whirlpools, and a 1945 lodge. A naturalist leads excursions and activities; (800) 346-2203, www.golden-eagle.com.

On the Upper Gunflint, Gunflint Lodge is a full-service resort with modern townhouse units that have VCRs, fireplaces, and whirlpools or saunas. Throughout the year, it offers theme weekends—horseback riding, culinary adventures, snowshoe-making, women's retreats. Rates are lowered in the off-season, and go to rock bottom during November and April work weekends, at which guests perform a morning's worth of chores; (800) 328-3325, (800) 362-5251, www.gunflint.com.

Just down the road, also on Gunflint Lake, Gunflint Pines has a nice lodge and A-frames; (800) 533-5814, www.gunflintpines.com. Heston's Lodge has woodsy lakeshore log cabins, some rustic; (800) 338-7230. Moosehorn Lodge, formerly Borderland, has cabins and B&B rooms; (888) 238-5975.

In the middle part of the trail, along the Banadad Trail, Boundary Country Trekking rents a cabin and yurts equipped with wood-fire stoves; (800)

A wooden mascot oversees the activity at Bearskin Lodge.

322-8327, www.boundarycountry.com. Old Northwoods Lodge, on Poplar Lake, has knotty-pine cabins with fireplaces; (800) 682-8264.

Accommodations (Summer Only). In addition to the resorts above, Clearwater Lodge is a 1926 classic halfway up the trail. The lodge is made of whole logs, and the cozy interior includes handmade furniture of diamond willow, with distinctive black cavities on the pale, polished wood. Upstairs, two B&B suites and three rooms with shared bath are lined with split pine; there's also a tepee and log cabins along Clearwater Lake, from which guests, outfitted by the lodge, can explore the Boundary Waters Canoe Area Wilderness; (800) 527-0554, www.canoe-bwca.com.

Dining. The Gunflint Lodge serves sophisticated North Woods cuisine in its popular restaurant overlooking Gunflint Lake; reservations advised. Bearskin serves delicious fixed-price four-course meals; reservations are required; (800) 328-3325.

But don't miss dinner at the Trail Center's Black Bear Bar & Restaurant. The outside, built for a 1930s logging camp, isn't much to look at, but the inside is adorned with a hodgepodge of old tin signs, moose racks, loggers' saws, wooden wheels, and snowshoes. What's more, the food is very good—try the Jack Daniels porterhouse—and it's served in a hearty atmosphere that transcends the usual skier-snowmobiler divisions; (218) 388-2214.

Skiing. In the Central Gunflint, Bearskin and Golden Eagle share a 66-kilometer network of trails, 36 of them also groomed for skating, and three of them lighted. In Upper Gunflint, the Gunflint Lodge, Heston's, Gunflint Pines, and Moosehorn Lodge (formerly Borderland) share 90 kilometers, 24 of them groomed for skating and four lighted. The 29-kilometer Banadad Trail connects the central and upper systems and is used by Boundary Country Trekking and Old Northwoods Lodge.

Trails are groomed after Thanksgiving; call resorts for conditions. Rates are lowest early and late in the season. Pincushion, just up the ridge from Grand Marais, has 25 kilometers. "Guest of All" cards allow guests of any of these lodges to use the amenities of others and also a shuttle.

Excursions. Boundary Country Trekking organizes lodge-to-lodge skiing and hiking, dog-sledding trips, yurt-to-yurt skiing and canoeing, snowmobiling, snowshoeing, and mountain-biking trips; (800) 322-8327, www.boundarycountry.com.

Hiking. Two half-mile trails provide lovely views of this pristine wilderness. Thirteen miles from Grand Marais, the Northern Light Lake Trail climbs Blueberry Hill to its bald basalt pate and a panorama of the lake and Brule River stretching into the distance. Many varieties of lichen grow here, as well as blueberries. Sixteen miles farther, turn off on County Highway 66 and drive 2 miles, just past the Flour Lake Campground. From here, the Honeymoon Bluff Trail climbs wooden steps to an iron-streaked cliff high above the labyrinthine waters of Hungry Jack Lake and, beyond, West Bearskin Lake. It's especially lovely at sunset.

Background Reading. Read Justine Kerfoot's fascinating autobiography, *Woman of the Boundary Waters*. Kerfoot was a 20-year-old student at Northwestern University when her mother bought a summer fish camp on Gunflint Lake in 1927. The young Justine came to stay for good in 1930, when a bank crash ruined her father and forced the family to sell their houses in Illinois. She turned out to be a scrappy outdoorswoman and an ingenious improviser, with a reverence for the wilderness that inspired readers of her books and her columns in the *Cook County News-Herald* of Grand Marais.

More Information. (800) 338-6932, www.gunflint-trail.com.

13. Grand Portage: Crossroads for Half a Continent

Two centuries ago, the Grand Portage meant two things to a voyageur—the most riotous few days of the year, but also the most wretched.

Paddling their laden 36-foot Montreal canoes down the St. Lawrence River and through Lakes Ontario, Erie, and Huron, they finally crossed Lake Superior and reached a palisaded stockade on a protected bay.

This was the depot of the North West Company, where goods imported from around the world were exchanged for furs trapped by the Cree, Assiniboine, and Ojibwe who lived in the interior. When the *mangeurs du lard,* or pork eaters, arrived from the East in July to meet the *gens du nord,* or north-

The stockade at Grand Portage National Monument is a re-creation of one that stood on the site until 1803.

men, who had brought in furs from posts in the West, it was time for rendezvous.

This was the time for cutting loose, as the *bourgeois,* or boss, was busy trading. Spending their wages on rum and tobacco, they sang obscene ditties, danced, told tales, fought, and—boasting being a favorite pastime—competed to see who could paddle fastest, carry the heaviest pack, and throw a hatchet hardest.

But afterward came the dreaded *Kitchi Onigaming,* or Grand Portage. First marked by Indian travelers, this great carrying place was 8.5 miles of muck and mosquitoes around the lower 22 miles of the Pigeon River, a series of cataracts and unnavigable chasms. Beyond it was a virtually unbroken water highway into the vast northwestern interior, full of beaver, whose barbed fur could be made into felt for the top hats that were all the rage in Europe. But first came this bottleneck, and the trip wasn't pleasant.

When Pierre de la Verendrye, the European who pioneered the traders' route, arrived in 1731, his men "mutinied and loudly demanded that I should turn back." Starting from a bay six miles south of the Pigeon's mouth, the path heads uphill to the north and then west, meeting the Pigeon at what today is the Ontario border.

A voyageur walked the 8 miles—that's 2,720 rods, the unit used to measure portages—balancing two or even three 90-pound bales on his back, the lowest being held by a leather tumpline that passed across his forehead. When the trade goods were across, the northmen paddled them west, spending the winter in the interior, while the pork eaters, some as young as 14, returned to Montreal with the furs.

Between 1731 and 1803, this spot was the nerve center of the Great Lakes fur trade. It was an unparalleled juncture of cultures—the French Canadian voyageurs, British Canadian clerks and partners, and the Indians who made the whole thing possible, guiding the Europeans along water routes, showing them how to build lightweight canoes, feeding them, and collecting and cleaning the furs.

From 1784, it was the headquarters of the North West Company, which became the most profitable fur-trade operation on the Great Lakes. Within the palisade of cedar pickets—meant to protect the trade goods from unruly voyageurs and animals, not Indian attack—were 16 buildings, including an office, warehouses, and living quarters for partners and clerks. During rendezvous, the northmen lived outside in tents, the pork eaters under their canoes, and the Ojibwe in tepees.

In 1803, however, the Scottish partners, being on American territory and subject to American licensing and taxes, moved the post 42 miles north, to the mouth of the Kaministiquia River and a new water route. Grand Portage reverted to the Ojibwe, to whom it still belongs.

The stockade, however, has been re-created as the Grand Portage National Monument, where the colorful era is preserved in and around a painstakingly rebuilt Great Hall. Costumed interpreters lead walking tours to birch bark tepees and wigwams and to the canoe warehouse, which houses a 36-foot Montreal canoe, which could hold three and a half tons, and the smaller north canoe, which could be carried over portages and could hold one and a half tons. Demonstrators fire black-powder muskets and work on canoes of birch bark. In August, the monument and the Grand Portage Band of Lake Superior Chippewa hold one of the region's most authentic rendezvous, along with a tribal powwow.

The band's Grand Portage Lodge and Casino is just down the road, occupying a prime spot on the bay, also the jumping-off spot for ferries to Isle Royale National Park, 22 miles away. The waterfalls that were the bane of voyageurs are 6 miles farther up Highway 61, next to the U.S.-Ontario border checkpoint.

The 120-foot High Falls, on the Pigeon River in Grand Portage State Park, is Minnesota's tallest waterfall.

At Grand Portage State Park, managed in cooperation with the band, visitors get to see the Pigeon River's 120-foot High Falls, a torrent that cascades over a sheer basalt cliff. A half-mile trail leads to overlooks on High Falls, and the 3.5-mile Middle Falls Trail takes visitors farther up the gorge, over ridge tops, providing more views of the river and Lake Superior.

The Grand Portage itself, meanwhile, is still open to anyone who wants to hike it. The national monument staff puts a few wood planks over swampy spots, but aside from that, the trail is preserved just as it was, a gauntlet of mud and bugs. Hikers can go the whole 8.5 miles and camp overnight at the site of old Fort Charlotte, but most walk a mile or two and come back.

Trip Tips

Accommodations. Grand Portage Lodge and Casino is on the lakeshore and has pleasant standard rooms, $66.50–$76.50, and a pool and restaurant; (800) 232-1384, www.grandportagemn.com. Naniboujou Lodge, 21 miles south, has nice rooms, $70–$90; (218) 387-2688, www.naniboujou.com. Grand Marais, 36 miles south, has many types of lodgings, (888) 922-5000, www.grandmaraismn.com.

Grand Portage National Monument. The stockade is open from Mother's Day to Columbus Day; (218) 387-2788; ranger station, (218) 475-2202, www.nps.gov/grpo. The Grand Portage is open year-round; there are two large primitive campsites at the other end, on the site of old Fort Charlotte.

The birch bark wigwams at Grand Portage are replicas of those that housed the Ojibwe who once inhabited the area.

Grand Portage State Park. Open year-round for day use only. The half-mile trail to High Falls is handicapped-accessible. The 3-mile-long trail to Middle Falls has magnificent views from the ridge that splits the park; (218) 475-2360.

Grand Portage Rendezvous. Along with the Grand Portage Powwow, it's held the second weekend in August; (218) 387-2788.

Grand Portage Passage Sled Dog Race. The 100-mile, eight-dog race from Old Fort William to Grand Portage and the 330-mile, 12-dog race from Grand Portage up the Gunflint Trail, into the Canadian wilderness and back, is usually held the third weekend in January.

Cruises. Day long and overnight narrated cruises go through Wauswaugoning Bay and past the Susie Islands and the 400- or 500-year-old Little Spirit Cedar Tree, a twisted tree at the tip of Hat Point that is sacred to the Ojibwe. It's known as the Witch Tree to tourists, who came by the thousands to see it, treading on its roots and stripping its bark, until the band closed off access. Cost is $40, $30 for those 12 and under. Cruises are booked through the casino, (888) 746-2305.

Hiking. The 1-mile round-trip Mount Rose trail starts at the parking lot of Grand Portage National Monument. It's asphalt but very steep, and provides good views of the stockade and bay. The steep, 2-mile round-trip Mount Josephine trail provides an even wider panorama; it starts from a small parking area off County Highway 17, 1.5 mile east of the monument.

Background Reading. Carolyn Gilman's *The Grand Portage Story* (Minnesota Historical Society Press, $9.95) is a wonderfully readable history.

More Information. Tip of the Arrowhead Information Center, (800) 622-4014.

14. Isle Royale National Park: Communing with the Moose

Measuring 9 miles at its widest point and 45 miles long, Isle Royale belongs to Michigan, though it's much closer to Minnesota and closer still to Ontario. It's a seven-hour ferry ride from Grand Portage to Rock Harbor, on its northeastern end, and the season is short, which may explain why it's the least-visited national park.

Solitude, however, is what many of its visitors crave, and they can get it on 165 miles of hiking trails, the longest of which, the 42-mile Greenstone Trail, follows the island's central ridge. In the early or late season, hikers may be more likely to run into a moose than a person. The moose population fluctuates from 500 to 2,500, depending on the severity of the winters and the numbers of wolves, but generally is the densest in the Lower 48.

Within the park are 42 lakes, including Siskiwit, the biggest lake on the biggest island in the world's biggest lake. Nearly all of the park's 36 campgrounds occupy scenic spots on lakes, bays, or coves. Those who don't want to backpack can stay at Rock Harbor Lodge and explore the island through day hikes and by attending naturalist programs. Rangers lead walks and cruises to sites all over the island, including Suzy's Cave, the 1881 Passage Island Lighthouse, the 1855 Rock Harbor Lighthouse, the historic Edisen Fishery, the site of the *Monarch* wreck, and the old Minong Mine, one of the remnants of the island's copper-mining days.

Sport fishermen come for the pike, walleye, and brook trout on inland lakes and trout and salmon on Lake Superior. Commercial fishermen once had small settlements here, and the island was a stop for the steamers that serviced the North Shore. One of them, the *America,* sunk in 1928 in less than 100 feet of water after hitting a rock pinnacle just off Washington Harbor. Today, the wreck is a popular site for sport divers who can withstand the 40-degree waters of Superior.

Another wreck on the north coast of the island wasn't found until 1977. All 20 aboard the freighter *Kamloops* died when it sunk in 1927, during an early December snow squall. It's in 170 to 250 feet of water, and only experienced divers with advanced certification can explore the wreck, whose engine room contains the preserved remains of at least one seaman.

Trip Tips

Getting There. From Grand Portage, the *Wenonah* makes daily round trips, two and a half to three hours each way (plus the stop), to Windigo on Washington Harbor. Trips, $33 each way, run from early June to mid-September. The *Voyageur II* makes stops around the island; the one-way trip from Grand Portage to Rock Harbor takes about seven hours, $54, and runs from mid-May through late October. Reservations required; (888) 746-2305, www.grand-isle-royale.com.

When to Go. July and August are peak months. The park is open from mid-April through October, but spring and fall can be harsh. Black flies are worst in June.

Accommodations. Rock Harbor Lodge is run by National Park Concession; call (906) 337-4993; between October and April, (270) 773-2191. Rates in the lodge, including three meals, are about $228 for two persons sharing a room, including utilities and tax. The lodge is open from early June through the Friday after Labor Day. Housekeeping cottages, available from Memorial Day, are about $146 per night for two. Reserve several months in advance for peak season.

Camping. Permits for tent sites at 36 campgrounds and 88 screened, three-sided shelters can be obtained at the ranger stations on the island.

Fees. There's a daily user fee of $4 for everyone 12 and older.

Activities. Rangers lead hikes and give programs on natural and cultural history from the Rock Harbor and Windigo visitors centers, which are open from early June through Labor Day. Tours that include a boat trip charge a fee.

Background Reading. Nevada Barr's mystery novel *A Superior Death* draws heavily on her experiences as a National Park Service ranger on the island and includes fascinating details about sport diving. Jim DuFresne's *Isle Royale National Park: Foot Trails and Water Routes* ($12.95) and other guides, books, and videos can be purchased from the Isle Royale Natural History Association, (800) 678-6925, www.irnha.org.

More Information. (906) 482-0984, www.nps.gov/isro. The Web site at www.isle.royale.national-park.com is useful.

Lake Country North

15. Lake Resorts: Starting a Cherished Tradition

There's nothing more hallowed in Minnesota than a week at the lake. Lazy afternoons on the beach, boat rides, marshmallow roasts, catching a string of sunnies—these are memories children savor their entire lives.

But not every family has a cabin. So if you want that vacation at the lake, you'll have to choose among Minnesota's 1,300 resorts—a choice that can seem daunting. But if your idea of a classic Minnesota lake experience includes a resort with an indoor pool, meal plan, on-site golf course, and supervised children's program, you won't have too much trouble picking one, mainly because the state doesn't have many of these kinds of resorts.

The big, full-service ones include Arrowwood in Alexandria; Ruttger's Birchmont Lodge in Bemidji; Breezy Point in Pequot Lakes; Grand View, Cragun's, and Madden's near Brainerd; Ruttger's Bay Lake Lodge in Deerwood; Izatys on Mille Lacs; Fair Hills, in Detroit Lakes; Gunflint Lodge on the Gunflint Trail; and Ruttger's Sugar Lake Lodge in Grand Rapids. But weekly rates are high—$2,500 to $4,000 or more for a family of four.

There are also a few small, family-run but more luxurious resorts, where guests can expect newer accommodations as well as various amenities, such as a pool, tennis courts, and supervised children's activities. They include quiet Lost Lake Lodge in Nisswa, which specializes in gourmet food, and Driftwood in Pine River, which offers many family activities and a nine-hole golf course. At these resorts, a family of four can expect to pay about $2,300 a week in peak season.

A Place in the Woods in Bemidji has newer log cabins with fireplaces and whirlpools and an extensive naturalist program for children. Near Park Rapids, Brookside has a nine-hole golf course, a miniature golf course, and free waterskiing. Many other resorts around Park Rapids offer extra amenities.

But most of Minnesota's 1,300 resorts offer the traditional amenities— housekeeping cabins, a lodge, a sandy beach, a playground, and use of canoes and paddleboats. For many families, that's all that's required for a wonderful vacation. At these resorts, expect to pay $600 to $800 for a two-bedroom cabin, though the more modest resorts may charge as little as $400. Here are a few things to consider when choosing a resort.

Decide when you want to go. The weather is most reliable from late June to mid-August, which is peak season. Try to reserve by February or, if you know which cabin you want, a year in advance. If you want to book a cabin for earlier or later in the season, nearly every resort offers discounts. Most resorts offer Memorial Day and Labor Day weekend specials, and some offer 10 days for the price of seven the week before Labor Day.

Consider the kids. If you have a toddler, pick a resort with a big, sandy beach and a gradual drop-off into the water. Teens will want an area where they can congregate with other teens, a game room, or a pool. What grade-school children love most is the freedom of running around on their own, and they can do that best at a small, family-oriented resort. But first . . .

Be honest about what you want. If "vacation" means a vacation from child-raising, choose a larger resort that offers a supervised children's program. If vacation means no cooking, choose a resort with a restaurant or a meal plan.

Target one region. Each has the basics—lakes, golf courses, state parks. Beyond that, each caters to a different kind of vacationer, so this is the best way to narrow down a search. The Brainerd-Nisswa–Pequot Lakes area has a lively atmosphere and brand-name golf courses; this is where die-hard golfers want to go, and its resorts and shops are increasingly catering to an upscale, urban visitor. For children, there are go-cart courses, miniature golf, and an amusement park; families can shop in the busy little town of Nisswa and bicycle on the 100-mile Paul Bunyan State Trail, whose southern trailhead is in Baxter, next to Brainerd.

You might want to avoid this area if you hate personal watercraft, unless you're careful to find a quiet resort on a small lake. And if you like boating but in a less bustling area, head east, to the Whitefish Chain and Crosslake; (800) 450-2838, www.brainerd.com, www.nisswa.com, www.pequotlakes.com.

Farther north, Park Rapids is an old-fashioned resort town, near Itasca State Park and at the western trailhead of the 45-mile Heartland State Trail. It's got lots of shopping and has a nice variety of full-service family resorts of medium size; (800) 247-0054, www.parkrapids.com.

Walker is on the shores of Leech Lake, the state's third-largest lake. It's a fishing mecca that's becoming a bicycling hub, and the downtown is full of

At Minnesota resorts, activity revolves around the lake.

galleries and boutiques; (800) 833-1118, www.leech-lake.com and www.Great
TimesNorth.com. Grand Rapids is known for moderate-priced family
resorts and is the western trailhead for the paved Mesabi Trail. The town also
has a children's museum and the Judy Garland birthplace, and it's a good
place to find golf bargains; (800) 472-6366, www.grandmn.com.

Bemidji, farther north, has a nice mix of resorts, and the town is a fun
place to hang out—it's a college town with a professional summer theater
and old-fashioned amusement park next to the famous statues of Paul and
Babe, on Lake Bemidji; (800) 458-2223, www.visitbemidji.com.

Just south of the Canadian border, the Lake Kabetogama and Voyageurs
National Park area is a giant playground for people who *really* like lakes.
There are lots of motorboats, tour boats, houseboats, and canoes—and
plenty of room for everyone. Call (800) 524-9085, www.kabetogama.com;
Rainy Lake, (800) 325-5766; Crane Lake, (800) 362-7405, www.crane
lake.org; and Ash River, (800) 950-2061, www.ashriver.com. For more big
lakes, call (800) 535-4549 or check www.lakeofthewoods.com.

To the east, big Lake Vermilion is sometimes called the Lake Minnetonka
of the North, for its shoreline—1,200 miles of it—and many bays, but also
because it has heavy boat traffic and includes the estates of many wealthy
people. It also has 365 islands; (800) 648-5897, www.lakevermilion.com. or
www.lakevermilionresorts.com.

Ely is a playground for canoeists, being near the Boundary Waters Canoe Area Wilderness, and is the home of the International Wolf Center; (800) 777-7281, www.ely.org. To the east, the Gunflint Trail links the lakes of the BWCAW with the North Shore and has luxury and rustic resorts; (800) 338-6932, www.gunflint-trail.com. The area around Mille Lacs is traditionally a fishing haven, with many inexpensive, ma-and-pa resorts; (888) 350-2692, www.millelacs.com.

The 1902 Driftwood Resort, run by the same family since 1959, is one of Minnesota's last family-run, full-service resorts.

Alexandria is the Brainerd of western Minnesota; it's known for its golf, speedboats, and NASCAR races and has many modest resorts on outlying lakes; (800) 235-9441, www.alexandriamn.org. Just to the north is Otter Tail County, which has more lakes than any other county in Minnesota. Along with old-fashioned Detroit Lakes, it's known for small, traditional resorts and a rolling forest-meets-prairie terrain that lends itself to bird watching; (800) 423-4571, www.ottertailcountry.com, and (800) 542-3992, www.visit detroitlakes.com.

And closest to the Twin Cities is the lakes region around Spicer, on the shores of Green Lake, and New London, where the local waterski team puts on shows on Friday evenings in summer; (800) 845-8747, www.kandiyohi.com.

Collect information. Call for regional visitors' guides and start looking at ads and Web sites. Consult the staff at local tourism bureaus. Minnesota Office of Tourism counselors can also help; (651) 296-5029, (800) 657-3700,

Minnesota State Parks

Fees. Daily passes are $4 and are good for two days; annual passes are $20.

Events. Open house, first Sunday in June.

Campsite Reservations. They can be made 90 days in advance by calling the Connection, (800) 246-2267, (952) 922-9000. The reservation fee is $7 and sites cost $7–$14.50 per night. About 30 percent of sites are kept open on a first-come, first-served basis. For the best chances of getting a weekend site in a popular park without a reservation, arrive on Monday or Tuesday. Between November 1 and April 1, all sites are first-come, first-served.

Lodging Reservations. They can be made a year in advance. The guest houses are very popular: Bear Head Lake's has three bedrooms and sleeps 10, $90; St. Croix's has six bedrooms and sleeps 15, $140; Savanna Portage's has one bedroom and sleeps six, $70; Scenic's has four bedrooms and two baths and sleeps 10, $90; and Wild River's has two bedrooms and a wood-burning fireplace and sleeps eight, $75. St. Croix also has five cabins with half-baths that sleep two, $50, that are open from mid-May to mid-September.

Log cabins at Tettegouche rent for $60 to $90, and Itasca has lodge suites, cabins, and a clubhouse, renting for $50 to $350. Two tepees at Upper Sioux Agency rent for $20. Camper cabins are $30 with electricity and $27.50 without; none has running water. Heated cabins are available at Bear Head Lake, Jay Cooke, Lake Maria, Lake Shetek, Mille Lacs Kathio, Minneopa, Savanna Portage, and Wild River. Camper cabins at Banning, Crow Wing, Glendalough, Hayes Lake, Maplewood, Myre Big Island, Sakatah Lake, Whitewater, and William O'Brien are available between April and October. For group centers at Flandrau, Lake Carlos, Lake Shetek, St. Croix, Sibley, Whitewater, Itasca, and Myre-Big Island, call the individual parks.

Special Programs. The most popular events book up quickly. Contact individual parks or consult the Traveler, a seasonal guide that is mailed to annual-pass holders.

More Information. The Minnesota Office of Tourism, (651) 296-5029, (800) 657-3700, will send out park guides, as will the Department of Natural Resources (DNR) Information Center, (651) 296-6157 or (888) 646-6367 from outstate Minnesota, www.dnr.state.mn.us/parks.

www.exploreminnesota.com. The *Explore Minnesota Resorts Guide* is available from the Office of Tourism and is on-line at www.hospitalitymn.com. The Congress of Minnesota Resorts guide includes an easy-to-use table of amenities at its 200 member resorts; call (888) 761-4245, www.minnesota-resorts.com.

(One tip: The word *modern* usually means only that the cabin has up-to-date plumbing, heating, and appliances. The words *newly built* or *recently remodeled* are more specific.)

Ask questions. The personality of the owners dictates the atmosphere of the resort, so chat away. Ask if it's the kind of informal resort where children can run around, or if it caters more to couples who keep to themselves. Ask if there's much drinking, and if people on wave-runners like to buzz the beach. Ask if the beach is weedy. If you're at all unsure, ask for references. Also, describe what you're looking for, and ask whether the owners think you'd be comfortable at their resort. If a certain resort isn't for you, most owners will tell you so: They'd rather save the space for a guest who will be happy and return year after year.

16. Ely: Scenery That Makes 'em Swoon

There's something about the lakes around Ely that just screams "Minnesota." It's a starkness not found on lakes farther south, a stripped-down essence of the north. There's nothing but sky, pines, and lichen-covered rock sliding cleanly into water.

Once, there was more. But the last glaciers ground up the softer rock and carried it down to southern Minnesota and Iowa. They got the sweet corn. Ely got the scenery.

Today, firs and spruce cling to a few inches of soil atop the remaining out-croppings of greenstone and granite, among the hardest and oldest rock on Earth, forced through its crust as lava two billion years ago. Their boughs contrasting sharply with the blue of the sky and water, these trees fringe the shore and the islands that pop up by the thousand. It makes a pretty picture, one that has brought tourists here for decades. Now, beckoning from computer screens like a North Woods mirage, it brings visitors from every corner of the world.

Once, Ely was the mining capital of the Vermilion Range, with four iron-ore mines operating within city limits. The last mine closed in 1967, and only a few vestiges of those days can be seen—in the bars lining Sheridan Street, at the old Pioneer mine headframe on Shagawa Lake, in the clapboard Ely Speed Wash, where one washing machine is marked "Mining Cloths Only."

Those were the good old days to many in Ely, a time when a fisherman could motor into any of the lakes around Ely, no permit needed. Those days ended in 1978, when the 1.1 million-acre Boundary Waters Canoe Area Wilderness was created, condemning many small fishing camps and resorts and driving a wedge through Ely that still divides it.

Today, Ely is the springboard into a vast playground for nonmotorized sports—canoeing and hiking in summer, cross-country skiing and mushing in the winter. Its proximity to the BWCAW has exerted a magnetic pull on people all around the nation, drawing them to Ely to play—and often stay,

The Dorothy Molter Museum pays tribute to the ``Root Beer Lady,'' the last person allowed to live in the Boundary Waters.

earning livings by opening restaurants, bed & breakfasts, outfitters, and shops.

Thanks to them, tourists who are just passing through can live very well in Ely. They can walk through a gallery filled with images from the state's best-known photographer, who now lives in Ely, but grew up in the only county in Minnesota that doesn't have a natural lake. They can treat themselves to superb homemade ice cream at Sherry's, operated by Indiana entrepreneurs who spend the summers in Ely. They can stay at the Blue Heron B&B, whose proprietor forsook the Twin Cities for "a million-acre front yard." Her chef gave up a career as a TV producer to produce sushi and strawberry-chardonnay pie.

The main draw still is the pristine waters and forests. But the town of Ely, population 4,000, is a destination in itself. The International Wolf Center, opened in 1993, is a must-stop. Exhibits explore the symbolic power of the wolf on human folklore—from Little Red Riding Hood to the Three Little Pigs—and the social dynamics among wolves, once exterminated in every state except Minnesota and Alaska.

But the biggest draws are the five resident wolves, who live in a wooded enclosure next to the center but can be watched from a glass-walled viewing room. There's Lucas, who, as the alpha male, runs the show; MacKenzie, the alpha female; and Lakota, an omega female who is larger than MacKenzie but is picked on by both of her siblings. As naturalists point out, it's not size that matters, but attitude.

The three, born in captivity in South Dakota in 1993, were joined in 2000 by two pups, Malik and Shadow, who spent 12 hours a day with human nannies during the first three months of their lives, to get them used to life around people. And the people come by the thousands, to learn about wolves inside the center but also to take hikes into the woods, to see abandoned dens, learn how to howl, and find out how researchers track and study wolves.

Down the road, another museum sits in a grove of red pines. Its two cabins were dragged by dog sled from Knife Lake, near the Canadian border, after the 1986 death of Boundary Waters legend Dorothy Molter. A Chicago nurse who came to Ely in 1930, Molter was the last person allowed to live within the BWCAW, supporting herself by brewing root beer, which she gave to passing canoeists for donations. Today, the legend lives on at the museum in a video featuring the feisty outdoorswoman, "Dorothy Molter, Root Beer Lady." The bottles she used and reused now are collector's items.

And everyone ends up in downtown Ely. The corner of Central and Sheridan is home to a trinity that few visitors miss—the log Chocolate Moose, a culinary pioneer; Piragis Northwoods Company, a store and outfitter; and, across the street, the Brandenburg Gallery. Along with Arctic explorers Will Steger and Paul Schurke, photographer Jim Brandenburg is Ely's most famous citizen. A native of the southwestern Minnesota prairie, he's known for his work in exotic places for National Geographic. But it is Brandenburg's ability to capture the outrageous beauty of "ordinary" nature—the luminous peach underskin of birchbark, ravens in the snow, a field of gayfeather—that will really impress a visitor to his gallery.

Down Central, Northern Grounds Café sells lattes, panini, tempeh melts, and other cuisine not indigenous to Ely. Mealey's Gift and Sauna Shop carries handsome Mission-style furnishings and attracts shoppers with a cheerful perennial garden. The next few blocks of Sheridan Street are lined primarily with outfitters and apparel shops. This is the place to gird for cold weather—with laced moosehide boots from the elegant, high-ceilinged Steger Mukluks store, or a fleece anorak from Susan Schurke's Wintergreen Northwoods Apparel.

Both shops sell through catalogs, which help them survive the long, frigid Ely winters. Thanks to these winters, Ely never will become an overrun boutique town, like those in the Rockies; unfortunately, the winters make it hard for small, tourist-oriented businesses to stay afloat, especially when there's not enough snow to bring in the skiers, snowmobilers, and mushers.

The main street for the locals is a block away, paralleling Sheridan. Chapman is a shopping street, too, mostly for necessities—hardware, furniture, auto parts, pharmaceuticals, and comfort food, served at Britton's Café—but also includes little nooks that sell espresso, antiques, and books.

But on a beautiful day, few want to hang around town. Hiking trails surround Ely—Bass Lake, a 6-mile loop along the side of a lake that dropped 60 feet in 1925; Secret-Blackstone, where 5 miles of trail, often on greenstone, wind around three lakes; or, closer to civilization, the Trezona Trail, a 4-mile asphalt path around Miner's Lake, just north of downtown.

Those who want to camp in the Boundary Waters need to obtain a permit, often far in advance for peak times at popular entries. But permits for day use are easily obtained at any outfitter; one of the most popular day trips is to the Hegman Lake pictographs, red-ocher Indian paintings on a lakeside cliff not far from the Echo Trail.

Other non–BWCAW lakes, such as picturesque Burntside, have public boat launches or resorts that rent canoes from their marinas. The 1913 Burntside Lodge, whose burnt orange log cabins probably are the most photographed in Minnesota, is an easy jumping-off spot for canoe trips across the lake and up the Dead River, which is named for an Indian cemetery and nearby village and has two scenic campsites.

Another way to see this 12-mile-long lake and some of its 125 islands is via pontoon, on Emily Wahlberg's Burntside Heritage Tours. Wahlberg, a retired science teacher from Illinois whose grandparents lived in Ely, points out dozens of points of interest: the spirit houses on Indian Island; author Sigurd Olson's lichen-covered Listening Point; the worn-out boiler of the logging tug *Bull of the Woods;* the eagle's nest on Miller Island; and Polka Dot Island, star of the Hamm's "Land of Sky-Blue Waters" commercial.

She's a bottomless source of lore about Ely. But Wahlberg says what people most want to know is, "Do you know of any property for sale on this lake?" One glance at those shimmering waters, and they're smitten.

The late Charles Kuralt also fell in love with Ely, and in his book *America* named it one of his 12 favorite places. "Anyone who has known the deep woods and the blue lakes for a week or a season," he wrote, "puts himself to sleep ever afterwards with memories of Ely."

Trip Tips

When to Go. July and August are peak season for canoeing. January, February, and March are peak for winter sports, though snow can be unpredictable. Hiking is best in September and early October, after frost kills off bugs. June is peak season for blackflies.

Accommodations. Blue Heron B&B, 8 miles east of Ely on South Farm Lake, has it all. From its dock, guests can take the inn's canoes into the BWCAW and return for a sauna and one of the inn's fine dinners. Proprietor Jo Kovach knows all about the flora and fauna; her attractive rooms go for

At Silver Rapids Lodge, a point juts into White Iron Lake.

$115–$125, less for stays of more than one night; (218) 365-4720, www.blueheronbnb.com.

In town, the 1896 Trezona House has five attractive theme rooms that share three bathrooms, $85–$110. The Cabin and Angler's rooms are nicest, and there's a sauna in the basement; Ken and Tracy Simkins, (218) 365-4809, www.trezona.com.

There are many resorts around Ely, most of which offer daily rates. The oldest and best-known is Burntside Lodge, 5 miles west on Burntside Lake. Its lodge and most of its distinctive orange cabins, originally painted with a pigment derived from dried pine needles and now with custom-made paint, are on the National Register of Historic Places. There's a sauna and sand beach, and history and naturalist programs are offered. Cabins go for $115–$180 nightly and $805–$1,925 weekly; (218) 365-3894, www.burntside.com.

Silver Rapids Lodge is a nicely maintained resort with a restaurant right off Highway 16 as it crosses White Iron Lake, 6 miles east of Ely. Cabins are $569–$1,452 weekly during peak season. The eight-bedroom Retreat House, with two kitchens and sauna, sleeps up to 24 and costs $2,490. Open in winter; (800) 950-9425, www.silverrapidslodge.com.

Holiday Inn Sunspree is an attractive, newer inn north of downtown, on a ridge above Shagawa Lake. Rooms start at $119 in peak season; ask for specials; (800) 365-5070, www.elyholidayinn.com.

The 1917 Camp Van Vac, on a point in Burntside Lake, is very rustic but beloved by its guests. Cabins, some made of stone, start at $280 per week in summer and go up to $800 for a cabin large enough to sleep 10. There's a sauna; (218) 365-3782, in winter (218) 365-6064.

There are many motels along Sheridan Street. The newer Super 8 is very nice and includes a whirlpool and small breakfast, $80 for a standard room in peak season; (218) 365-2873. Older, motel-court lodgings with nice but basic rooms include the West Gate, $60, (800) 806-4979; and Paddle Inn, $58, (888) 270-2245.

Lake Vermilion, whose eastern shore is half an hour west of Ely, has many resorts; (800) 648-5897, www.lakevermilionresorts.com.

One of the best-known resorts is Ludlow's Island Resort, where all the cabins have fireplaces, (800) 537-5308, www.ludlowresort.com. Other resorts

Boundary Waters: Canoeists' Promised Land

Along Minnesota's northern border with Canada, more than 200,000 people a year find an increasingly rare commodity—absolute wilderness. The million-acre Boundary Waters Canoe Area Wilderness is not much changed since voyageurs used its chain of lakes and rivers to push deep into the continent's interior. Today, the foot trails over which they carried their canoes and 90-pound packs are used by modern-day canoeists, who wind their way from lake to lake in search of the perfect combination of woods, water, and solitude.

As they paddle along the glassy waters of more than 1,000 lakes, they keep their eyes peeled for moose, lynx, otters, owls, and even beaver, who have rebounded from near-extinction at the hands of trappers. In the evening, at nearly 2,200 campsites, they listen for the trill of loons and the howl of wolves, whose numbers also have rebounded.

It's the stuff of memories, to be fondly savored back in civilization.

Trip Tips

When to Go. Early June generally is the height of blackfly season, depending on how early spring arrives. Bring hats with netting, available at outfitters. July and August are peak season. May and September can be sunny and warm, or it can snow; anything is possible.

Who Can Go. Nine people and four watercraft are the maximum allowed per party.

Camping. It's allowed only at designated sites, which have fire grates and wilderness latrines and are first-come, first-served.

include Elbow Lake Lodge, (800) 441-1620, www.elbowlake.com; Pike Bay Lodge, on the former estate of a mining industrialist, (800) 474-5322, www.uslink.net/~pikebay; and Vermilion Dam Lodge, (800) 325-5780. www.vdl.com.

Dining. At the Blue Heron, chef Roy Misonznick presides over a dinner-party atmosphere, serving such dishes as wild mushroom ravioli with lobster and pecan-crusted walleye as well as inexpensive stir-fries and pastas. Open to the public Wednesdays–Sundays. Reservations required; (218) 365-4720.

The Chocolate Moose was an outpost of fine dining when it opened and still is a fine place to eat, with such dishes as sesame-glazed Atlantic salmon and grilled duck with blackberry coulis; (218) 365-6343.

Entry Points. There are 62 overnight-entry points from the perimeter of the BWCAW, including the North Shore, the Gunflint Trail, Ely, and the Lake Vermilion area.

Reservations. Reservation requests for entry on specific dates from specific access points are accepted beginning November 1 via mail, fax, or Internet and will be processed by lottery, regardless of when they are received, beginning January 15. Telephone reservations can be made starting February 1. Write BWCAW Reservation Center, P.O. Box 462, Ballston Spa, NY 12020; phone (877) 550-6777; fax (518) 884-9951; www.bwcaw.org. A $20 deposit is required.

Fees. The reservation fee is $12 for overnight trips or day-use motorized trips to designated lakes. The user fee is $10, $5 for children to age 17, per trip.

Permits. Permits can be picked up at 80 resorts, outfitters, YMCA camps, bait shops, and Forest Service offices, as specified by the person making the reservation. These stations also issue nonreserved permits, if available. Credit cards are required for balance due; only Forest Service offices can accept cash and checks.

Forms for self-issuing permits, for day use, or overnight trips between October 1 and April 30, can be picked up at main entry points, at outfitters, and Superior National Forest offices and by mail. Carry a copy during the trip.

Maps. A Fisher or McKenzie map, available at outfitters, is a wise investment.

More Information. For the complete rules and wilderness protocol, contact the Superior National Forest; (218) 626-4300, www.snf.toofarnorth.org.

Burntside Lodge's airy, bleached-pine dining room is lined with windows overlooking the lake. It's known for walleye, but also serves such dishes as jerk pork, duck papardelle, and steak salad; (218) 365-3894, www.burntside.com.

The screened-in porch of Minglewood Café on Sheridan Street is a fine place for pancake breakfasts and lunches of salads and sandwiches, including tasty gyros. Stony Ridge Resort, off Shagawa Road just above Semers Beach, is renowned for its 22 kinds of hamburgers. Closed Mondays.

Near the Kettle Falls dam, visitors can look southward into Canada.

Events. Blueberry Arts Festival, last full weekend in July. Harvest Moon Festival, weekend after Labor Day. Voyageur Winter Festival, first through second weekend of February.

Educational Weekends. Vermilion Community College offers weekend programs year-round on such topics as rock climbing, birding, sea kayaking, and winter sports such as dog-sledding. Cost of $365 (more for dogsledding) includes lodging, meals, and instruction; (800) 657-3609.

Tours. Emily Wahlberg's two-hour Historical Pontoon Boat Rides on Burntside Lake, $20, are an interesting window into Ely past and present. Call (218) 365-5445, www.cpinternet.com/~emilyw.

Voyageurs National Park: A Playground of Lakes

Just west of the Boundary Waters Canoe Area Wilderness, there's another labyrinth of waterways, much like the BWCAW, with one important difference: Motors are allowed here, and green and red buoys point the way to vacationers in launches, pontoons, and houseboats.

Established in 1975, Voyageurs is Minnesota's only national park. Its establishment caused some acrimony, mainly from resort owners, but nearly everyone agreed the historic wilderness should be preserved.

Two hundred years ago, it was traversed by convoys of short, tough men recruited from villages near Montreal. Each summer, they paddled canoes full of European trade goods into the Canadian interior, and in spring they paddled back to Grand Portage with beaver pelts, using the stars, the sun, and crude maps to find their way around hundreds of islands and channels.

Voyageurs National Park, which took their name, hasn't changed all that much since then. It's still wild, it's still big, and there are still many ways to get lost. Sitting on the northern border of the Land of 10,000 Lakes, Voyageurs is a giant playground for people who really like lakes. Curled around a 26-mile-long peninsula lie four big ones: 15-mile Kabetogama on the south, 17-mile Namakan and 7.5-mile Sand Point to the east and, on the northern border with Ontario, 60-mile-long Rainy Lake, rendezvous of the voyageurs and just about everyone else ever since.

It's not so pristine as the BWCAW, the better-known area to the east that requires entry permits, but canoeists can explore its nooks and crannies for weeks without a single portage. Hikers into the Kabetogama Peninsula, where the park provides free use of canoes and rowboats on six interior lakes, will encounter few people, if any.

But motors allow visitors to experience the sheer sweep of Voyageurs. On the *Sight-Sea-Er* pontoon boat, passengers pass a succession of islands, bays, and narrows that makes the park feel like an immense maze.

They'll also pass plenty of wildlife. On the 26-mile ride to Kettle Falls, they may see bald eagles, a loon performing a territorial dance on the water's surface, a whitetail deer peering from a cove, or pelicans on a rocky spit. Beavers have bounced back from near extinction and are often seen by canoeists. Two hundred black bears are in residence, along with moose, timberwolves, and the nation's largest population of river otter.

Of course, it's what's under the water—walleye, especially—that is the traditional draw. In the 1920s, thousands of 100-pound crates of fish were auctioned each week on the docks of the Kettle Falls Hotel, on a narrow channel of Rainy Lake that straddles the U.S.–Canada border. The hotel is on land that's a longtime crossroads: To the Ojibwe, it served as summer fishing grounds, and

(Continued)

International Wolf Center. Check in advance for the many on- and off-site programs, such as animal tracking, twilight hikes, howling trips, and two-hour Discovery Camps for children. The wolves' weekly feeding of roadkill deer, on Saturdays, is an on-site program. Register for programs by calling (218) 365-4695 (ext. 25, Monday—Friday, ext. 30, Saturday and Sunday). The regular schedule is also packed; check for guided exhibit tours, story time for kids, and free special programs, such as wolf bingo or talks on voyageur history. Open daily from May through October, Friday–Sunday from November through April. Admission is $5.50, $8 with on-site program and $11 with off-site program. Children 6–12 are half-price; (800) 359-9653, www.wolf.org.

Dorothy Molter Museum. Open weekends in May and daily from Memorial

(Continued)

to the voyageurs, who met wintering traders on Rainy Lake, it was the end of a 47-portage paddle from Lake Superior. In 1893, the discovery of gold on Rainy Lake brought an influx of fortune hunters.

After the hotel was built in 1913, it was a favorite meeting spot for loggers, commercial fishermen, and bootleggers. Now owned by the National Park Service, the white-frame hotel has been restored to look as it did in its heyday, complete with red-and-white striped awnings, a bearskin pelt on the lobby wall, and bar with a sloping funhouse floor and color prints of "the girls," gauzy nudes from the 1930s and 1940s. It's popular with boaters, who pull up for a meal or a drink on the old-fashioned screened veranda.

Life is quieter these days around Kettle Falls, as it is everywhere around the park. The swashbucklers are gone, and recreation rules. At three visitors centers and a campground, naturalists lead canoe trips and hikes and talk about nature; tour boats set out to visit historic sites and look for wildlife.

Amid the vast acreage, all the boats create barely a ripple. It's just what the park's founders had in mind.

Trip Tips

Accommodations. There are many resorts on Kabetogema, (800) 524-9085, www.kabetogama.com; Rainy Lake, (800) 325-5766, www.rainylake.org; Crane Lake, (800) 362-7405, www.cranelake.org; and Ash River, (800) 950-2061, www.ashriver.com.

The Kettle Falls Hotel has 12 nice rooms that share three baths, $45 per person, $15 children under 12, continental breakfast included. Villas, some with

Day through mid-September. Admission is $3, $1.50 children 6–12; (218) 365-4451, www.canoecountry.com/dorothy.

Ely-Winton History Museum. On the campus of Vermilion Community College, the center has exhibits on fur trading, logging, Native Americans, Will Steger's and Paul Schurke's North Pole expedition in 1986, and Schurke's Siberian expedition in 1989. Open daily Memorial Day to Labor Day. Admission is $2, $1 children 6–15; (218) 365-3226.

Vince Shute Wildlife Sanctuary. Volunteers and student interns from around the world usher visitors to the observation deck of this haven for bears, where naturalists explain the behavior of the beasts who come out of the woods to feast on apples, dates, dog food, sunflower seeds, and other

---

kitchenettes, are $140–$170 and sleep six. Suites sleep eight, $250; three-night minimum; (888) 534-6835, www.kettlefallshotel.com.

Camping. Designated campsites in the park are first-come, first-served, with no fee.

Boat Tours. From the Kabetogama Lake Visitor Center, the *Sight-Sea-Er* offers five-hour cruises to Kettle Falls Monday, Thursday, and Friday, $30, $20 children 2–15, and two-hour sunset wildlife cruises Sunday, Tuesday, and Wednesday, $12, $8 children. Reservations are a must, and other boat tours are available, (218) 875-2111 in the summer, (218) 286-5258 in the winter.

Houseboat Rentals. From May to October, Dougherty's Rainy Lake Houseboats, (800) 554-9188, www.rainylakehouseboats.com, and Northernaire Houseboats, (800) 854-7958, www.northernairehouseboats.com, rent boats out of Rainy Lake, and Ebel's Voyageur Houseboats rents out of Ash River, (888) 883-2357, www.ebels.com.

Naturalist Programs. From Woodenfrog Campground on Kabetogama, there are morning canoe trips, afternoon explorations for kids, and campfire talks. From Rainy Lake, there are voyageur canoe trips, explorations for kids, and beaver pond paddle-hikes. Check for times.

More Information. Voyageurs National Park, (218) 283-9821, www.nps.gov/voya. The book *Voyageurs National Park: Water Routes, Foot Paths & Ski Trails*, by Jim DuFresne ($9.95, Lake States Interpretive Association), is helpful, especially for planning camping trips.

In early evening, bears converge on the Vince Shute Wildlife Sanctuary for dinner.

treats. It's located 14 miles west of Orr, along Highway 23. Open from 5 P.M. to dusk Tuesdays–Saturdays. Pets and motorcycles are not allowed. Admission is free, but donations are appreciated. For more information, contact the Orr Information Center, (800) 357-9255, www.orrareavacations.com; or visit www.americanbear.com.

Canoeing and Kayaking. Outfitters offer all kinds of day-trip and overnight packages at varying rates. If you even think you might buy a boat, use of canoes or kayaks is free on Tuesday evening paddles with the friendly staff of Piragis; (218) 365-6745, www.piragis.com. Many resorts, including Burntside Lodge, rent canoes by the hour from their marinas.

Swimming. Sand beaches of any size are in short supply around Ely. The town itself has perhaps the best one: Semers Beach on Shagawa Lake, complete with lifeguard and playground. To get there, take Central 3 blocks north from Sheridan and turn left onto Shagawa Road (which may be unmarked).

Golf. The nine-hole Ely Golf Course is just up Central Avenue; (218) 365-5932.

Casino. Fortune Bay Resort and Casino on Lake Vermilion, run by the Bois Forte Band of Chippewa, has one of the state's more attractive gaming halls and hotels; (800) 555-1714, www.fortunebay.com.

More Information. Ely Chamber of Commerce, (800) 777-7281, www.ely.org.

17. Mille Lacs:
The Walleye Factory

For more than a thousand years, Lake Mille Lacs has provided unlimited bounty to those who come to its shores.

The first to arrive were the ancestors of today's band of Mdewakanton, the "people who live by the water of the Great Spirit." The waters they called Spirit Lake were renamed by French fur traders—*Mille Lacs,* or One Thousand Lakes, referring to the whole region. The French also mistranslated the Spirit Water that flowed from the lake, calling it the Rum River.

This Dakota band fished for walleye and pike, hunted in the rolling, wooded hills, and tapped maples for their sugar. There was wild rice in the marshes and smaller lakes; when the people learned to parch green rice for storage, around 800 A.D., they began to establish year-round villages. At the largest village of Izatys, explorer Daniel Greysolon, Sieur du Lhut, planted the French arms in 1679.

The Ojibwe arrived in the 1700s and, according to their oral tradition, forced the Dakota out of northern Minnesota in an epic 1745 battle. The Ojibwe spent the next two centuries trying to hang onto the land, as white loggers and settlers made their own claims.

Today, they share the shoreline with fishermen, who claim their own spiritual connection to this 20-by-4-mile lake, affectionately known as the walleye factory. In the spring and summer, armadas of small boats make the bays look like the beaches of Normandy. In the winter, more than five thousand icehouses pop up, forming a village known as Frostbite Flats.

Here, fishing is a way of life. The smells of gasoline, minnows, and frying oil perfume the one hundred miles of highway that hug a shore lined with giant fiberglass walleyes, boat launches, ma-and-pa resorts, and shacks advertising Bait-Gas-Grocery—the true essentials of life. Tiny Garrison is the nominal capital, with its motels, restaurants, and 15-foot walleye at water's edge.

Ojibwe land starts to the south, past Wigwam Bay. Into the 1950s, local Ojibwe stationed themselves along the road in summer, making a meager living by selling handmade baskets, blueberries, and souvenirs to tourists, displaying their wares on lines running between trees.

They're still making a living from tourists, but now their source of income is the blinking, neon-lit Grand Casino Mille Lacs, which lights the night sky from a hill above the highway. The casino, which includes a hotel and restaurants, has earned millions, which the band has plowed into tribal schools, clinics, and roads in the spirit of *shawanima,* the common good.

Children are fascinated by exhibits at the Mille Lacs Indian Museum.

Across the road, Ojibwe culture is splendidly preserved and displayed at the Mille Lacs Indian Museum, run by the Minnesota Historical Society in cooperation with the Mille Lacs Band. It tells the story of the band's legal struggles to stay on their land, which earned them the name "Non-Removables." Ojibwe artisans often work at the museum, demonstrating the arts of beading, sweetgrass basketry, or flute making. Videos show fancy dancers at powwows and wild ricers thwacking the grain into canoes. A computer that translates English words into the soft, cushioned syllables of Ojibwe is a huge draw for children, who watch, fascinated, as it turns "candy" into *ziinzibaake-wadooz(n)s* and "blueberry pie" into *miinan,* blueberries, and another 85 letters that explain how the pie is made.

But the Four Seasons room is the centerpiece. Life-size figures enact the seasonal cycle, tapping and stirring syrup over a fire in the spring sugaring camp, making nets of stinging nettles in the summer fishing wigwam, gathering and parching rice in the fall wild-rice camp, and carving pipes and mending inside the winter tepee, insulated with cattail mats and banked in snow and leaves.

Overhead, geese honk and owls call according to the season. Guides, some of whose relatives were the models for the figures, tell about Ojibwe innovations, from early wildlife conservation to the first disposable diapers, lined with dry moss and completely biodegradable.

The museum also includes exquisite examples of Ojibwe artistry—birchbark tobacco trays, basswood boxes, beaded bandolier bags—many from the collection of Harry and Jeannette Ayer, who ran a trading post on the reservation from 1918 to 1959. Next door, their restored 1925 Trading Post now is the museum gift shop, with contemporary craftwork for sale.

Three miles farther south on Highway 169, clusters of colorful tents at Mille Lacs–Kathio State Park echo the many wigwams that once stood here. The park—Kathio is a corrupted version of Izatys—straddles the Rum River as it begins its twisting run down to the Mississippi, and remnants of villages from 800 A.D. have been found along Ogechie, Shakopee, and Onamia lakes, through which it runs. On Ogechie, the park has re-created a palisaded village from traces found in one place, one of 19 prehistoric sites in the park.

Ojibwe or Chippewa?

Minnesota has two main tribes, the Dakota and Ojibwe. The Dakota were living in the forests of northern Minnesota when the Ojibwe arrived from the East, pushed out by the Iroquois. Annual buffalo hunts on the prairies south and west already were part of the Dakota lifestyle at the time, but the better-armed Ojibwe, in a series of battles, forced the Dakota into southern Minnesota for good by the middle of the eighteenth century.

Sometimes, tribal names cause confusion. The Ojibwe were called the Chippewa by French traders, and Chippewa still is used to describe formal and political institutions, especially by Wisconsin bands. The name Anishinabe, or "the original people," has more spiritual meaning and is what one Ojibwe calls another. The term Ojibwe is used most often when referring to tribal culture and tradition.

The term Dakota—also Lakota and Nakota, on the prairies farther west—is the tribe's own word for "allies." But historically, they have been known as the Sioux, which is derived from the Ojibwe word *nadowesioux,* or "little snakes." Although the name Sioux was meant to be derogatory, it has become associated with courage and bravery over the years, and many Dakota, especially elders, still bear it proudly.

Skiing at Mille Lacs–Kathio State Park is among the best in the state.

In 1680, Father Louis Hennepin spent six months here with the Dakota, who captured him and members of his expedition while they were camping on Lake Pepin. He spent the time taking notes for an adventure book, which became a best-seller in France.

Today, hikers and skiers flock to the state park, Minnesota's fourth-largest. It has 35 miles of hiking trails, but it really becomes a playground in winter, when skiers head out on 18 miles of tracked cross-country trails. Snowmobilers have 19 miles of groomed track, nearly all at a healthy remove from the ski trails. There's a popular sledding and tubing hill just outside the park trail center, where logs crackle merrily on a raised round hearth.

Its annual candlelight ski under a full moon, when volunteers set out more than 400 luminaries along 3.25 miles of trails, is one of the best-attended events in Minnesota parks. Hundreds of people show up to glide through bogs and glens, given a fairy-tale aura by the glowing bags.

The 11-mile paved Soo Line Trail connects Mille Lacs–Kathio to Father Hennepin State Park, just outside the town of Isle on the lake's southeast corner. It's a smaller park, but its shady lakefront campsites, within earshot of the lapping water, are highly prized. Boat access and a long swimming beach are just steps away.

The little town of Wahkon has blossomed along the Soo Line, with a log-look motel, restaurant, and seven shops. An old Soo Line depot houses Susi's

Nordic Station—"Gifts from the Lands of Long Winters"—and Evangeline's Depot Studio, where local weavers make and sell their rugs. Pepperberry's sells gifts, as well as ice cream to take down to the lakefront park. Isle is at the lake's southeast corner, where another fiberglass walleye proclaims "The Walleye Capital of the World." It's a claim that's not refuted around here.

Trip Tips

Accommodations. The glittery Grand Casino Mille Lacs is adjacent to the museum and has a full-service hotel, $35–$166; (800) 468-3517, www.grand casinosmn.com. There are many lakeside resorts. Two of the larger ones that cater to fishermen and snowmobilers are Eddy's Lake Mille Lacs Resort, a half-mile from Kathio, $69–$129; (800) 657-4704, www.eddysresort.com, and McQuoid's Inn east of Isle, with motel rooms, some with whirlpool, $50–$125, and cabins and condos, $115–$295; (800) 862-3535, www. mcquoids.com.

Izatys Golf and Yacht Club, on the south shore, is centered on two 18-hole golf courses and a full-service marina. Rates go from $80 for a lodge room in winter to $476 for a four-bedroom lakeside townhome on a summer weekend. Ask for package specials. There are indoor and outdoor pools and a supervised children's program; (800) 533-1728, www.izatys.com.

Northern Inn in Wahkon is a spiffy newer motel with a coffee bar, half a block from the Soo Line Trail and two blocks from the lake. Rooms are $49–$59; (320) 495-3332.

The best place for families on a budget is Camp Onomia, a retreat center with an indoor pool and two saunas that's 4 miles south of Mille Lacs–Kathio on County Highway 26. It caters to groups—it's in high demand for family reunions—but rooms, all with private bath, may be available to individual families on weekends. The rate for two nights and four meals is $67 adults, $50.25 children 12–16, $33.50 children 6–11, and $16.75 children 2–5. Bedding and towels are not provided but can rented; (320) 532-5251.

Dining. Woodlands Steakhouse at Grand Casino is a well-regarded restaurant. Headquarters Lodge, 1 mile south of Garrison, and the Blue Goose Inn in Garrison also are good places to eat. In Wahkon, the covered patio of Mugg's Main Street Saloon is a pleasant place to have a burger.

Nightlife. Grand Casino Mille Lacs frequently presents nationally known performers in concert.

Mille Lacs–Kathio State Park. The annual candlelight ski is held on the Saturday closest to the February full moon. Other naturalist programs include snowshoe hikes and archaeological walks. Skis and snowshoes can be rented. The park is a half mile off Highway 169 on Highway 26; (320) 532-3523.

Father Hennepin State Park. It's just west of Isle on the southeast corner of the lake and has a swimming beach, fishing pier, and lakefront campsites; (320) 676-8763.

Mille Lacs Indian Museum. It's 3 miles north of Mille Lacs–Kathio State Park on Highway 169. Demonstrations and classes are held on weekends. Open daily mid-April through Labor Day, Thursdays–Sundays in winter. Admission is $5, $3 for children ages 6–15; (320) 532-3632, www.mnhs.org.

Events. Walleye opener, second weekend in May. Onamia Days, early June. Wahkon Days, mid-August. Mille Lacs Band of Ojibwe Powwow, mid-August.

Bicycling. The paved, 11-mile Soo Line Trail cuts through countryside between the old depot behind Onamia's Main Street to the playing field in Isle. Six miles of county road connect Mille Lacs–Kathio State Park with Onamia and 1 mile connects Father Hennepin with Isle. The lake frontage road between Cove and Sha Bosh Kung Point also is good for bicycling.

More Information. (888) 350-2692, www.millelacs.com.

18. Brainerd Lakes: From Fishing Holes to Golf Holes

Brainerd, gateway to the first lakes region north of the Twin Cities, is the home of big. Big resorts on big lakes. Big-name golf courses with big greens fees. Big crowds for hot-rod racing. A big Paul Bunyan.

Once, the verdant shores of Gull Lake, as well as the other 464 lakes within 25 miles of Brainerd, were the hunting and fishing grounds of the Dakota and Ojibwe. The site of Brainerd was known only as the Crossings until the Northern Pacific came through in 1870. Soon, thousands of lumberjacks were milling in the streets between dozens of saloons, which also served workers at the railroad's big repair shops, at paper mills, and at the mines in the nearby Cuyuna Range, where iron ore was discovered in 1904.

Through it all, the vacationers came, especially after 1899, when the train reached Nisswa and resort guests could take steam-powered launches through a chain of lakes to Gull. In the 1920s, guests came in automobiles to the grand new resorts, such as Grand View Lodge, built on Gull in 1919, and Breezy Point, which was built in 1922 on Pelican Lake and had a casino gambling operation that drew movie stars and other celebrities.

Many of the more affluent resort guests later built their own cottages in the area. In the 1930s, Floyd B. Olson became the first of several Minnesota governors to build a home on Gull Lake, which became the most prestigious address in Minnesota after Lake Minnetonka.

While the area always has attracted a well-heeled clientele, it also drew everyone else. The common denominator was fishing, but there was recreation for the whole family: go-cart tracks, miniature-golf courses, and amusement parks, including the Paul Bunyan Amusement Center, founded in 1950 around a 26-foot seated Paul who winks and calls children by name. Farther up the highway, the Colonel's Brainerd International Raceway draws crowds of 26,000 to its grandstand for drag racing, motocross competitions, and muscle-car contests where "the bad boys of the blacktop battle it out."

But in the 1990s, another kind of visitor began to make an appearance. Grand View and other resorts began building top-quality golf courses, designed by the biggest names in the business. Today, there are more golf holes than fishing holes in the Brainerd lakes region, and it draws hard-core golfers from around the country to its courses, where greens fees can cost $100.

The kind of vacationer who can afford those prices also can afford a pretty nice cabin. Lakeshore property in the Brainerd area now is worth so much that the small, mom-and-pop resorts on the bigger lakes have disappeared, to be replaced by $2 million mansions. Lear jets make frequent appearances at the Brainerd airport, and limos mix with minivans on forested county roads.

The Brainerd lakes haven't been a true North Woods–type destination for a while. But there are still pockets of serenity—at the hundreds of smaller lakes scattered between Brainerd and Mille Lacs, in Pillsbury State Forest, and even along the Paul Bunyan State Trail, whose first 15 miles out of Brainerd traverse a maze of roads that link little mom-and-pop resorts that draw their guests back year after year.

Nowadays, people with big money are making the waves. But the ordinary folk who have always come to Brainerd are still enjoying the water.

Trip Tips

Accommodations. Lodgings at the larger resorts generally include a mix of rooms, cottages, cabins, and townhomes, some on the lake, some on fairways. In addition to luxury accommodations, expect such amenities as indoor sports centers, indoor pools, elaborate children's programs, and a variety of restaurants.

At the three big Gull Lake resorts—Grand View, Madden's, and Cragun's—a family of four would pay $3,000–$4,000 a week during peak season, including two meals a day, supervised children's programs, and golf on social and executive courses. Rates drop significantly in the off-season, and always ask for packages.

Grand View Lodge, on the northern shore of Gull Lake, was built in 1919 and has lovely, old-fashioned grounds packed with every modern amenity. It's the hub of Brainerd-area golf, with 54 holes of its own, including the Pines, the Preserve, and the new Deacon's Lodge, designed by Arnold Palmer. Its indoor pool complex has a 110-foot slide; (800) 432-3788, www.grand viewlodge.com, www.thepines.com.

Madden's, on a peninsula in Gull Lake's south shore, is a longtime golf resort. It has 63 holes of golf on four courses, including The Classic, and offers the Chris Foley "For Women Only" Golf School throughout the summer. It also has a tennis and croquet club; (800) 642-5363, www.maddens.com.

Cragun's, on the southern tip of Gull Lake, is a sprawling resort with 45 holes of golf, including The Legacy, and a large indoor sport center. In the winter, it offers special theme weekends that include poolside buffets and

Built in 1919, Grand View Lodge helped introduce a look that became standard for North Woods resorts.

many activities for children with cabin fever; (800) 272-4867, www. craguns.com.

Quarterdeck Resort, on the west side of Gull Lake, is a mid-size resort with luxury units, the Boathouse restaurant and supervised children's activities in summer; (800) 950-5596, www.quarterdeckresort.com.

Kavanaugh's, on Sylvan Lake, just south of Gull Lake, has a variety of luxury accommodations and an indoor pool complex; (800) 562-7061, www.kavanaughs.com.

Breezy Point, on Big Pelican Lake, is a large resort with a variety of accommodations, including the historic Fawcett House, and two golf courses, Whitebirch and The Traditional. Built by magazine publisher Billy Fawcett, it became the benchmark of the good life on the lakes until the lodge burned in 1956. Today, it's a modern resort community, with some of its units time shares; (800) 432-3777, www.breezypointresort.com.

Ruttger's Bay Lake Lodge, a full-service resort east of Brainerd, is still run by members of the family that founded it in 1898. It's large, with villas, condos, and cottages on lake and fairways, but has a more traditional feel. It has a championship course, The Lakes, as well as Alec's Nine, and indoor and outdoor pools. In peak season, the American Plan includes two meals a day, golf on Alec's Nine, kids' camp, and such activities as pontoon cruises, wine tastings, and water skiing. There's an Oktoberfest the third weekend in October, with entertainment and an arts and crafts fair; (800) 450-4545, www.ruttgers.com.

Driftwood, on the southwestern shore of Upper Whitefish Lake, is a smaller, friendly, full-service, family-run resort with lots of do, including daily pony rides, paddleboats, tennis, children's activities, museum, evening entertainment, and golfing on its own nine-hole Norske Course, all included in the rates. There's an outdoor swimming pool and flowers everywhere. In peak season, rates include fine meals in the Norwegian-accented dining room; (800) 950-3540, www.driftwoodresort.com.

Boyd Lodge, on the southern shore of Whitefish Lake, is a family-run resort on property that includes two lakes, five miles of trails, and luxury lodgings; (800) 450-2693, www.boydlodge.com.

Manhattan Beach Lodge near Crosslake is a hotel with the homey touches of a B&B. The 12 attractive rooms, $69–$139, and six suites, $129–$199, with views of Big Trout Lake, are a good value; suites have gas fireplaces, fridges, and microwaves, and two have double whirlpools. It's a nice retreat in winter. Breakfast is included Mondays–Saturdays; (800) 399-4360, www.mblodge.com.

The AmericInn is a handsome new log hotel two miles north of Pequot Lakes, right on Highway 371 and the Paul Bunyan State Trail, with pool, hot tub, and sauna. Rooms and suites, some with whirlpool and fireplace, go for $80–$210; (888) 568-8400, www.upnorthlodge.com.

Dining. Iven's on the Bay, halfway between Nisswa and Brainerd on Highway 371 on North Long Lake, serves fine seafood and meat entrees and has a nice wine list; (218) 829-9872, www.brainerd.com/ivens.

Manhattan Beach Lodge, whose dining room has a view of Big Trout Lake, serves steaks, ribs, fish, and pasta prepared in fresh ways; (218) 692-3381.

Antlers, on County Highway 11 in Breezy Point, has attractive North Woods décor and overlooks the Whitebirch golf course at Breezy Point Resort. It does a nice job with a traditional menu of ribs, burgers, and pasta; (218) 562-7162.

Grand View's Sherwood Forest, in a historic lodge between the west shore of Gull and Margaret Lake, is an atmospheric place for dinner; (218) 963-0225. Sibley Station, on the Paul Bunyan Trail in Pequot Lakes, serves pizza, pasta, and daily specials. Closed Sundays; (218) 568-4177.

Black Bear Lodge & Saloon, a quarter mile north of the intersection of Highways 210 and 371 in Baxter, serves an American menu in a North Woods atmosphere; (218) 828-8400. Poncho & Lefty's, two blocks north of the intersection of Highways 210 and 371 in Baxter, is a pleasant place to have fajitas, quesadillas, and tacos; (218) 829-0489.

Nightlife. In summer, Chris Olson's outdoor Elvis concerts at Breezy Point are popular, (800) 432-3777; he also performs at the Exchange Nite Club in Crosslake, (218) 692-4866. His schedule is on www.espking.com.

Shopping. Nisswa, with dozens of small shops, is the browsing hub on overcast summer days. Pequot Lakes also has many small shops, as well as the large Silver Creek Traders, which sells classy gifts, furnishings, and gourmet foods (there are always plates of samples) as well as a coffee bar, where it sells cones, baked goods, and deli sandwiches. Kinzie Candles, on County Highway 11 on the edge of town, offers tours of its factory, (218) 568-8828.

Swimming. Gull Lake Recreation Area, run by the U.S. Army Corps of Engineers on the southeast end of the lake, has a sandy beach, $1 for those over 12; (218) 829-3334. Its campsites, $18, are also popular; reserve at (877) 444-6777. There's also a beach on the south shore of Pelican Lake, east of Nisswa off County Highway 118.

Cruises. The 65-foot *Knotty Bear* paddleboat offers narrated lunch and dinner cruises on weekends from its dock on the southeast end of Gull Lake, $20–$35; (218) 828-8444, www.knottybear.com.

Amusements. Paul Bunyan Amusement Center, at the corner of Highways 371 and 210 in Baxter, has a midway, bumper cars, miniature golf and, of course, Paul himself, www.paulbunyancenter.com. The Nisswa Family Fun Center, at the corner of 371 and 77, has a 400-foot water slide, hot tubs, and a pool; (218) 829-6342.

Auto Racing. Colonel's Brainerd International Raceway holds sanctioned races plus street-rod and muscle-car weekend events. Camping is available on 525 acres; (218) 824-7220, www.brainerdrace.com.

Skiing. The Brainerd area has some of the best cross-country skiing in the state. Five miles east of town, French Rapids, (218) 568-5016, attracts advanced skiers with 26 kilometers of trails, 10 of them groomed for skating. The Brainerd Nordic Ski Club also maintains the 26 kilometers of easier trails at Northland Arboretum, with 12 of them groomed for skating and 6 that are lighted.

Cass County grooms more than 32 kilometers of trails along the south shore of Gull Lake, with access from Cragun's and Kavanaugh's, that run into Pillsbury State Forest. It also maintains two fine networks of trails through pine forest 11 miles west of Pine River, the 16.5 kilometers at Cut Lake and the challenging 20 at Spider Lake, (218) 947-3338. Maps can be downloaded from www.GreatTimesNorth.com.

Ski Gull on the west side of Gull Lake, has 8 downhill runs, 60 percent of them for beginners, and a vertical drop of 280 feet; (218) 963-4353.

More Information. (800) 450-2838, www.brainerd.com; www.GreatTimes North.com.

Historic Lodges: Minnesota's Golden Oldies

It didn't take long for tourists to discover Minnesota and its lakes. They came as soon as steamboats pushed up the Mississippi in the 1820s, and they followed the railroads into western Minnesota. When the loggers left northern Minnesota, they poured in to fish from denuded shores.

After World War I, they explored in their new automobiles, on newly built highways. The 1920s were the golden age of resorts, when the classic, leisurely "at the lake" vacation was born. During this era, log-cabin architecture became popular, and the look—massive beams, fieldstone fireplaces, boulder foundations—became synonymous with the North Woods.

Times have changed. But many of Minnesota's classic resorts are still around, giving tourists a chance to reconnect with a bygone era.

Naniboujou, 15 miles east of Grand Marais on the shore of Lake Superior, is one of a kind. Opened in 1929 as an exclusive private club—Babe Ruth and Jack Dempsey were among its charter members—it foundered after the stock market crash just a few months later. But it's still gorgeous, with its weathered cypress shakes and red and cream window frames. Inside, a fine restaurant occupies the Great Hall, brilliantly painted with geometric Cree designs. Quiet is the word here—there's a solarium for board games and reading, and phones and televisions are absent in the attractive rooms; (218) 387-2688, www.naniboujou.com.

Gunflint Lodge, on the Gunflint Trail at the edge of the Boundary Waters Canoe Area Wilderness, looks like a modern conference center, and it is. It's also legendary, thanks to the writings of scrappy outdoorswoman Justine Kerfoot, who came to help her mother run the resort in 1927; her son, Bruce, and his wife, Sue, run it now. The original lodge burned, but the 1953 replacement is a classic, with a stone fireplace and big windows overlooking Gunflint Lake, which straddles the U.S.-Canada border. Its restaurant is renowned, and the resort offers all the amenities. All cabins have fireplaces and saunas or hot tubs; (800) 328-3325, www.gunflint.com.

Clearwater Lodge, midway up the Gunflint Trail, was built of whole logs in 1926 by outdoorsman Charlie Boostrom, and his diamond-willow furniture still is used in the classic, homey lodge, which has a big stone fireplace and long porch. Log cabins line the shore of Clearwater Lake, from which guests, outfitted by the lodge, can explore the BWCAW; (800) 527-0554, www.canoebwca.com.

Burntside Lodge, started as a hunting camp after the turn of the century, became a resort in 1913, making it the oldest resort in the Ely area. The resort's log lodge and cabins are painted burnt orange, which provides a striking contrast with the bright blue of lovely, 12-mile-long Burntside Lake and the 125 pine-covered islands. Its charmingly old-fashioned restaurant is open to the public; (218) 365-3894, www.burntside.com.

Douglas Lodge, built in 1905, is saturated with the history of Itasca State Park, Minnesota's oldest and most-loved park. From its steps, guests can set off for nature hikes, boat trips, or bicycle treks through the state's largest stand of virgin white pine or to the headwaters of the Mississippi, at the other end of Lake Itasca. Its four rooms and three suites are quite attractive; the lodge includes a restaurant. They and other Itasca lodgings can be reserved through the Connection at (800) 246-2267.

Grand View Lodge was one of the first big log lodges when it was built in 1919. Its varnished log walls, stone hearth, and mounted stag heads are impressive, though the action today is on the golf courses and at the pool and water-slide complex, connected to the lodge by a cobblestone path lined by flower boxes and Arts-and-Crafts lampposts. The Nisswa resort offers every amenity and accommodations in 12 lodge rooms, 65 cottages and cabins, town-homes, and clubhouse suites around Gull Lake; (800) 432-3788, www.grand viewlodge.com.

Lutsen was the oldest family-run resort in the state until the Nelsons sold it in the 1980s; it began life as a North Shore hunting and fishing camp on land homesteaded by Swedish immigrant Charles Axel Nelson in 1885. Its 1952 timber lodge is cozy and inviting, with its big stone hearth, polished leather chairs, and picture windows overlooking the lake. There are 32 old-fashioned rooms upstairs, and cabins, villas, and condos nearby; (800) 258-8736, www.lutsenresort.com.

Ruttger's Bay Lake Lodge was founded as a fishing camp in 1898 by a young German man who had come to America to escape service in Bismarck's armies. Joe and Josie Ruttger's grandson Jack and his son Chris now run the full-service resort north of Mille Lacs, the state's oldest resort still operated by the same family. The original 1901 cottage has been absorbed into the main lodge, which includes the 1922 log dining room; a hallway gallery is lined with historic photos; (800) 450-4545, www.ruttgers.com.

Ruttger's Birchmont Lodge, spread along the west shore of Lake Bemidji, still has a feel of old-fashioned gentility. Its 1921 white-frame lodge holds the dining room and, with the beach and indoor pool complex, is the center of activity. The Ruttger family bought the 1915 resort in 1936; today, Randy and Tina Ruttger offer all the amenities; (888) 788-8437, www.ruttger.com.

Driftwood Resort, near Pine River, is an anomaly for the Brainerd area; it's full-service but medium-sized, and happy to stay that way. The Leagjeld family

(Continued)

(Continued)

has run the 1902 resort since 1959. Meals are in the gabled dining room; there's also a pool, a nine-hole golf course, and nightly entertainment. The Minnesota Resort Museum, a collection of artifacts from early resorts, is on the grounds; (800) 950-3540, www.driftwoodresort.com.

The Kettle Falls Hotel became the often-raucous social center for loggers, fishermen, and bootleggers after it was finished in 1913. Now part of Voyageurs National Park and owned by the National Park Service, the white-frame hotel has been restored to look as it did in its heyday. Lodgers stay in old-fashioned hotel rooms or newer villas; (888) 534-6835, www.kettlefallshotel.com.

Two other lodgings are among the state's most historic: The Fawcett House, built in 1925, was once the summer home of Minneapolis magazine publisher Billy Fawcett and housed the famous, including Clark Gable and Carole Lombard. The log mansion now is part of Breezy Point Resort near Pine River. The 10-bedroom, eight-bath mansion includes a spiral staircase, a loft, field-stone fireplace, and—some say—Fawcett's ghost; (800) 432-3777, www.breezy pointresort.com.

Peters Sunset Beach Resort, on the shore of Lake Minnewaska in Glenwood, was built in 1915 by former Soo Line conductor Henry Peters, who admired the lake from his train. Today, the Peters family still runs the resort, and activities revolve around golf; (800) 356-8654, www.petersresort.com.

19. Nisswa: Speeding Turtles and Power Shoppers

For many decades, the village of Nisswa has been Kid Heaven.

For children vacationing at nearby resorts, this three-block oasis in the woods was the place to go for glorious junk—slingshots, magic ink, rabbit's feet, arrowheads, exploding golf balls. Covered sidewalks connect the shops, each with something to catch a child's eye. Inside a glass case at the Totem Pole, the mechanical Mathondis, his long white beard curling out of a hooded black robe, leans over a glitter-encrusted light fixture and promises to predict the future for fifty cents.

Across the street, wooden barrels filled with candy stand in the window of the Nisswa Country Store, where signs advertise Ice Cream! Fudge! Children in the know head for Zaiser's, a few doors away, where an inner room is stocked with the cheesy souvenirs they like best.

On Wednesday afternoons, crowds materialize for the turtle races that have been held every year since 1966. It's a ritual that doesn't vary: Local turtle impresarios show up with boxes full of writhing reptiles, which the children study, trying to figure out which will be fastest. (Tip: Bigger is better; the bigger turtles have a longer stride.) Those who haven't brought their own turtles rent one, and everyone heads for the parking lot behind the Chamber of Commerce, on which big red circles are painted. At the beginning of the races, children kneel inside the inner circles, pounding the pavement and shouting their turtles on to victory. Winners receive $1, and winners of each heat compete for the grand prize—$5 and his or her name announced on the radio. Everyone else gets another chance in races for button-holders, out-of-staters, resort guests, and "mighty midget" turtles.

Excited children will always set the tone in Nisswa, which includes the surrounding 36 square miles. But its complexion has changed over the last decade, with the opening of top-flight golf courses nearby. Now, people who can afford to spend $500 for a day's lodging and golf at neighboring Grand View Lodge can come into town and easily spend that much at the fifty shops of Nisswa. There are even sophisticated shops for children. On a gray day, they love to spend time in Rainy Days Bookstore and, next door, at Golden Turtle Toys.

The Paul Bunyan State Trail, which cuts through town on a corridor once used by logging trains, is a beauty of a trail. From downtown Nisswa, it heads south into old-fashioned lake country, passing Lake Hubert, then Mollie and North Long lakes, and a line of little resorts around Merrifield. From there, the trail traverses a corridor of green, ending near Northland Arboretum and the Paul Bunyan Amusement Center.

On Wednesdays in the summer, tiny Nisswa is packed with turtle racers and spectators.

To the north, the trail follows the highway, separated by trees, seven miles north to Pequot Lakes, which has shops, cafés, and a nice trail center. Three miles north of Pequot, the trail opens to the highway, not to disappear until Backus. The seven miles from there to Hackensack, past meadows and wetlands, are the prettiest of the trail's southern half.

Today, with bicyclists and shoppers filling the boardwalks, Nisswa is a busier place than ever. But those who listen can still hear the trill of a loon, wafting over the crowds.

Trip Tips

Accommodations. The Nisswa Motel downtown has clean and pleasant rooms, $49–$99; (800) 254-7612.

Two small resorts are within walking distance of downtown Nisswa and along the Paul Bunyan Trail: Good Ol' Days, (218) 963-2478 or (800) 229-4501, and Eagle's Nest, (218) 963-2336. There are many other traditional resorts nearby.

Lost Lake Lodge, 10 minutes west of downtown Nisswa, is a small, quiet boutique resort on 80 acres between Lost Lake and the Upper Gull Lake Narrows. It's known for its fine food; breakfast and dinner are included in its rates, $2,500–$3,000 a week in peak season for a family of four. Supervised children's activities, naturalist programs, and daily maid service also are included; (800) 450-2681, www.lostlake.com.

Dining. The Nisswa Grille and Raw Bar serves soups, sandwiches, and espresso drinks, as well as oysters and shrimp upstairs.

Gantley's and the Country Cookin' Café are pleasant places for breakfast or lunch.

Lost Lake Lodge serves excellent prix-fixe dinners to the public, with such entrees as rosemary-garlic steak, mahi-mahi, and roast Cornish game hen, served with cornbread baguettes and cracked-wheat rolls made with flour from the resort's own grist mill. Reservations required, (800) 450-2681.

Events. Nisswa Flea Market, Saturdays from Memorial Day to Labor Day. Nisswa Naturally, third Saturday in June. Majestic Pine Arts Festival, fourth weekend in July. Crazy Days, second weekend of August. Fall Harvest Festival, fourth Saturday in September.

And, of course, there are the turtle races, held at 2 P.M. every Wednesday from the second week in June through the third week of August. Cost is $2, with a refund of $1 when turtles are returned.

Paul Bunyan State Trail. The trail starts in Brainerd (actually, Baxter) just east of the Paul Bunyan Amusement Center, off Highway 371 at Excelsior Road. The asphalt ends in Hackensack but eventually will stretch to Bemidji. The Web site is www.paulbunyantrail.com.

Bicycle Rentals. Bicycles and in-line skates can be rented in Nisswa at Martin's, $15 half day and $25 full day for both, (218) 963-2341, and bikes at Trailblazer Bikes, $15 half day, $25 full day, (218) 963-0699.

More Information. (800) 950-9610, www.nisswa.com.

20. Grand Rapids: Lumberjacks and Legends

It's warm and sunny in Grand Rapids, but at the nearby Forest History Center, it's a freezing day in December 1900. Miss Minnie the "cookee," or cook's assistant, shows wide-eyed visitors around the logging camp under the baleful glare of her boss, Miss Rebecca. They walk by a giant rut cutter, used to make grooves in the ice roads for the logging sleighs. They visit Miss Nettie in the clerk's cabin, where loggers buy socks and long johns: "They don't take them off all winter," she says. "If they go in the hospital with a serious injury, sometimes the nurses have to shave them off; the hair just grows right through them."

They visit Miss Rebecca, who hands out freshly baked sourdough biscuits. Miss Rebecca is a very important person here: "Men choose a camp based on the kind of cook it's got. If the cook's a belly robber, they won't stay very long." They visit the bunkhouse and Oscar the bull cook, whose job includes waking up the men.

"Daylight in the swamp!" he shouts, demonstrating, then breaks character: "It's been one hundred years since daylight came through those trees, and it's our job to cut them down. It's actually not a very good idea, but we think it is."

The Minnesota Historical Society's reconstructed camp is a remnant of the days when magnificent pines blanketed northern Minnesota. That is, until men with such names as Weyerhaeuser and Pillsbury put up 300-man camps like this one to clear-cut timber and, a year or two later, move on.

The second part of the story is told at the end of a forest path, on a channel of the Mississippi. There, it's May 1901, the second month of a log drive, and a bargelike shack called a wanigan has moored for the night. Inside, cooks provide for the 30 "river pigs" who dance with cleated boots on 130,000 floating logs, positioning them with pike poles or, failing that, dynamite.

Today, lumber—aspen, mostly—still rolls through this town of eight thousand, on flatbed trucks headed downtown to the Blandin Mill, Grand

Edge of the Wilderness National Scenic Byway

One of the most interesting and scenic drives in Minnesota starts at the foot of a paper mill, its flat roof studded by smokestacks unleashing plumes of white smoke into the air.

From Grand Rapids, the 47-mile Edge of the Wilderness National Scenic Byway winds northward past glittering, undeveloped lakes and pristine forests. In the fall, it's a favorite drive for its maples and aspen, which burst into color around the end of September. But this ribbon of asphalt, which locals called "Highway Loop-de-Loop," also is a slice of history. One of the first routes to be designated a national scenic byway, it's lined by interpretive displays that populate this wilderness with faces from the past.

The highway skirts Suomi Hills, a Chippewa National Forest recreation area known for its 21 miles of skiing and hiking trails. Named by its earliest settlers for their homeland, Finland, it became the site of a Civilian Conservation Corps work camp in 1933 and, a decade later, a prisoner of war camp.

The site is just south of the Laurentian Divide, a worn-away mountain range that now divides Minnesota's rivers between those that flow north and those that flow south. Four miles farther along, motorists are directed to a scenic overlook on North Star Lake, in which weathered timbers from an old rail trestle provide shelter for muskie.

This was, and still is, logging country, though the railroads are gone. Once, there were 40 of them, hauling logs out of the woods. Another stop is at the old Pine Station on the Minneapolis and Rainy River Railway, which the locals called the "Gut and Liver Line." Why? Perhaps because those were the only meats left aboard by the time it reached its northern terminus, or because every logging camp served liver sausage.

The highway's towns still are logging towns—Marcell, moved from Turtle Lake during 1911 and 1912; Bigfork, where a wood-carved "river pig" stands with hook in hand before City Hall; and Effie, where the forest thins and farming is possible, though hard. Effie's North Star Stampede became the biggest rodeo of its kind, and still takes place every July.

There are also chances to hike amid bogs and stands of cedar and anyone who brings a canoe can slide it into the water at one of the many landings. The pines may be gone, but the wilderness is back.

Trip Tips

Dining. There are several cafés along the route. Or stop a block from the starting point at Craiglow's Cake Kingdom and Bakery, where children will delight in a raised-doughnut "yummy worm" with jelly-bean eyes or a "hamburger" with a thick patty of chocolate frosting.

(Continued)

(Continued)

Events. North Star Stampede in Effie, last weekend in July. Fall Festival of Colors in Marcell, second weekend in September. Color Tour in Marcell, Bigfork, and Effie, fourth weekend in September.

Recreation. On a warm day, the city beach outside Bigfork would be a nice stop. There's a lifeguard and changing rooms.

Rapids' largest employer since 1902 and a pioneer of coated paper for magazines.

Grand Rapids is surrounded by lakes, as well as forests, and it's also part of the Iron Range. But its true lot in life, it seems, is to keep legends alive. Along with such larger-than-life lumberjacks as Gunnysack Pete and Tamarack Joe, a four-year-old named Frances Gumm left her mark on the town before her family moved to California in 1926.

Baby Gumm, who loved the spotlight so much her father had to carry her off the stage after her debut at age two, singing "Jingle Bells"—nine times, she recalled later, while her father hissed "Come on!" from backstage—became the famous Judy Garland. Of course, fame eventually ran away with her— "I've never looked through a keyhole without finding that someone was looking back," she once said.

In June, Grand Rapids becomes a shrine for fans from all over the nation, who flock to town for its annual Judy Garland Festival. The Wizard of Oz Munchkins, a loyal threesome who invariably remember her as "a terrific teenager," have faithfully appeared, and Mickey Rooney and Lorna Luft, Garland's daughter, have made appearances.

Three permanent sites allow fans to immerse themselves in Judy lore year-round. In the Old Central School downtown, above two floors of shops, the Itasca Heritage Center includes an exhibit on the star. It proves that Garland, who can hardly be expected to remember much about a town she left at age four, was at least a good sport: Three times, she posed for photos that showed her reading copies of home-state newspapers, and she was quoted in a 1960 interview saying, "I do know that is the only time I ever saw my mother and father happy, you know, in that wonderful town . . . for such a mixed-up life later, it started out beautifully."

The 1895 Central School, by a happy coincidence, is yellow brick, with brownstone accents. A newer yellow-brick path winds across the lawn, flanked by patches of cornstalks.

But ground zero for Judy fans is south of town, on Highway 169, where the star's 1892 white frame childhood home has come to rest on donated land. Next door, the Children's Discovery Museum is set to open in late 2001, with exhibits of memorabilia that include a silver Winkie sword, from the Wicked Witch of the West's fortress, and one of the bell-bottom coats from the Emerald City.

At the Judy Garland Birthplace, fans get to see where Judy and her sisters lived. None of the furniture is original, though the staff is careful to note that the pieces are authentic to the era—circa 1925—and arranged based on family photos and the recollections of family friends. Sheets of paper lie everywhere, explaining that here is the landing where Baby Frances and her sisters rehearsed, and here is where Esther Gumm would have sewed her daughters' costumes.

Other sheets fill in the gaps in the story of Baby Gumm: the darling toddler who loved going to the vaudeville theater her parents ran in Grand Rapids, who grew up to be Dorothy; the terrific teenager schooled on Hollywood backlots; then Judy, the sad star who married five times, became addicted to the benzedrine pills the studio provided to help her lose weight, and, at 47, died of an accidental overdose of sleeping pills.

It's an affecting display. As recordings fill the house with Garland's distinctive voice, full of that famous vulnerability, visitors read that the star's father died of spinal meningitis at age 49, a sister by her own hand at age 50, and her mother and other sister of heart attacks at ages 59 and 60.

It was an extraordinary life, led almost entirely on stage, full of hard work and triumph but also pathos and disappointment. No wonder her fans can't let her go. On one of the yellow rectangles stamped onto the nylon walkway outside, one fan has scrawled, "I came 1,500 miles by bus to show tribute to the greatest star of all time . . . Always loved, always remembered."

Trip Tips

Accommodations. Seagren's Pokegama Lodge B&B has a sandy beach on Pokegama Lake, 10 minutes south of downtown. Five comfortable lakefront rooms, one handicapped-accessible, share four bathrooms, boats, office, TV rooms, $63–$75; two cabins, $95–$125. Good swimming, pleasant proprietors Alan and Jean Seagren; (888) 326-9040, www.seagrens.com.

Ruttger's Sugar Lake Lodge, a newer full-service resort 15 minutes southwest of town, has attractive lakefront townhouses, lodge rooms, and cottages, $79–$415 in summer, and an 18-hole golf course, Sugarbrooke. The resort offers well-priced golf specials, some of which include play at the other golf courses nearby; (800) 450-4555, www.ruttgerssugarlake.com.

The information center in the old depot downtown has a photo album of area resorts.

The Country Inn & Suites is next to the Judy Garland Birthplace on Highway 169, (800) 456-4000 or (218) 327-4960. The Sawmill Inn is next to the Country Inn, (800) 804-8006, www.sawmillinn.com.

Dining. Otis's, at Ruttger's Sugar Lake Lodge, serves fine food with a flourish and a view of Sugar Lake; (800) 450-4555.

The Home Town Café, across from Central School, is a pleasant place for breakfast or lunch, while the Taste of Goodness, in a house overlooking McKinney Lake on Third Avenue (Highway 38), is a good spot to have a treat on the front-lawn picnic tables.

Events. The Judy Garland Festival is usually held the fourth weekend in June. Mississippi Melodie showboat performances, last three weekends in July. Tall Timber Days, first full weekend in August, with parade, Scheer's Lumberjack Show and arts and craft fair. White Oak Rendezvous, first weekend in August, with a reenactment of fur-trade days at a reconstructed 1798 North West Company fur post just outside nearby Deer River; (218) 246-9393.

Forest History Center. It holds special events on summer Saturdays—Children's Days and many programs on such topics as log-home building, Bunyan-style tall tales, weather lore, and orienteering—and ski events in winter, including candlelight skiing. Its Woodcraft Festival in mid-July is the year's biggest event; the Metalsmithing Festival is in early August. It's 2 miles southwest of town and open daily from June to mid-October. Admission is $5 adults, $3 children 6–12; (218) 327-4482, www.mnhs.org.

The barn boss picks up a water can from the cook at the Forest History Center's replica of a 1900s logging camp.

Judy Garland Birthplace. It's open daily from mid-May to mid-October. Admission is $3; (800) 664-5839, (218) 326-1900, www.judygarland museum.com.

Children's Discovery Museum. It's open year-round. Admission is $3; (800) 664-5839.

Itasca Heritage Center. Open daily in summer and Monday–Saturday in winter. Admission is $4 for adults, $2 for children; (218) 326-6431.

Bicycling. The Mesabi Trail starts at the fairgrounds, off Third Avenue north of downtown, and goes 13 miles east to Taconite; eventually, it will be 132 miles and go to Ely.

Golf. Four courses—Sugarbrooke, Eagle Ridge, Pokegama, and Wendigo— are touted as Grand Rapids' "Grand Slam"; www.grandslamgolf.com.

Casino. The new White Oak Casino, owned and operated by the Leech Lake Band of Ojibwe, is 15 miles west of Grand Rapids on Highway 2, (218) 246-9600.

More Information. (800) 472-6366, www.grandmn.com.

21. Bemidji: City of Behemoths

In Bemidji, three faces tell much of the town's story. One, Chief Bemidji stands facing the lake the Ojibwe called *Bemidgegumaug,* or "river flowing crosswise." His real name was Shay-Now-Ish-Kung, and he fed the white people who settled on the lake's shores in 1888. Their settlement became the first town on the Mississippi, which starts 35 miles south in Itasca State Park, winds north to Bemidji, flows through its lake, and turns south again.

A stern, square-shouldered Paul Bunyan stands a block away, at the edge of the old-fashioned amusement park. When he and his blue ox, Babe, were built for Bemidji's first Winter Carnival in 1937, the town's lumberjacks were still around, still telling stories of the logging camps that, not long before, had fed the area's magnificent white pines into the maw of the sawmill.

The concrete-and-plaster duo were an immediate sensation when they were built, sparking a mania for giant mascots that continues today. As a piece of Americana, they're irresistible. Over the generations, very few tourists have left Bemidji without a photo of Paul and Babe.

A third giant figure stands across Bemidji Avenue, next to Morell's Chippewa Trading Post. Known at the shop as "Injun Joe," he's naked from the waist up, has a single feather stuck in a headband, and raises a stiff arm in a "How" salute. With his presence, unwelcome to many in Bemidji, Injun Joe speaks volumes about the historically uneasy relationship between the town and the Ojibwe residents of the nearby White Earth Reservation.

For a town with a population of 11,500, Bemidji has many layers. One of the last towns in Minnesota to be settled, it retains a frontier feeling despite the presence of a university and the main campus of Concordia Language Villages, which pulls in students, counselors, and visitors from around the world.

It's still a logging town, and the home of hard-core fishermen and snow-mobilers, but it also has some of the best cross-country ski trails in the state. Lake Bemidji State Park is a center for silent sports, with naturalist programs, swimming at a long beach facing town, and the northern trailhead of the

Built in 1937, the plaster-and-concrete images of Paul Bunyan and his blue ox, Babe, became instant North Woods icons.

100-mile-long Paul Bunyan State Trail, popular with bicyclists.

In the summer, no matter what the activity, visitors fill their lungs with the bracing air beloved by generations of windswept North Dakotans and heat-fleeing Southerners. In the forests, there's a rich, woodsy tang born of balsam fir, pine resin, and moist earth; Thoreau called it "the moulding of odors of the soil."

During the long winters—average ice-out on Lake Bemidji is April 26— the snow-draped forests are threaded with trails. At Three Island County Park, skiers glide along 20 kilometers of trails, many of them alongside the rushing Turtle River. At Movil Maze, 11 kilometers take advanced skiers on a roller-coaster ride. There are gentler trails in Hobson Memorial Forest, through stands of red pine and along small lakes and bogs across from Concordia Language Villages.

At Lake Bemidji State Park, 17.5 kilometers of ski trails wind through forest and along a ridge above the beach; during two candlelight ski tours, the lights of the city, glittering from across the black lake, add to a magical atmosphere. And Buena Vista Ski Area has 25 kilometers of trails, on which the Finlandia Ski Marathon is held every February.

Buena Vista, which straddles the Laurentian Divide, is a friendly ski area run by a family that's been living next door for more than a century, since there was a logging boomtown of Buena Vista. Owner Earle Dickinson, clad

At Concordia Language Villages, the Waldsee campus welcomes students of German. Eleven other languages are taught.

in plaid flannel, greets skiers, and his sister, Muffy, often plays rollicking show tunes on the bright red piano next to the chalet's café, which serves home-baked desserts along with the usual burgers and chili.

Four chairlifts serve 15 trails, all starting at the top of the ridge that determines whether a raindrop flows to the Arctic or to the Gulf of Mexico. The view, obviously, is spectacular. And at the bottom of the hill is Earle Dickinson's pet project, a re-created logging town with a church, a schoolhouse, a lumberjack hall of fame, and a wanigan, a floating cook shack used during log drives. In February, Logging Days pay tribute to the area's logging history.

Bemidji's downtown is a modest collection of brick storefronts, with a few surprises. On Beltrami Avenue, a cream-and-peach building that looks as if it should be on the Italian Riviera houses Tutto Bene, whose ivy-shaded patio is northern Minnesota's best spot for dinner al fresco. Next door, the marquee of the renovated 1918 Chief theater blinks year-round, with concerts, dance, and community theater performances in winter and, in summer, the musicals, comedies, and farces of the professional Paul Bunyan Playhouse. The playhouse was started in 1951 by an impresario who brought in a troupe of New York actors for a season but went broke in a month.

It was long enough to hook Bemidji's citizens, who raised enough money to pay the actors' room and board while they performed the rest of the season's plays and to pay for their tickets home. Then, the town raised enough to pay for a season the next year, and the year after that. Now, the Paul Bunyan is Minnesota's oldest professional summer-stock company. Other plays and concerts are put on at the lakeside Bemidji State University, whose influences can be seen around town—at the body-piercing parlor, the whole-foods store, and at Cyber Bugs Paradise Café, an Internet-wired coffee shop where all the screensavers sport scenes of palm-shaded beaches.

At the southern edge of downtown, a renovated 1910 depot houses Union Station, an attractive wood-paneled restaurant, and the shops of Union Square. It was the first of a wave of renovations and openings in Bemidji, including the Headwaters Science Center, where children carry out their own experiments, and the Bemidji Community Art Center, in the old Carnegie library on the lake. The Prairie-style Headwaters School of Music and the Arts—whose motto is "Seek music, engage the arts, build community"— houses the Fly By Night Artspace, which shows and sells the work of local and regional artists, and hosts frequent concerts by local performers. Next door, the Uptown Caffe shows other works on its slick, contemporary walls.

But not everything in Bemidji is modern. The family-run Bemidji Woolen Mills has been going strong since 1920, still famous for its plaid Paul Bunyan jackets, ear-flap caps, and other warm items made in the back, where short tours are given on weekdays.

New is good. But there's no sense in throwing out the Babe with the bathwater.

Trip Tips

Accommodations. Ruttger's Birchmont Lodge, on the northwest corner of Lake Bemidji, has a feel of old-fashioned gentility. It's a full-service resort with a long beach, indoor pool complex, dining room, and supervised children's program in summer. Rates drop in the shoulder seasons, and it's a nice place for groups in the winter; (888) 788-8437, www.ruttger.com.

A Place in the Woods, 12 miles northeast of Bemidji on Turtle River Lake, includes attractive log cabins, built in 1991, with cathedral ceilings, decks, and woodstoves; some have Jacuzzis and fireplaces, and there's a common sauna and outdoor hot tub. Summer rates include supervised children's activities and range from $555 for three nights in a honeymoon cabin to $1,795 for a week in a four-bedroom deluxe cabin; (800) 676-4547, www.aplaceinthewoodsresort.com.

The Edgewater Inn has motel-court rooms on a sandy beach just south of downtown, with a spa. Rooms go for $51–$82, $149–$195 for suites; (800) 776-3343, www.visedgewaterinn.com. There are many other resorts in the area, and many franchise motels along Highway 2.

Dining. Tutto Bene, (218) 751-1100, serves fine, garlicky mostaccioli and other pastas, as well as steaks, shrimp, and such traditional Italian dishes as cacciatore and veal marsala. Union Station is a pleasant place to have dinner, and the Coachman Café, Raphael's Bakery, and the Keg 'n' Cork are decent lunch spots.

Events. Brrrmidji Polar Daze, third week of January.

Concordia Language Villages. The children's summer camp is open to kids as young as seven. First-time campers attend a one-week camp for the first year only, and subsequent sessions are two weeks, except for four-week credit courses for high schoolers. Cost is $470 for one week, $950 for two. For adults, one-week Spanish, Finnish, French, Norwegian, and German camps are offered. Cost of $460 (Finnish, $395) includes dormitory accommodations, instruction, materials, and three excellent daily meals in the cuisine of the country studied. For detailed information, call (800) 450-2214; www.concordialanguagevillages.org.

Paul Bunyan Playhouse. Call (218) 751-7270, www.paulbunyan.net/pbp.

Lake Bemidji State Park. A year-round naturalist organizes nature programs Wednesdays through Sundays in summer and on weekends in winter, including snowshoe hikes and candlelight skiing; (218) 755-3843.

Cross-Country Skiing. Pick up maps at the visitors center or any business.

Downhill Skiing. Lift tickets at Buena Vista, 15 miles north of downtown on County Highway 15, are $8–$24; (800) 777-7958, www.bvskiarea.com.

Sports Rentals. Bemidji State University (BSU) rents canoes, kayaks, sailboats, and bikes on the lake side of its football field, just south of Diamond Point Park at the end of Fifteenth Street; (218) 755-2999.

More Information. (800) 458-2223, www.bemidji.org.

22. The Iron Trail: Mining the Past

They would have preferred gold. But the iron made them rich, too.

In 1865, reports of gold brought a rush of prospectors to the shores of Lake Vermilion. What they found, instead, was red earth. Those who didn't go home disappointed stayed to develop one of the world's richest deposits of iron ore into an industry that would give rise to dozens of towns, help the nation win two world wars, and create a distinctive piece of Minnesota's cultural fabric.

The first mine was on the shores of Lake Vermilion, on the end of a body of ore that stretched from Tower to Ely. The Vermilion Range ore sat in layers, requiring extraction from deep underground shafts.

Just to the south, an even larger vein lay along a wooded ridge of hills, an exposed stretch of the Laurentian Divide that the Ojibwe thought of as the sleeping giant, or *Mesabi*. It ran nearly 120 miles, from Coleraine to Hoyt Lakes, and the soft ore was so shallow it could be dug from open pits. It produced up to a third of the world's iron ore before the high-grade ore began to run out in the 1950s, after which lower-grade ore began to be produced in the form of taconite pellets.

The thousands of unskilled jobs drew a wave of immigrants that included Finns, Slovenes, Italians, Swedes, Croatians, Poles, Germans, Serbs, and many other nationalities, who became incorporated into the lumpy melting pot on the Range. Vestiges are apparent today, in bakeries that sell the Slovenes' walnut potica, at halls where the Slavs' polkas are danced, and at government centers all over the Range, whose populist politics were profoundly influenced by the Finns, who included longtime U.S. Communist Party secretary Gus Hall, born Arvo Halberg in Cherry, a rural area between Hibbing and Virginia.

Once, nearly 400 ore pits operated on the Mesabi Range. The days when the whole Range hummed with industry and excitement are over, but mining still is its economic backbone, both past and present. Today, tourists can watch operating mines from the edge of giant pits, and see abandoned ones from close-up. Museums recall mining's heyday, and the Ironworld theme park in Chisholm pays fond tribute to its culture and history. In Hibbing, visitors see the skeleton of a town that got in the way of the shovels, as well as a palatial high school paid for by the mining companies and a famous bus company that began life as a mining shuttle.

But there is recreation, too—bicycling along the paved 132-mile Mesabi Trail, which links attractions and 22 towns between Grand Rapids and Ely, and golfing on one of the state's most scenic courses, at Giants Ridge in Biwabik, which is able to retain snow for Alpine skiing and cross-country racing longer than anywhere else in Minnesota.

Today, this stretch is known as the Iron Trail. One of the most interesting stops is at its western edge, virtually in the back yard of Calumet. This was the Hill Annex Mine, from which 63 million tons of ore were taken between 1913 and 1978 on land leased from the state, which now runs it as a state park.

Its centerpiece is an emerald green lake, surrounded by birch and jack pine and frequented by ospreys and loons. Once, it was an open pit, where the grinding of giant shovels filled the air and explosives shook the earth three times a day. Guides drive a little trolley bus around the rim of the lake and point out an old steam drill, blasting shacks, and a 1951 electric shovel. Gleaning usable ore left mountains of waste rock, created by running train cars full of waste onto a high scaffold and dumping. It was dirty work, and it was also dangerous, especially for the blasters and the truck drivers who spent their days at the edge of 500-foot precipices.

The gaping red craters and detritus of open-pit mining are everywhere along the Mesabi Range. Just up Highway 169, the towers and conveyor belts of National Steel Pellet Company loom over little Keewatin, giving it the air of a rust-tinted Emerald City. In 1919, when the mine got too close to Hibbing, the mining company moved the town.

Today, all that's left of the old town are a few lampposts and street signs in a grassy meadow at one edge of the vast Hull Rust Mahoning Mine, the world's largest open-pit ore mine. Crawling through the red dirt two miles away, giant dump trucks look like Matchbox toys. Retired employees man the observation center at pit's edge, talking about the Range's heyday, when mine companies made sure every church in town was freshly painted and that schools had nothing but the best.

Hibbing High School, built in 1920 for nearly $4 million, is palatial even today, with its marble, murals, and chandeliers; tours are given in the summer. A miner's shuttle made Greyhound Lines famous; a few blocks away, the Greyhound Bus Origin Center traces its evolution from its 1914 start in Hibbing.

Down Highway 169, Ironworld USA celebrates the people of the Range with living history, exhibits, and a summer-long series of ethnic festivals.

In Hibbing, the Greyhound Bus Origin Center traces the evolution of the bus line from its start as a miner's shuttle in 1914.

Electric trolleys skirt the rim of the Glen Mine on their way to the old Glen Depot, where costumed interpreters talk about life in 1915. Other interpreters demonstrate ethnic crafts and occupy a Sami camp, trapper's cabin, wigwam, and pioneer cabin, telling what life was like at each one. In the restaurant, visitors can sample the hearty Old World food that came over with the miners—sarma, pierogi, pasties, kielbasa.

In Virginia, the Mineview in the Sky gives visitors a look at the three-mile-long Rouchleau mines, which started shipping ore in 1893 and soon became one of the many Minnesota mines swept into the financial empires of John D. Rockefeller, Andrew Carnegie, and J. Pierpont Morgan. Today, volunteers staff the observation complex, talking about the pit in the distance, but mostly about the big yellow vehicle that looms over the parking lot, a Tonka truck on steroids called King of the Lode. It's 300,000 pounds and 44 feet long and was retired in 1998, worn out after 10 years of hard labor and too expensive to overhaul: Each tire costs $29,000, and a chain $60,000.

Another kind of mining was practiced on the Vermilion Range, where the rich ore is in hard vertical layers of hematite. The Soudan Mine was the first in the state when it began operating in 1884. It became an underground mine in the 1890s, with a shaft that eventually reached 2,400 feet, or seven football fields, into the earth.

Today, it's the Soudan Underground Mine State Park, and visitors can take a three-minute ride in an elevator cage to the bottom, where they get into electric trains and ride to a stope, part of a crossword-puzzle maze of excavations created when miners drilled and blasted into fingerlike veins. It's cold and dark, and miners suffered hearing loss from the noise, but this was considered "the Cadillac" of mines: Only 13 men died in 79 years.

There are still many tons of ore left, but excavation costs became prohibitive. The mine closed in 1963, only four years before the closing of the Pioneer Mine in Ely marked the end of mining on the Vermilion Range.

It was a hard life. But it was one that made the people of the Range proud.

In Virginia, a 20-foot fiberglass loon floats on Silver Lake.

Trip Tips

Accommodations. The new Lodge at Giants Ridge at the foot of the slopes has 93 suites, many with fireplaces and whirlpools, $79–$265. Giants Ridge also offers reasonably priced golf and ski packages at many nearby motels; (877) 442-6877, www.lodgeatgiantsridge.com.

The Villas at Giant Ridge are on Wynne Lake. Rates range from $75 for a studio in the off-season to $480 for a four-bedroom villa with sauna and hot tub during prime time; (800) 843-7434, www.thevillasatgiantsridge.com.

Bear Head Lake State Park, 18 miles east of Tower, has a three-bedroom guest house, $90, that comes with a boat or canoe. To reserve, call the Connection at (800) 246-2267. The park is at (218) 365-7229.

In Biwabik, the Dane Family Inn B&B, in a 1908 Victorian, has five rooms, two with shared bath, $65–$105; (888) 432-5915; www.danefamilyinn.com.

McNair's B&B in Side Lake, 20 miles north of Hibbing, is an attractive French Colonial frame house with two suites with fireplaces and a two-person whirlpool, $140–$150; Louise McNair, (218) 254-5878, www.bbonline.com/mn/mcnairs.

Dining. In Gilbert, the very popular Whistling Bird serves Caribbean specialties, pasta and steaks. Reservations highly advised, (218) 741-7544.

Events. Land of the Loon Arts & Crafts Festival in Virginia, third weekend in June; Field of Dreams Festival in Chisholm, second weekend of July; Mines & Pines Jubilee in Hibbing, second week of July; Calumet Miner's Day at Hill-Annex State Park, third Saturday in July; Merritt Days in Mountain Iron, first weekend of August; Weihnachtsfest in Biwabik, first Saturday in December.

Ironworld. It's open daily from early June to early September. Summer events include Blues on the Range and Polka Festival in June, Scandinavian Day, Festa Italiana, and Festival Finlandia in July, All-Slav Days in August, and the Button Box Festival in September. Admission is $8 adults, $6 children 7–17, $30 per family, more for some events. Weekends, when the most is going on, are the best time to visit; (800) 372-6437, www.ironworld.com.

Hill-Annex Mine State Park. Hour-and-a-half tours are given daily Memorial Day–Labor Day. Admission is $6 adults, $4 children 5–12; (218) 247-7215, www.dnr.state.mn.us/parks.

Soudan Underground Mine State Park. Tours are given daily Memorial Day through September. Bring a coat and wear sturdy shoes. Admission is $6 adults, $4 children 5–12. There are also 5 miles of hiking trails among open-pit mines; (218) 753-2245, www.dnr.state.mn.us/parks.

Hull Rust Mahoning Mine View. Open daily mid-May through September. Admission free.

Minnesota Museum of Mining. The Chisholm museum is open daily in summer; $3–$2. (218) 254-5543.

Bicycling. The 132-mile, paved Mesabi Trail will connect Grand Rapids and Ely when completed. The longest finished section is the 28-mile stretch between Nashwauk and Kinney, passing the Hull Rust mine and Ironworld. There's also an 11-mile section between Mountain Iron and Gilbert, past

Mineview in the Sky in Virginia, and a 13-mile stretch between Grand Rapids and Taconite. A Wheel Pass, $10 yearly, $5 weekly, can be bought from local businesses and visitor centers; (877) 637-2241, www.mesabitrail.com.

Golf. The course at Giants Ridge, deep in Superior National Forest, is considered one of the best and most scenic in the state; (800) 688-7669, www.giantsridge.com.

Skiing. Giants Ridge has 34 downhill runs and 70 kilometers of well-maintained cross-country trails groomed for striding and skating, including 3

Embarrass: Stronghold of the Finns

It took plenty of *sisu* to settle Embarrass.

It's the consistently coldest spot in the Lower 48; arctic blasts blow up against the Laurentian Divide and pool over the township, which set a record of –64 in 1996. The soil is poor, allowing farmers to do little more than grow potatoes and raise a few cows.

The very word *embarrass* is French for obstacle, and comes from French voyageurs' opinion of the local river: curvy as a corkscrew and usually too low to navigate.

The Germans left. The Irish left. But the Finns stayed. They had *sisu*— Finnish for stubbornness and a can-do spirit—in spades. When they arrived at the start of the twentieth century, many to work at nearby mines and logging camps, they had to settle for leftover land. But they knew how to get by and, especially, how to build.

Today, the buildings they raised out of tamarack, pine, and poplar have become enduring symbols of these tenacious early pioneers, many of whom were blackballed for union organizing at the mines and turned to their farms for subsistence. There, they built sturdy houses, barns, and saunas with the same skill and care they had used to hew the timbers that kept mines from collapsing.

Their dovetailed corners and double-notched joints, pointed out on daily tours, make architects swoon. Not long ago, volunteer firefighters, with the blessing of landowners, were torching Finnish buildings for practice. Now four structures are on the National Register of Historic Places, and they and other sites are visited by thousands every year.

Tours leave from the log Visitor Center, which, with the café across the highway, is as close as Embarrass gets to a downtown. Visitors follow guides to the

kilometers that are lighted; (800) 688-7669, www.giantsridge.com.

Near Tower, Bear Head Lake State Park has 15 kilometers of trails. For trail conditions, call (800) 777-8497.

Snowmobiling. The Taconite and Laurentian trails are part of a 2,000-mile network.

More Information. Iron Trail Convention and Visitors Bureau, (800) 777-8497, www.irontrail.org.

Hanka homestead, with a tamarack barn built in 1915, and to the silver-painted Nelimark sauna, made large to accommodate the family's 11 children. There's the 1906 Apostolic Lutheran Church, a craft co-op known as Sisu Tori, and the Timber Hall community center, a Taj Mahal of Lincoln Logs. The Seitaniemi Housebarn is the pièce de résistance; built between 1907 and 1913, combining a house, hay barn, and cattle barn under one three-peaked roof, it's the last of its kind still standing in the United States.

Trip Tips
Accommodations. Finnish Heritage Homestead is a restored 1901 farmhouse on picturesque grounds that include many wooden outbuildings, including a 1936 hipped-roof barn, a 1907 log barn, and a wood-fired sauna. Five attractive rooms, three that share a bath, go for $78.50–$105, including large breakfast. Buzz Schultz and Elaine Braginton; (800) 863-6545, www.bbonline.com. There are also ten campsites at Heritage Park on the Embarrass River, first-come, first-served.

Dining. The Four Corners Café, across from the Visitor Center, is open daily.

Events. Finnish-American Summer Festival, second Sunday of June; Embarrass Region Fair, last weekend of August.

Sisu Homestead Tours. Three-hour guided tours from the Visitor Center at Highway 135 and County Highway 21, 15 miles north of Biwabik, given 10 A.M. and 2 P.M. daily between Memorial Day and Labor Day, $5 adults, $2 children; (218) 984-2106 and (218) 984-2084.

More Information. Town clerk, (218) 984-2084, www.embarrass.org.

23. Park Rapids: First Stop for Vacationers

Ever since it was settled, Park Rapids has been a crossroads for tourists.

The trains that hauled out white pine at the turn of the century brought in summer guests, who were met at the depot by resort owners and taken to the lakes in wagons. When highways were built, Park Rapids became the gateway to Itasca State Park, 20 miles to the north. After the rail line was abandoned, it became the western trailhead of the Heartland State Trail, one of the nation's first paved bicycle trails. As birding became the nation's fastest-growing pastime, it became the eastern portal to Tamarac National Wildlife Refuge, where birds from the prairies mix with those from hardwood and pine forests.

But Park Rapids has always made its living from more than tourism, and it has an old-fashioned, small-town feel that's appealing. Cars park in the center of the wide downtown streets, in front of the confectionery, the movie theater, and the MinneSoda Fountain, a longtime teen hangout that seems frozen in time since the 1950s.

On summer Saturdays, tourists pour in on their way to the cabins, resorts, and campgrounds on the lakes that ring Park Rapids. Two of the largest are potato-shaped Fish Hook Lake and fish hook-shaped Potato Lake; thanks to a mapmaker's error, their names were switched. From Fish Hook Lake, the Fish Hook River flows through downtown Park Rapids, where a lacquer-red footbridge marks a path that leads into Heartland Park and the beginning of the 27-mile Heartland Trail.

The Heartland is one of the state's most interesting trails because of the towns it traverses. Each lays a claim to a record: Dorset claims to have the world's largest number of restaurants per capita, and Nevis the world's largest tiger muskie. Akeley is the home of Minnesota's largest Paul Bunyan, and Walker holds the world's largest eelpout festival.

The county roads that wind around the lakes north of Park Rapids also are a popular place to ride, and the town's Headwaters 100 Bike Ride and Race in September, which winds up to Itasca and back through Lake George,

Itasca State Park: Mecca on the Mississippi

Ever since the French paddled into Minnesota, explorers have tried to find the true source of the Mississippi River. In 1832, a Sault Ste. Marie Indian agent named Henry Schoolcraft became the first white man to find it, with the help of an Ojibwe named Ozawindib. Schoolcraft, who spoke Ojibwe and later chronicled Ojibwe culture around Lake Superior, named the lake Itasca, combining the Latin *verITAS CAput,* for true head.

It's a good thing someone told the tourists, because they come from all over the world to see the narrow point where the mighty Mississippi begins its 2,552-mile run to the Gulf of Mexico, becoming a flowing superhighway as countless rivers and streams add to its girth. In Itasca, however, it's a placid little stream, and tourists like to teeter across the string of boulders through which it flows, or even wade, so they can brag, "I walked across the Mississippi."

But Itasca has a bigger place in the hearts of Minnesotans. It was the first state park and is home to the largest remaining stand of old-growth white pines, which makes visitors feel reverential, especially when they're standing in the hushed Preachers Grove.

In 1891, a far-sighted surveyor named Jacob Brower used his own salary and hard-won legislative permission to start piecing together the park. Logging in the area didn't stop until 1919, but even so, a quarter of the old-growth pines that escaped loggers in northern Minnesota are on Itasca's 32,000 acres.

In the summer, Itasca is a hive of activity. It takes days to investigate everything: Twenty hiking and nature trails. Seventeen miles of paved biking trails. A sandy beach. A pioneer cemetery and ancient burial mounds. Narrated cruises on the *Chester Charles.* A natural history museum with a small amphitheater where naturalists put on daily programs in summer. And, for a view of a beautiful sunset, Peace Pipe Vista.

The Douglas Lodge, which sits above the East Arm of Lake Itasca, has served lodgers since 1905, when they arrived on foot or horseback. It's a privilege to stay in a well-appointed suite in the middle of Minnesota's favorite park, so a reservation there is a real plum. Campsites, too, are highly prized.

Itasca is even more beautiful in the winter, when 275-year-old red pines and old cedars stand out against a stark white backdrop. Thirty miles of cross-country ski trails, groomed weekly, sweep past dozens of smaller lakes and along Lake Itasca to the headwaters. Skiers may see porcupines, fishers, whisky jacks or, if they're very lucky, a moose or a glimpse of the resident pack of wolves.

The 1.8-kilometer Schoolcraft Trail, near the headwaters, and the 3.5-kilometer Dr. Roberts Trail, near the Forest Inn, are groomed for snowshoes, which can be rented at the Forest Inn. A 31-mile snowmobile trail winds along the park's periphery, with a parking lot on the lake near park headquarters. Free

(Continued)

(Continued)

programs, such as snowshoe hikes, are held most winter weekends. With reservations, use of snowshoes is free.

Winter visitors can also stay right in the middle of the park, at the handsome Mississippi Headwaters Hostel. Part of the Hostelling International network, the 1923 former park headquarters was renovated and reopened in 1992 with six carpeted dorm-style rooms, three bathrooms, a gleaming kitchen, and a stone fireplace surrounded by sofas and upholstered chairs. Skiers and ski clubs book up weekends early, but weekdays are slow, and guests often can have a room to themselves.

Trip Tips

Accommodations. The three suites in Douglas Lodge have private baths, a double bed, and two single beds; $77. Four rooms share two baths; $50 double. Cabins, some with kitchens, are $77 to $138. The Club House, a 1910 log building with 10 bedrooms, six baths, and a fireplace, rents for $350. Reserve rooms and campsites as early as possible by calling the Connection, (952) 922-9000 or (800) 246-2267. Lodgings and food service operate from Memorial Day weekend through the first weekend in October.

Bert's Cabins is a private resort on Wilderness Drive, with outdoor swimming pool. One- to three-bedroom cabins are $56–$110, and five are winterized, four with fireplaces, $77–$110. Open January–February and May–October; (218) 266-3312.

The handsome Mississippi Headwaters Hostel, near the park headquarters, is open all year. Rooms hold four to six bunk beds each; guests share three bathrooms and have access to a kitchen and a living room. It's $15–$19 per person, $9 for children; bedding and towels are not included. Family rooms can be reserved; (218) 266-3415, www.himinnesota.org. For information on lodgings around Itasca, call the Itasca Area Lakes Association, (888) 292-7118, www.itascaarea.net.

Dining. The dining room at Douglas Lodge serves food that can be good, but eating three meals a day there would be expensive. The Brower Inn, near the beach, serves snack food, such as pizza, hot dogs, and popcorn.

More Information. (218) 266-2114, www.dnr.state.mn.us/parks.

Emmaville, Dorset, and Nevis, has become one of the state's most popular bicycle tours.

But in the summer, Park Rapids has the face of a classic resort town. On sunny days, the tourists stay near the water, at the area's exceptionally good

selection of family re-
sorts. When the skies are
overcast, they come into
town, to pet the animals
at Deer Town and ride
the go-carts and bumper
boats at World of Christ-
mas Evergreen Park and
Kartland.

The main magnet for
shoppers is Summerhill
Farm, started in 1981 on
a hillside five miles north
of town. Brick pathways
connect seven gift and
apparel shops and a
restaurant, housed in a
pretty collection of slate
blue farm buildings with
white trim. Strolling
around the pond and
browsing in the shops is a
pleasant way to spend
any afternoon, but power
shoppers come on Labor
Day weekend, when the
annual sale brings in so
many people the com-
plex has to hire traffic
directors. And those who
miss that can try to hit
the town's big craft fes-
tivals, held in July and
November.

**A string of boulders marks the point where the
Mississippi River flows out of Lake Itasca and begins
its journey to the Gulf of Mexico.**

Downtown, the traditional fudge shops and souvenir stores have been
augmented in recent years by hipper shops, such as Third Street Market, a
health-food store and café, and Emily's Harvest, a coffeehouse that provides
Internet access along with bagels and biscotti. In late July, it sponsors a street
dance, with bands performing folk, Celtic, country-western, and swing
music atop a flatbed truck.

These days, vacationers can check their e-mail over a jolt of espresso—
and be back on the lake by mid-morning. Park Rapids is a nice town—but
with so many gorgeous lakes nearby, there's not an hour to lose.

Trip Tips

Accommodations. The area is particularly rich in family resorts that offer amenities beyond the basics. Here are just a few.

On Long Lake, Timberlane Lodge has an indoor pool, sauna, whirlpool, tennis, and supervised playroom. It's open in winter, (800) 662-0262, www.timberlanelodge.com. Edgewood Lodge has a 1996 cabin that sleeps 23 and a 2001 cabin that sleeps 40, and it rents personal watercraft; (800) 593-4664, www.edgewood-resort.com.

On Potato Lake, Northern Pine Lodge has a sauna, waterskiing, tennis, and supervised children's activities, (218) 732-5103, www.northern pinelodge.com; and Papoose Bay Lodge has a reunion house that sleeps 16–30, (800) 535-8800.

On Two Inlets Lake, Brookside Resort has a nine-hole golf course, tennis, pool, sauna, waterskiing, and supervised children's activities; (800) 247-1615, www.brookside-resort.com; and White Pine Resort has newer cabins with fireplaces and whirlpools and a Hot Tub House, (218) 732-4973, www. whitepineresort.com.

On Bad Axe Lake, Isle O' Dreams has a swimming pool and waterskiing, (800) 700-3349, www.isleodreams.com.

On Fish Hook Lake, there's a nice B&B with a beach. The handsome stone-and-log Wildwood Lodge is 2 miles north of Park Rapids and includes the attractive Eagle's Nest, $150–$160, which is above the carriage house and has a deck and double whirlpool. Two other rooms, $115–$125, are off one of two beautifully decorated living areas shared with the owners. Phil and Liz Smith, (888) 995-6343, www.wildwoodbb.com.

Fourteen miles northwest of town, the Lady Slipper Inn has five attractive rooms, most with whirlpools and fireplaces, $85–$115, and a Friends room, $25. Dinners are $20 apiece; sleigh rides, $30 a couple. Pat and John Corbid, (800) 531-2787, www.ladyslipperinn.com.

There are other bed and breakfasts and many franchise motels in Park Rapids.

Dining. Gilbert's on Third Street East serves imaginative dishes, (218) 237-6190. The Third Street Market serves lunches of soups, sandwiches, and pies. The MinneSoda Fountain on Main Street is a wonderfully old-fashioned place for lunch or a treat.

Summerhill Farm. It's open daily from mid-May (the walleye opener) to the week after Labor Day. The year's biggest event is the Labor Day weekend sale; (218) 732-3865.

Golf. The 18-hole Blueberry Pines Golf Club is 8 miles south of town: (800) 652-4940.

Once a rail village, Dorset now is a stop on the Heartland State Trail.

Dorset: Oasis on a Bicycle Trail

Stuck out in the countryside, 6 miles from Park Rapids, Dorset should be a ghost town. Thanks to chimichangas and hyperbole, however, it's not. The one-block-long hamlet, 1.5 mile off Highway 34, is not on a lake. It has virtually no houses.

It does, however, know how to promote itself. In the 1920s, it tried "land of clover, the big white potato and the dairy cow." It tried boasting of "the shortest state highway in Minnesota running through its downtown," and, until 1986, was "the smallest town in the United States with a bank." But Dorset didn't hit its stride until the first Taste of Dorset festival in 1987, at which its restaurants—one for every four residents—supplied food. After that, it became "Restaurant Capital of the World" and "Boom Town with a Burp." Today, its restaurants keep people milling around town far into the night during summer.

Once, Dorset was a real town, a stop on the Great Northern Railway. But it had virtually disappeared by the time the 27-mile Heartland Trail opened on the old rail line. The Heartland, one of the nation's first paved recreational trails, brought tourists back to town. A gift shop and tearoom opened, then a

(Continued)

135

(Continued)

popular Mexican restaurant, a stained-glass studio, and a craft shop. A potter built a gallery, the schoolhouse became a B&B, and a bookstore and antiques shop opened.

But Dorset is most famous for its restaurants: During the day, the porch swing outside the Dorset House, built in 1894 as a general store, is usually occupied by a bicyclist eating an ice-cream cone, and at night, the restaurant puts on a buffet. The Dorset Café and La Pasta Italian Eatery have their fans, and at Companeros, the crowds keep waitresses in red peasant dresses rushing around the maze-like restaurant, which has had to be expanded five times.

The biggest day of the year is Taste of Dorset, held the first Sunday in August, when thousands of people fill the street to eat Mexican mudballs, barbecued ribs, calzone, and quesadillas. The ladies from the First English Lutheran Church sell pie, bands play, and there are wagon rides, minnow races, a bean toss, and a dunk tank. Visitors with political aspirations can pay $1 to enter the raffle that elects Dorset's mayor.

A block away, Dorset's 1920 white-frame schoolhouse now is the Heartland Trail B&B, where guests can literally go back to second grade—rooms are named for grades—and check breakfast times on the hallway blackboard. Breakfasts are large, calculated to get bicycling guests to the next town. That is, if they don't want to shop first.

Trip Tips

Accommodations. Heartland Trail B&B has six attractive rooms, with high ceilings and deck, $65–$80. John and Pat Corbid, (218) 732-3252, www.heartlandbb.com.

More Information. Park Rapids Chamber, (800) 247-0054, www.parkrapids.com

Events. Headwaters of the Mississippi Rodeo, Fourth of July weekend. Mid-Minnesota Arts and Crafts Celebration, third weekend in July and second weekend in November. Headwaters 100 Bike Ride/Race, last weekend in September.

More Information. (800) 247-0054, www.parkrapids.com.

24. Walker: Where the Muskies Are

Even before the lumbermen had finished divesting its shores of their magnificent pines, Leech Lake's reputation as a magnificent fishing hole had reached beyond the state's borders. Soon, the fishing tales were growing as tall as the trees—except they were mostly true. Leech Lake, with 640 miles of shoreline and bays filled with sandbars and weed beds, is a muskie factory, and the walleye, northern, and bass are pretty good-sized, too.

Though a resort owner was the founder of Walker, the town that grew up along the lake's southern shores, a lumber baron was the source of its name. The townspeople hoped T. B. Walker would build his sawmill there, but Mrs. Walker, shocked by the new town's many saloons, intervened. Faced with a

For anglers, shoppers, and bicyclists, all paths lead to Walker.

choice—jobs or whiskey—the town fathers kept their saloons but also Walker's name, since they'd already sent in the incorporation papers.

The mill was built in nearby Akeley, a dry village that didn't stay dry for long. Akeley boomed—Mrs. Walker having given up trying to separate lumberjacks from liquor—and the sawmill became one of the world's largest, spawning the first written Paul Bunyan tale and a fortune that was plowed into a famous Minneapolis art collection.

But the forsaken village did all right. Other sawmills were built there, and tourists arrived by rail, taking excursion steamers to Federal Dam, the Indian agency at Onigum and Ottertail Point for picnics. Hotels were built, along with hundreds of small resorts.

Today, fishermen are still pulling four- and five-foot muskies out of Leech,

In Hackensack, the 17-foot-tall Lucette Diana Kensack is billed as Paul Bunyan's sweetheart.

the state's third-largest lake, often assisted by the fishing guides who operate out of Walker and nearby resorts.

And in the winter, there are all the eelpout anyone wants to catch. That's a lot during the International Eelpout Festival, a goofy festival launched in 1979 to poke fun at the pout, a notoriously ugly roughfish that twists out of the depths to spawn in time for the February bacchanal. The eelpout is nothing to look at, with its squashed face and pudgy white belly, but it's actually pretty tasty, being the only freshwater member of the cod family. It's the fish's behavior that is revolting; when a fisherman pulls it out of the water, it tends to wrap its slimy, eel-like tail around his arm.

Still, the pout has been good to Walker, drawing ten thousand people not just to ice fish but to build a whole party town on the frozen lake, where they dance, play ice baseball, race snowmobiles and, of course, drink—though in recent years, the town has put a few brakes on *that*.

Fishing has been the county's bread and butter since the end of logging, along with snowmobiling in winter. Now, the county is increasingly catering to a different kind of outdoors people, the kind who like bicycling, hiking, cross-country skiing, and snowshoeing.

Walker is the seat of Cass County, which is the land of big lakes—Winnibigoshish, Cass, and Gull, in addition to Leech—and big woods. It includes most of Chippewa National Forest, a heavily wooded patchwork of lakes, streams, and bogs left by the advances and retreats of the last glaciers. It's the size of Delaware, with a northern boundary in Big Winnie and a southern panhandle that reaches the Crow Wing River near Brainerd.

The woods are creased by trails. A 68-mile section of the North Country National Scenic Trail, which eventually will stretch from North Dakota to

Paul Bunyan in Minnesota

The origins of Paul Bunyan are lost in the wood smoke of long-ago logging camps. The mighty lumberjack most likely was born in the camps of Maine or Nova Scotia. Nevertheless, northern Minnesota towns have taken the legend and run with it.

The little town of Akeley, 10 miles southwest of Walker, calls itself Paul Bunyan's birthplace, and it's got a good claim—it was the headquarters of the Red River Lumber Company, where, in 1914, a publicist named William Laughead is said to have written the first Paul Bunyan story in a company brochure. Today, Minnesota's largest Bunyan, a fiberglass 33-footer, kneels with outstretched hand outside the town's Paul Bunyan History Museum, where a 28-pound fish is labeled "Paul's Minnow."

But Bemidji was first to catch the world's attention. In 1937, the local Rotary Club built an 18-foot, plaid-shirted Bunyan and a blue Babe for the town's first Winter Carnival. Coverage in newspapers and national magazines brought crowds to Bemidji, and a family photo with Paul on Bemidji's lakefront still is de rigueur for tourists.

But in 1949, Brainerd built a 26-foot seated Bunyan and began a rivalry by laying claim to the legend. Its Bunyan lives at the Paul Bunyan Amusement Center, where he winks, calls children by name, and invites them to sit on his boot. The two Pauls now are linked by the 100-mile Paul Bunyan State Trail.

The oddest Paul lives at the midpoint of the trail, in Hackensack, about 10 miles south of Walker. He's a plaid-shirted midget Paul Jr., waving to gawkers next to his buxom 17-foot mother, Lucette Diana Kensack, who is billed as Paul Sr.'s sweetheart. And one town even lays claim to Paul's bones. In Paul Bunyan Park in Kelliher, a large mound is marked by a headstone that reads, "Here lies Paul, and that's all."

New York, goes through Chippewa National Forest south of town; 9 miles of it are used by runners in the North Country Marathon in September. There's mountain biking in Paul Bunyan State Forest, to the west. The cross-country skiing is superb, on the 12 kilometers at Shingobee Hills south of town and on many other trails nearby.

The town also became the number one bicycle junction in the state after plans were made to extend the 27-mile Heartland Trail another 18 miles to Cass Lake and the 50-mile Paul Bunyan Trail another 50 miles to Bemidji, crossing the Heartland in Walker. On Main Street, bicyclists find rows of shops that get more sophisticated every year. The candle-scented Northern Exposure gift shop set the tone for recreational shopping when it opened in 1993. Discerning shoppers also like to browse for Icelandic sweaters at Lundrigan's, crystal and linens at the Liten Hus, and pottery at Walker Art Gallery. Many smaller gift shops also vie for their attention, and Walker Bay Coffee Company is a good place to pick up a muffin or a sandwich.

On overcast days in summer, downtown streets are jammed with refugees from lake resorts and cabins, in for a day of shopping. Special events crowd the town, too: In addition to the Eelpout Festival, there's Moondance Jam, which draws up to 50,000 rock fans in July, and August's Cajunfest, a bonanza of bayou music and food.

Snowmobiling still is the top sport in winter. In summer, golfers flock to Tianna County Club, a hilly classic built in 1922, and to the new Longbow Golf Club, carved out of the woods north of town. Children like to spend a day at Moondance Ranch and Wildlife Park, where they can whoosh down the water slide, go on trail rides, and pet the deer and goats that walk around a hilly, wooded park. In fact, in Walker there's nearly anything anybody wants to do for fun.

Yes, Akeley got the sawmill and the state's biggest Paul Bunyan. But Walker got the tourists.

Trip Tips

Accommodations. There are dozens of resorts around Leech Lake, some catering to families and others to fishermen. If you don't want a resort that has a bar, be sure to ask.

An AmericInn is near the Heartland trailhead and walking distance to downtown, $72–$100 in peak season; (218) 547-2200, (800) 634-3444. A Country Inn & Suites is outside town, $69–$109 in peak season; (218) 547-1400, (800) 456-4000.

Peace Cliff B&B is a Tudor-style house overlooking the lake on a bluff east of town, five attractive rooms, $75–$125. Dave and Kathy Laursen, (218) 547-2832.

Dining. Giuliana's Italian Ristorante in downtown Walker is friendly, inexpensive, and serves good food. Café Zona Rosa has a big menu and an outdoor patio. The Outdoorsman Café is a venerable breakfast spot, and the Wharf is a comfortable place to have a burger.

Events. Moondance Jam, third weekend of July, www.moondancejam.com. Muskie/Northern Derby Days, last weekend of July. Cajunfest, second weekend of August, www.walkercajunfest.com. Leech Lake Regatta, third weekend of August. Ethnic Fest, second weekend of September. Walker/North Country Marathon, which includes a two-person relay option and a 10K, fourth weekend of September. Eelpout Festival, the closing weekend of walleye season, around mid-February. In Akeley, Paul Bunyan Days is held the fourth weekend in June.

Attractions. Moondance Ranch and Wildlife Park is 3 miles south of town, $6 with park and mini-golf, $11 with water slide, $15 with trail ride, $17 with ride and slide; (218) 547-1055, www.moondanceranch.com.

The Cass County Museum & Pioneer School House & Indian Art Museum, at the east edge of downtown, is open Monday–Saturday, $3; $6 per family. It's a good place to hear about the local Ojibwe—the land east of Walker, including Leech, Cass, and Winnibigoshish lakes all the way to Deer River, is the Leech Lake Reservation—and the 1898 Battle of Sugar Point, the United States' last armed conflict with Indians.

Bicycling. Back Street rents bikes from its shop near the trailhead, just west of the junction of Highways 34 and 371; (218) 547-2500, www.backstreet bike.com.

Fishing. Downtown, Reed's Sporting Goods is fishing central and lists guides, including those of the Leech Lake Guide Coalition, who charge $225 per day, boat and equipment included, (218) 547-3212.

Golf. Tianna Country Club is on Highway 34 just south of town, (218) 547-1712, www.tianna.com. Longbow Golf Club is six miles north on 371, (218) 547-6336.

Casinos. The Leech Lake Band of Ojibwe runs Northern Lights Casino on the east edge of town, (800) 252-7529, as well as The Palace Bingo and Casino, a larger complex with an attractive hotel, 25 miles north outside Cass Lake, (800) 228-6676.

More Information. Leech Lake Area Chamber of Commerce, (800) 833-1118, www.leech-lake.com. Cass County is a good source of information on events and trails, (218) 568-7302, www.GreatTimesNorth.com.

Lake Country West

25. Alexandria: Many Lakes and One Mysterious Stone

There are many colossal lumberjacks, voyageurs, and Indian chiefs scattered around Minnesota, all paying tribute to a colorful past. But there's only one Big Ole. He stands at the end of Alexandria's Broadway Street, 28 feet of glowering Viking, brandishing a spear and clutching a glistening silver shield that reads, "Alexandria, Birthplace of America."

The past he represents is so fantastical it's been debated for more than a century. Were Vikings roaming Minnesota 130 years before Columbus touched land? The claim is based on a 202-pound stone slab found 23 miles away in Kensington, wrestled from the roots of an aspen tree in 1898 by a barely literate Swedish farmer named Olof Ohman. Scratched into the stone were ancient runes that, depending on the translation, read, "8 Goths and 22 Northmen are on this acquisition business from Vinland, far to the west. We had an encampment by shelters one day's time north from this stone. We were fishing one day. After we came home I found 10 men red from blood and dead. Hail Mary deliver from evil." On the side was a date—1362—and hidden within the inscription were the words, "Eivar composed me."

Scholars of the time immediately debunked the stone, claiming that Ohman, who had six weeks of formal education, faked it. So the farmer took it home and, for six years, used it as a stepping-stone outside his granary. He certainly never profited from his find. His 16-year-old daughter fled home to escape the taunts; his son committed suicide.

But in 1907, a visiting amateur historian from Door County, Wisconsin, saw the stone, proclaimed it authentic and spent the rest of his life as its

Resplendent in mukluks and miniskirt, Big Ole defends Alexandria's claim to being the ``Birthplace of America.''

champion. Few in academic circles were won over, but thanks to Hjalmar Holand, the debate continues.

It's just as well, because Alexandria is heavily invested in the legend. Dozens of shops and businesses are named for the Vikings, and even the schools operate as the Runestone Area Education District. There's usually a tour bus idling outside the Runestone Museum, and children posing for pictures at Big Ole's mukluk-shod feet.

Alexandria's lakes, however, are the real draw. Two hug the city's downtown, and seven of Douglas County's largest lakes flank it on three sides. In fact, Douglas and adjoining Otter Tail County have Minnesota's densest concentration of lakes, thanks to vast chunks of ice that dropped off the last glacier and formed hundreds of lakes amid a rolling landscape of glacial gravel and sand.

They're deep, clean, and usually full of fish, though they're not wilderness lakes—the pinelands are northward, and prairie begins just to the west. Farms replaced the hardwood forests long ago, and in the outlying areas, grain elevators often occupy the same block as resorts. Alexandria's lakes are just over two hours from the Twin Cities via interstate, making them the closest for most city dwellers.

Tourists have reveled in these lakes since the late 1870s, when the railroads pushed through to the wheat fields of the Red River Valley. The Hotel Alexandria opened on Lake Geneva in 1883, one of the first resort hotels north of the Twin Cities. In the following decade, cottages were built by well-to-do outing clubs from Chicago, Minneapolis, St. Paul, Kansas City, and Monmouth, Illinois.

They sailed and fished, but golf fever took hold early; one of Alexandria's biggest events, the weeklong Resorters Golf Tournament, has been held since 1923. Theater-goers have had a venue on Lake Le Homme Dieu since 1961, when faculty from St. Cloud State University began staging a summer season of light musicals and comedies. Cast members, a mixture of professional actors from the city and college actors from a five-state region, stay in large cabins on the theater's lakeshore site and put on six plays in eight weeks.

At Viking Speedway on the county fairgrounds, NASCAR races draw crowds on weekends. Junior speed demons hop onto the "Naskarts" at Casey's Amusement Park, which also has bumper boats and miniature golf.

Life is quieter at Lake Carlos State Park, a 1,210-acre patch of nature that wraps around the deep lake's northern tip. Its sandy beach, rimmed by waving reeds, is one of the prettiest in the area, a fact not lost on the park's campers, who make Lake Carlos the state's third-busiest camping park, after Itasca and St. Croix. Hikers can walk along 13 miles of hiking trails through a glacial moraine of meadows, marshes, and forested ridges.

Not far from the western flank of Lake Carlos, the Carlos Creek Winery invites visitors into the cool of its tasting room and gift shop, where they can taste a crisp, summery Johannesburg Riesling and a full-bodied cabernet sauvignon as well as chardonnays, rosé, and merlot. Forty percent of the grapes are grown on the winery's acreage, which includes 7,000 apple trees that produce fruit for sparkling cider and apple wine.

Started in 1999 by former Arizona residents Deb and Bob Johnson, the vineyard and grounds are an oasis of order. Picnic tables sit in the shade of trees; those who bring a picnic can accompany it with a full glass of wine from the tasting room, a bargain at $3. And few visitors fail to visit the horse barn, the remarkably posh and immaculately clean home of the family's purebred Arabians, all of which can be petted.

It's fun to stop at the gift cottages that pop up along the roads that twist to and around Alexandria's lakes, but the best selection of shops are right downtown, behind the 1880s brick storefronts and pillared concrete bank buildings that housed the town's early businesses. One side of Broadway Street is antiques row, with Now & Then Antiques, Grandma's Treasures, Alexandria's Antiques, and Yesterday's providing as many rhinestone brooches, vintage birdhouses, and bedroom sets as anyone could want.

On the other side of the street, the Garden Gallery carries a classy selection of April Cornell dresses, hand-painted pillows, and cotton sweaters; the Scandinavian Gift Shop has a full complement of Finnish glass, Swedish linens, and Norwegian sweaters. And the Daily Grind is a real find—a cool, quiet haven where customers can sit in an upholstered wingback chair, sip a cappuccino, and gaze out the big picture window in front.

At the end of Broadway, tourists stream into the Runestone Museum. Inside, volunteers and a video fuel speculation that the Vikings *could* have made it to middle America. What about the blond hair and blue eyes early explorers found among the Mandan Indians in North Dakota, and the 1440 map of "Vinland" that showed a corner of northeast America? How about those medieval firesteels and axes also found in Minnesota? And didn't the Norwegian baron Magnus Erickson commission an expedition to Greenland from which nine men returned in 1364, two years after the runestone was supposed to have been written?

Perhaps the most compelling question is, if poor Olof Ohman faked it, why? And how? "Nobody could believe he'd do such a thing," intones the narrator of the video.

There's a replica of a Viking house at the museum, furnished with straw berths, a loom, and sheepskins. Elsewhere, there's a tepee and Indian gallery, a diorama full of wildlife, and a corner dedicated to golfer Tom Lehman, who grew up in Alexandria, which locals call Alec. Outside, there's Fort Alexandria, a village of pioneer buildings—a schoolhouse, a church, a general store, and a shed filled with vintage tractors, sleighs, and boats. In Alexandria, history covers many bases.

Trip Tips

Accommodations. Arrowwood is a large, country-club-style resort on the shores of Lake Darling with attractive units, $184 for a standard room in peak season and $299 for a one-bedroom suite with fireplace, kitchen, and whirlpool. There's an 18-hole course, stable, indoor tennis, marina, indoor and outdoor pools, and kids' crew for children 5–12. Rates go down in winter, when the resort offers guided snowmobile trail rides, sledding, horse-drawn sleigh rides, ice fishing, and cross-country skiing; (320) 762-1124, (800) 333-3333, www.Radisson.com/alexandriamn.

The area has many modest, family-run resorts; to choose one, look at the looseleaf preview book at the chamber of commerce, just inside the Runestone Museum.

Lake L'Homme Dieu B&B is a 1999 cedar and brick inn with four attractive rooms with whirlpool tubs and VCRs, $165–$195, and a four-season porch, outdoor hot tub, and living room with gas fireplace for guests. There's no beach, but guests can bring boats. Steve and Judy Radjenovich, (800) 943-5875.

In town, the 1900 Tudor-style Cedar Rose Inn has four rooms, two with double whirlpool and one with fireplace, $75–$130. Florian and Aggie Ledermann, (888) 203-5333, www.echopress.com/cedarose.

To reserve a campsite in Lake Carlos State Park, call the Connection, (952) 922-9000 or (800) 246-2267. The park is at (320) 852-7200.

Dining. Downtown, Old Broadway has a pleasant atmosphere and a traditional steaks-and-seafood menu that also includes pasta, fajitas, and stir-fries. The Depot Express, around the corner from Big Ole, has a long patio overlooking Lake Agnes and serves a large traditional menu. It's best known for pizza and ribs. For lunch, the Daily Grind serves soups, salads, and sandwiches.

Runestone Museum. Open Monday–Saturday; daily in summer. Admission is $4–$2; (320) 763-3160.

Events. Ole Oppe Fest, the third week of May; Art in the Park, fourth weekend in July; Annual Resorters Golf Tournament, first full week of August; Festival of the Lakes concerts, Wednesdays in August; Douglas County Fair, third week in August.

Theatre l'Homme Dieu. For tickets, call (320) 846-3150 during the season; otherwise, (320) 762-4660, www.alexweb.net/theatrelhommedieu.

Carlos Creek Winery. It's open year-round. Special events include the Grape Stomp and Fall Festival in mid-September; (320) 846-5443, www.carloscreek winery.com.

Lake Carlos State Park is a tranquil oasis just north of Alexandria.

Public Beaches. There's a swimming area on Lake Le Homme Dieu, on its isthmus with Lake Geneva, and a shadier beach on Lake Latoka, just south of County Highway 82.

Parks. Small children will enjoy Noonans Park, at Nokomis Street and 10th Avenue, with its goofy little fairy-tale fun house and a matching footbridge over a pond with fountains.

More Information. (800) 235-9441, www.alexandriamn.com.

26. Little Crow Lakes: Easy Life in the Sun

There's nothing complicated about summers on the lakes that line the meandering course of the Crow River.

On a lake in New London, sun-bleached water-skiers flip and build pyramids for Friday-night crowds. On the long, broad beach of Green Lake in Spicer, packs of tanned teenagers play volleyball and take turns diving off two rafts. Bicyclists pedal from Spicer on the paved Glacial Lakes State Trail, pausing for an ice-cream cone in New London before riding on to Sibley State Park, which has a pretty beach on Lake Andrew and an observation tower atop the county's highest point.

The Dakota held powwows atop Mount Tom. They, too, spent summers along the shores of Green Lake, which they called Mdeto and still is clear and full of fish. The summer tradition continued through early settlement. With railroad baron James J. Hill, town founder John Spicer made Green Lake a stop on the St. Cloud–to–Sioux Falls rail line in 1886; Spicer shipped out grain, and Hill shipped in tourists. But the shores of Green Lake, the biggest in Kandiyohi County, soon became residential, and even today, the town of Spicer seems half-missing—everyone lives around the lake, making the downtown only a few blocks long.

This is not a region of log cabins and pine trees—there are cornfields squeezed in between the lakes—and it is largely overlooked by people from the Twin Cities. Yet it's easy to have a light-hearted, sun-drenched weekend here and feel much farther from the city than two hours.

In New London, the shows of the Little Crow Water Ski Team seem a throwback to the 1950s, with blaring oldies music accompanying the performances by dozens of skiers in brightly colored costumes, pulled by three-engine muscle boats. The team, which won the National Show Ski Championships in 1994 and 1998, puts on quite a show for the crowd gathered in Neer Park, cruising by in 20-woman dance lines, performing double flips on six-foot-long jump skis, skiing barefoot at 45 miles per hour and building pyramids, which can go up to four tiers and 42 people but are impressive with much less.

Between tricks, the announcer and a few helpers fill in with gags about fictional townsfolk, such as "Ole," who may blow up a grill, and the "queen candidates," whose hairy legs show from under sequined party dresses. But it's all part of the show, and it takes little away from the sheer athleticism on display. Every year, several team members go on to paying jobs skiing for Disney World, Sea World, or Tommy Bartlett's in the Wisconsin Dells.

But in Neer Park, they go into the crowd after the show and shake hands. This old-style wholesomeness is reflected elsewhere—at the Green Lake Bible Camp, where the crowds who attend the annual quilt auction are entertained by gospel-singing teen counselors; at the Green Lake beach, where two rafts bounce up and down under a constant stream of youths; on the peaceful Glacial Lakes State Trail, where the most frequently spotted form of wildlife is the bunny.

There are many modest resorts in the area, but one of the best places for families to stay is Sibley State Park, which has a sandy beach lined by shaded picnic tables and flanked by a fishing pier. A little stone store sells water toys, ice-cream treats, and basic groceries to campers from the campground on a little ridge nearby.

And there's plenty for campers and other visitors to do. Most walk up to Mount Tom, which is the highest point in 50 miles and has a sweeping view of the hills and woods that Henry Sibley, Minnesota's first governor, once used as his hunting grounds. There are 18 miles of hiking trails, and tree-identification plaques line the paved trail. From the Interpretive Center, naturalists lead night hikes and talk about turkeys, owls, whitetail deer, and other denizens of the park.

One of Minnesota's most unusual places to stay is on wooded grounds above 600 feet of Green Lake shore. It's John Spicer's 1893 home, a traditional Queen Anne that became known as Spicer Castle after 1913, when Spicer's daughter Jessie returned from Europe and had it remodeled, turning its peaked tower into a crenellated turret. Today, it's a B&B run by Spicer's descendants, who keep its genteel atmosphere as close to the original as possible. The wood floors may be scuffed, and the carpets threadbare, but the lovely afternoon tea is served on china, with coffee poured from silver pots, and sun streams in from galleries lined with windows.

Rooms are named for the Spicer children and furnished with their possessions, such as Mason's cavalry saber and Agnes's paintings; Jessie's room includes the octagonal tower she turned into a turret. Eunice's room has 14 windows; John's cottage has 15.

The house's days-of-yore feel make it a perfect place to hold murder mysteries, which are conducted during and between the five courses of a lavish dinner. In summer, guests who don't want to dress up in flapper dresses or top hats for mysteries set in 1920s Chicago or 1930s England can have a simpler dinner aboard the Spicer Castle Belle, as it takes a two-and-a-half-hour cruise around Green Lake.

Another unusual building is just down Indian Beach Road, across the street from Green Lake Bible Camp. It's a stave chapel, patterned after the wooden churches of medieval Norway. Its cool, vaulted interior suggests the hull of a Viking ship; outside, waterfalls tumble over tiers of boulders surrounded by gardens.

On the Little Crow Lakes, a weekend can be a simple as a day in the sun, with a beachside dinner of grilled hamburgers. Or it can include a nostalgic trip to eras and places around the globe. It's your choice.

The Little Crow Water Ski Team entertains crowds in New London's Neer Park.

Trip Tips

Accommodations. Spicer Castle has eight rooms and two cottages, $80–$145, with private but cramped baths. Of two cabins, the most popular is John's Cottage, with fireplace and whirlpool; Eunice's Room, $120, has a swinging bed and double whirlpool. Murder mysteries with dinner, $55.50 à la carte, are held Fridays, plus Saturdays in fall and winter. Dinner cruises, $36, are given Thursdays and Saturdays in summer; (800) 821-6675, www.spicercastle.com.

Indian Beach Resort on Green Lake is a tidy family resort with a harbor, lodge, and 23 cottages. Split weeks are available, (320) 796-5616. The Northern Inn, right across Spicer's Lake Avenue from the southern beach on Green Lake, is an attractive newer hotel with a pool and continental breakfast, $80; (800) 941-0423, www.northerninn.com.

Camping. County Park 5 is a pleasant, full-service park on Green Lake with a store, boat rental, and 45 campsites, $11. Call (320) 796-5564.

Dining. Little Melvin's, next to Green Lake beach in Spicer, is a fun place to have a beer or dinner; (320) 796-2195. On Spicer's Lake Avenue, Annie's Downtown Diner serves good comfort food, O'Neil's Food and Spirits serves a full menu that includes prime rib and burgers, and the Green Lake Emporium serves a good cappuccino. In New London, Agape Coffee House is a nice place to have a granita or sandwich, and the Riverside Café and Ice Cream Shoppe is open for breakfast and lunch and has a pleasant deck. The New London Bakery, across the street, makes very good croissants and doughnuts.

Events. Fourth of July weekend in Spicer. New London Water Days, third weekend in July. Green Lake Bible Camp Quilt Auction, third weekend in July. New London to New Brighton Antique Car Run, third weekend in August.

Water-Ski Shows. The Little Crow Water Ski Team puts on shows every Friday evening in New London's Neer Park, June through Labor Day, except when it's on the road for tournaments. They also perform at festivals. Admission is $4.

Bicycling. Glacial Lakes State Trail is paved along the 12 miles between Willmar and New London, and another 6 miles of compacted granite continues to Hawick. The 5 miles along County Highway 148 from New London to Sibley State Park is a very scenic, little-used stretch with a wide bike lane. The state park has a shady, 5-mile paved bike trail along Lake Andrew, from the interpretive center to the beach and beyond. Bicycles can be rented at Spicer Bike & Sports, (320) 796-6334.

Sibley State Park. It's 4 miles west of New London and has a beach, trails, campsites, and daily nature programs in summer. Call (800) 246-2267 for campsite reservations; the park is at (320) 354-2055.

Swimming. County Park 4, on the southern shore of Green Lake, is large and festive. County Park 5, on the north shore, is more quiet and geared to campers.

Golf. The 27-hole Little Crow Country Club is on Highway 23, between New London and Spicer, (320) 354-2296.

Nightlife. Little Melvin's and O'Neil's offer music on summer weekends.

More Information. (800) 845-8747, www.kandiyohi.com.

27. Detroit Lakes: Last Stop before the Prairie

More than any other place in Minnesota, Detroit Lakes looks like a resort town—vintage 1950.

A city park wraps around the north shore, where a strait once separated Little Detroit Lake and Big Detroit Lake, and a mile-long beach winds down the west shore from the park. Along that idyllic little stretch are all the landmarks of beach life: a dance pavilion; a waterslide; ice-cream shops; a boat-rental hut; a Key West–style bar under a candy-striped tent; and several vintage resorts, including the tiny, red-and-white Fairyland Cottages.

Detroit Lakes's mile-long city beach is the place to be on a summer day.

On balmy summer evenings, as teenagers begin to cruise along West Lake Drive, it's easy to imagine this town of seven thousand as it was in the 1950s. But there was live music and dancing every night then, and people pouring in from small resorts on the hundreds of nearby lakes, the last before the North Dakota prairie.

Today, people come to Detroit Lakes for many reasons. Birders come because the town sits not only at the edge of the prairie but also at the edge of the northern pine forest and the eastern hardwood forest. In one day at nearby Tamarac National Wildlife Refuge, a birder can see 150 of the 258 species listed in this unusual area of convergence.

During the town's annual Festival of Birds in May, birders head in all directions. They'll go west to Hamden Slough and Felton Prairie, to see loggerhead shrikes, chestnut-collared longspurs, and other birds of the Dakotas. They'll go south to Rothsay, to see the rare prairie chicken, perhaps still showing some of its bizarre courting behavior. And they'll go east to the 43,000-acre Tamarac and to the bogs, hardwoods, and old-growth pines of Itasca State Park.

Golf courses also bring visitors to Detroit Lakes; there are 108 holes within 10 miles, including Fair Hills' Wildflower Course and the championship course at Detroit Country Club, where the Pine to Palm amateur tournament is held in August. And, also in August, hordes of country-music

Skiers glide past one of the cabins at Maplelag resort.

Maplelag: A Treasure in the Woods

Twenty miles northeast of Detroit Lakes, there's a patch of hills and trees at the edge of the hardwood forest that, for some reason, catches snow from prairie storms and hangs onto it longer than nearly every other place in the state. This snow belt is the home of Maplelag, one of the best places to ski in the Midwest.

Founded as a maple-syrup farm in 1973, it soon was discovered by skiers, so proprietors Jim and Mary Richards built a lodge, turned two old Finnish saunas into cabins, and began developing more housing and a superb trail system that grew to 53 kilometers.

In December 1999, the original lodge, which housed Jim Richards' irreplaceable collection of railroad-depot signs, tin lunch boxes, and antique neon clocks, burned to the ground, horrifying the resort's intensely loyal guests. But it was replaced by a new, larger lodge, with dozens of new stained-glass windows that, like those in the old lodge, bathe the pine interior in warm rays of gold and apricot.

Despite temperatures and windchills that can drop far below zero, Maplelag is perhaps the warmest spot in Minnesota, thanks to the hospitality of its owners. There are always four bottomless cookie jars, bowls of fruit, and vats of coffee next to the kitchen, which serves three family-style meals a day—baskets of hot fry bread, bowls of Greek salad and scalloped corn, platters of roast chicken and pork, trays of cakes and bars—as well as a Scandinavian buffet brunch on Sundays, complete with gjetost cheese and herring.

The personable Richardses are always around to greet guests, along with their son Jay, the ski instructor; his wife, Jonell; and Lucky, a stray lab who showed up in the resort's driveway not long before the passing of Maplelag's gentle border collie, Laddie, who lived to be 16 and was beloved by every child who passed through the door. There's an enormous hot tub where guests gather after dinner, as well as a sauna in the lodge and a wood-fired sauna on the lake, where clothing is optional after dark. Patrons of this sauna who bake and then jump into a hole cut in the ice of Sugarbush Lake earn the right to buy a T-shirt reading, "I Took the Plunge."

Weekends are busiest, when the cabins, houses, and cabooses fill with families and ski clubs. There's a talent show every Saturday, with children performing everything from the Macarena to Beethoven's "Für Elise" and adults putting on various skits, often poking fun at the legendary Scandihoovians.

But even with 200 people beating paths between trails, coffee pot, saunas, hot tub, and cabins, Maplelag still retains the feel of a family reunion—not surprisingly, the lag in Maplelag, pronounced "log," is Norwegian for "community."

(Continued)

fans descend on the town. WE Fest, held just south of town at Soo Pass Ranch, brings in fifty thousand people a day, many in a noticeably festive mood that does not always endear them to townspeople.

Detroit Lakes first was a stop for fur traders and settlers. It was a French priest, traveling through with one of the Red River oxcart caravans, who named it for the narrow strait between the lakes, or *detroit*. The town called itself Detroit until 1926, when the inevitable postal mix-ups with its Michigan counterpart forced it to change its name.

It was a logging town until 1917, when the sawmill in nearby Frazee, once the second-largest in the world, was packed up and sent over the prairies to Montana. That was the end of virgin timber in Minnesota. Harvesting of ice from the lakes continued for decades longer, sent by rail from the town's depot, through which 50 trains a day, including Amtrak, still pass.

All along, the lakes have drawn vacationers. Today, those visitors see a resort town that is not so slick as others, but has a pleasantly low-key quality that's been lost elsewhere.

(Continued)

And even on weekends, the beautifully groomed web of trails through the resort's 660 acres and beyond are uncrowded. Children head out on Poki-Loki, Sap Run, and Mother Hen, the 1-kilometer beginner trails, and skaters on the 4-kilometer Skater's Waltz. Wavy Gravy, Twin Lakes, and Island Lakes trails wind westward, with 20 kilometers between them, and the 10-kilometer Roy's Run heads north into the woods. The scenic, 5-kilometer Bullhead Lake trail heads east, down Suicide Hill and through cattail marsh, and follows the up-and-down contours of the lake ridge. If they're lucky, skiers will spot a porcupine or a great gray owl.

During the summer, the resort is used as a Spanish-language immersion camp by Concordia College of Moorhead, which operates Concordia Language Villages. Elderhostels often are held in the fall, and in spring, the resort hosts birders during the annual Festival of Birds in Detroit Lakes.

Whatever the season, guests will feel lucky they found Maplelag. In a state full of great resorts, it's one of a kind.

Trip Tips

Accommodations. Reserve early for the Christmas holidays and Martin Luther King and Presidents' Day weekends. The weekend rate, for two nights and six

Trip Tips

Accommodations. Fair Hills Resort, 9 miles southwest of town on Pelican Lake, is a traditional, full-service, family-run resort that includes the championship Wildflower Golf Course. In the summer, rates include three meals a day, evening entertainment, golf on a nine-hole executive course, supervised children's activities, sailboats and instruction, windsurfing and instruction, and fishing boats. There's a pool, hot tub, and tennis courts, and use of golf clubs is free. A week for a family of four in peak season is about $2,500, a relative bargain compared with similar resorts in the Brainerd area; (800) 323-2849, www.fairhillsresort.com.

Half an hour south, on Spirit Lake near Vergas, the Log House & Homestead B&B has five elegant rooms in a restored 1902 house and the renovated 1889 home of the proprietors' great-great-grandfather. Furnishings, linens, and décor are exquisite. There's no beach, but canoes and rowboats are provided. Two rooms in the Log House, which has a nice screened porch, are $100–$120. Three rooms in the Homestead, which have fireplaces and double whirlpools, are $145–$195. Suzanne Tweten, (800) 342-2318, www.loghousebb.com.

meals, is $179–$205 adults; $124 children 8–14 and $98 children 4–7, with a 10 percent discount for families. The rate for three-night weekends, with nine meals, is $240–$270 adults, $146 and $114 for children. The rate for two midweek nights is $152 adults and $91 and $72 children.

There's a wide variety of rooms, with those who reserve year-to-year occupying the choicest ones on weekends. Tier 1 lodgings include restored pioneer cabins and a former chicken coop, which have stained-glass windows but no bathroom (guests use the ones in the main lodge). Tier 2 lodgings have shared bathrooms down the hall, and Tier 3 lodgings, including the cabooses, have private bathrooms. All guests bring their own sleeping bags, pillows, and towels.

Equipment Rental. Ski equipment in all sizes can be rented, as well as snowshoes and kicksleds.

Babysitting. Staff members are available to stay with small children while parents ski, at a rate of $3.50 per hour per child, plus $1 for every additional child. Advance notice is required.

More Information. (800) 654-7711, www.maplelag.com.

The Holiday Inn Lakeside has a nice beach on Detroit Lake, and rooms with balconies, (218) 847-2121; it's usually the Festival of Birds headquarters. There are many other hotels in town, such as the Best Western Holland House, (800) 338-8547, (218) 847-4483, and small, inexpensive resorts, such as Fairyland Cottages just across from City Beach, (218) 847-9991.

Dining. The Lakeside and Zorbaz are across from City Beach; the Fireside is across the lake on East Shore Drive, and the Hotel Shoreham is south of town on County Highway 22, between lakes Sallie and Melissa. Downtown, in Washington Square Mall, Sunflower Hill sells espresso drinks, soup, and sandwiches.

Events. Festival of Birds, usually the third weekend of May, with a full schedule of lectures and birding tours. Northwest Water Carnival, second week of July. Spirit Fest, second weekend of July. Arts & Crafts in the Park, fourth weekend in July. WE Fest, first weekend in August. Pine to Palm Golf Tournament, second week in August. Dick Beardsley Half Marathon and 5K Run/Walk, second Sunday in September. The Shady Hollow Flea Market, on Highway 59 south of town, is held Sundays during the summer.

Scuba Diving. Tri-State Diving, just outside town, holds group dives on summer weekends at nearby lakes, such as Bad Medicine and Pelican, as well as at mine pits on the Mesabi and Cuyuna ranges and larger lakes such as Leech and Bemidji. Equipment can be rented inexpensively; (888) 728-2236, www.tri-statediving.com.

Tamarac National Wildlife Refuge. The visitors' center is at the junction of Highways 29 and 26 and includes a diorama, exhibits, and auditorium; outside, visitors can watch marsh birds through a binocular telescope. Open Monday–Friday year-round, plus weekend afternoons in summer; (218) 847-2641, www.fws.gov/r3pao/tamarac.

More Information. (800) 542-3992, www.detroitlakes.com. The chamber of commerce's birding, fishing, and snow-conditions hot line is (800) 433-1888.

28. Otter Trails: Surprises along a Scenic Byway

The writer Sinclair Lewis was thinking about Otter Tail County when he chided Minnesotans for not knowing about their own "haunts of beauty."

Few know that Otter Tail County has more lakes than any other county in Minnesota—1,048—or even that it has lakes at all. It also has the state's densest concentration of giant mascots and roadside sculpture, as well as two state parks, a picture-postcard mill, and Inspiration Peak, the state's second-highest point after Eagle Mountain on the North Shore.

The rolling landscape was created by the back-and-forth scraping of glaciers from four ice ages, which left a glacial moraine of kames, piles of sand

The Otter Tail River flows through the Otter Tail County town of Fergus Falls, but its city mascot is on the shore of Grotto Lake.

and gravel dropped by glacial meltwater, and kettles, created when blocks of ice fell off the glaciers, pressed into the earth, melted, and filled up again as ponds and lakes.

It's the kettles the Nobel Prize–winning author saw when he climbed Inspiration Peak, a high kame atop the hilly moraine. His ode to the view of "a glorious 20-mile circle of some 50 lakes, scattered among fields and pastures like sequins fallen on an old paisley shawl" led people to begin calling it Inspiration Peak, and the name stuck.

Today, a short but steep asphalt path leads to the summit, cloaked with prairie wildflowers. From there, fields and woods undulate into the far-off haze; just to the west, the eastern hardwood forest gives way to what once, before the arrival of the plow, was a sea of tall-grass prairie.

Inspiration Peak is a prominent stop on the Otter Trail Scenic Byway, a 150-mile loop that passes through the most interesting parts of this big county. Citizens here think big—big as in a 22-foot otter, a 1,200-pound foot, and a 15.5-foot pelican. Big as in the 23-foot fiberglass warrior who looms over one of the county's many resort towns.

From the peak, the byway heads west, through Dalton, where the threshing days of the early 1900s are re-created every September, and to the new Prairie Wetlands Learning Center, where 4 miles of nature trails and boardwalks wind through 200 acres of restored grasslands and 38 acres of wetlands. The learning center is on the edge of Fergus Falls, where the giant otter crouches alongside Grotto Lake and a tree-lined riverwalk winds through a pretty downtown that includes the Center for the Arts, a 1921 vaudeville

Minnesota's Mascots

It all started in 1937, when the Bemidji Rotary Club built an 18-foot Paul Bunyan and Babe the Blue Ox for the town's first Winter Carnival.

The pair was a sensation, and coverage in newspapers and national magazines brought crowds to see them. Other towns jumped on the bandwagon. The nearby town of Blackduck was first, building a 16-foot wooden black duck the next year; like Paul and Babe, it toured the state. The 1938 original still lives in downtown Blackduck and has been joined by two smaller black ducks, one at a motel and one at a park.

Today, giant mascots are sprinkled all over Minnesota. Otter Tail County has so many it could start a zoo. In Fergus Falls, a 22-foot concrete otter sits at the edge of Grotto Lake. In Vergas, a 20-foot concrete loon trains its beady red eyes on Long Lake. Rothsay has a more exotic bird—a 13-by-18-foot concrete prairie chicken depicted "booming," a springtime mating ritual at the nearby booming grounds, where the birds stomp and whoop loudly by inflating orange air sacs. Nearby, a 15.5-foot concrete pelican stands in downtown

house that now is a venue for music, theater, and film.

From Fergus Falls, the route heads east to Phelps Mill Park. Set deep in lake country, it's a captivating place that evokes a nostalgia for a time most of us never knew. Above the dam, on nice summer days, teenagers swing from a tree into the Otter Tail River; below, families gather to fish. Inside the 1889 brick and clapboard mill, the video "River of Wheat" explains that the mill, once the center of a bucolic rural community, was made obsolete by the rise of the huge mills in Minneapolis and by the rails that brought local grain directly to them.

In Silver Bay, home of a taconite-processing plant, Rocky Taconite celebrates the resurgence of Minnesota's mining industry after high-grade iron ore ran out.

Pelican Rapids, at the foot of Mill Pond Dam. The real pelicans now stop at nearby Lake Lida on their way north in spring and south in fall. Still more fowl are just across the county border in Frazee, where a 7-foot fiberglass turkey peers around the business district and a 22-foot turkey sits in Lions Park.

On the western shore of West Battle Lake, stern Chief Wenonga salutes passersby. According to local lore, the chief was one of the few survivors of an Ojibwe war party that, in 1795, engaged the Dakota in battle near what is now the resort town of Battle Lake. The chief, known as "the vulture," is said to have loved telling about his war exploits.

And in New York Mills, a giant farmer on a tractor dominates a sculpture park along Highway 10. The farmer began his existence as a logo for the New York Mills Regional Cultural Center and was brought to life in sheet metal by Ken Nyberg, a retired construction foreman and self-taught sculptor. Nyberg also has turned the nearby village of Vining into a virtual sculpture garden,

(Continued)

161

A 25-foot serpent named Kanabec, named after the Ojibwe word for snake, undulates on the north shore of Serpent Lake, near downtown Crosby.

(Continued)
with a giant Big Foot, square knot, clothespin, and pliers, plus more tradition-al statues. His pièce de résistance is a coffee cup, suspended in air by a stream of molten coffee.

Other mascots are rooted in history. In the west-central town of Starbuck, a colorful 8-foot figure commemorates the jobless men who, during the Depression, gathered in a wooded area along the shores of Lake Minnewaska. Many townspeople befriended the men, and the gathering spot became known as Hobo Park.

In Bemidji, named for the lake the Ojibwe called *Bemidgegumaug,* for "river flowing crosswise," a statue has honored an Ojibwe man since the 1890s. Sha-Now-Ish-Kung, known as Chief Bemidji, fed the first white settlers in 1888.

Two other mascots are rooted in more ancient history. According to legend, a plague of grasshoppers once threatened the wild grapes that blanketed ancient Finland, but they were banished by a chant from St. Urho. Menahga, south of Park Rapids, was settled predominantly by Finns and pays tribute with a 12-foot fiberglass statue of the saint, holding a pitchfork impaling a grasshopper.

The mill closed in 1939 but now is the site of one of the region's most popular festivals, which is held in June and features a juried arts and crafts fair, children's activities, and music. In the old general store across the street, visitors can buy ice cream and gifts.

To the north, the byway skirts the southern border of Maplewood State Park, a big park with more than 20 kettle lakes amid a series of high hills, created when one glacier rear-ended another and dumped piles of debris. Stands of basswood, sugar maple, and oak mark the very end of the hardwood forest, and the park's overlooks are good places to spot fall color.

In Pelican Rapids, a giant concrete pelican stands in the froth from Mill Pond Dam, just off the main street. Early settlers saw pelicans feeding at the original rapids; now, the birds stop at nearby Lake Lida, which the scenic byway passes on its route east. Perham is the home of turtle races, held on Wednesday mornings in summer. From there, the byway heads south, around the eastern shore of big Otter Tail Lake and into Battle Lake.

An early resort town frequented by millionaires from Missouri and points west, the village of seven hundred has become a laid-back hub for the local cottagers and tourists, who can stop in the gift shops that line wide Lake Avenue. Just north of downtown, the stern, 23-foot-tall Chief Wenonga stands along the shore of West Battle Lake, named for a 1795 battle between the Dakota and Ojibwe, who were badly beaten and renamed the lake *Ish-quan-a-de-win-ing,* meaning "where but few survived." This area, a coveted hunt-

---

Alexandria's mascot has an even more tenuous hold on history. Big Ole, a 28-foot Viking who brandishes a spear and a silver shield reading "Alexandria, Birthplace of America," stands outside the town's Runestone Museum, which houses a slab of stone purportedly left in 1362 by a party of Vikings.

Mora, in east-central Minnesota, delved into more recent times for its mascot. The townspeople, many of Swedish descent, chose the Dala horse, hand-carved since the mid-1800s in the Swedish province of Dalarna, whose principal city also is named Mora. The 22-foot-tall, bright orange fiberglass horse now is a landmark.

Other townspeople honor hard-working predecessors. The workhorses of the fur trade are a favorite subject. Voyageurs can be found in Crane Lake, Cloquet, Two Harbors, and Pine City, where a 35-foot redwood figure in Riverside Park pays tribute to commerce on the Snake River and to a nearby wintering post, re-created as the Minnesota Historical Society's North West Company Fur Post.

On the Iron Range, outside Chisholm's Ironworld theme park, the 81-foot-tall Iron Man is a reminder of the glory days of mining. With his 150-ton base,

(Continued)

ing ground, was for many years thereafter part of the "war road" between the rival tribes.

Two miles east of the byway, Glendalough State Park includes six undeveloped lakes, two of them havens for waterfowl. Formerly a private game preserve, it's kept more primitive than most state parks.

To the east, construction foreman Ken Nyberg has turned the tiny village of Vining into a sculpture mecca. In his spare time, he's furnished the town with a whole set of quirky scrap-metal sculptures: a foot with an oversized big toe, a square knot, a coffee cup poised in mid-air, a 20-foot clothespin, and a pliers gripping a cockroach. There's a more traditional cowboy, too, and an Indian on a horse.

From Vining, the route dips down to Urbank, and back to Inspiration Peak. From there, it's just a short sprint to I-94—and the real world.

(Continued)

he's the third-largest free-standing statue in the nation, after the Statue of Liberty and the St. Louis Arch. And in Silver Bay, cartoonish Rocky Taconite, holding a pick in his red-gloved hands, celebrates the development of taconite, which allowed mining to continue after high-grade ore was depleted.

Farmers also get their due. In Embarrass, a 6-foot wooden farmer with a homemade hay rake is one of the emblems of this isolated northeastern Finnish community; he's joined by a miner, a logger, an old lady at a well, and two children. And in Olivia, a 25-foot corncob stands atop a park gazebo.

And then there are the fish. They're everywhere: in Garrison, where a 15-foot fiberglass walleye overlooks Mille Lacs Lake; in Orr, which has a 5-foot bluegill; and in Preston, where a 19-foot brown trout represents the "Trout Capital of Southeast Minnesota." Near the southern shore of Lake Winnibigoshish, just west of Bena, a 65-foot-long muskie stretches outside a supper club called—what else?—The Big Fish. Built in 1957, the muskie began life as a drive-in, with a window near its gills to serve customers.

There's other wildlife, too. On the shore of Serpent Lake, near downtown Crosby in north-central Minnesota, a 25-foot-long serpent named Kanabec, after the Ojibwe word for snake, is a favorite of vacationers. In the northeast Minnesota town of Virginia, a 20-foot fiberglass loon floats on Silver Lake, not far from downtown. A 26-foot Smokey the Bear stands in International Falls, gateway to Voyageurs National Park. In northeast Minnesota, Moose Lake has put a 9-foot fiberglass moose on Moosehead Lake, and an 18-foot fiberglass crow perches outside Belgrade, in central Minnesota near the Crow River.

Anything mssing? Oh yes, a giant mosquito. There's one in Effie, north of Grand Rapids.

Trip Tips

Getting There. From the Twin Cities, Inspiration Peak is the closest point along the 150-mile route. Get off I-94 at the Brandon exit, just west of Alexandria, and head north on Highway 7. If you want to take shortcuts or explore off the byway, bring a good map, preferably a DeLorme *Atlas & Gazetteer.*

Accommodations. There are many modest, old-fashioned lake resorts along the route.

Maplewood State Park rents an unheated camper cabin with a screened porch, and Glendalough State Park rents four, $27.50. Call The Connection to reserve, (800) 246-2267.

Aloft in the Pines is an attractive log home on Pickerel Lake, 4 miles north of Phelps Mill, and has three rooms, $70–$80. Mary and John Peterson, (888) 457-6301, www.bbonline.com/mn/aloft.

Bakketopp Hus, on Long Lake near Fergus Falls, has three rooms, one with fireplace and one with double whirlpool, $70–$105. Judy and Dennis Nims, (800) 739-2915, www.bbonline.com/mn/bakketopp.

Bergerud B's B&B and Bakery, 11 miles south of Fergus Falls, is an 1895 home with three rooms, two with shared bath, $45–$75. Jim and Sylvia Bergerud, (800) 557-4720, www.bbonline.com/mn/bergerud.

Xanadu Island B&B, 5 miles west of Battle Lake, is a 1920 stone and wood lodge on a seven-acre island, reached by bridge. There are five attractive rooms, one with fireplace, two with double whirlpools, and two that have private half-baths and share a shower, $90–$155. Bryan and Janet Lonski, (800) 396-9043, www.xanadu.cc.

Events. Battle Lake Flea Market, summer weekends. Summerfest in Fergus Falls, second weekend of June. Brews and Blues Festival in Fergus Falls, late June. Phelps Mill Festival, second weekend in July. Turkey Festival in Pelican Rapids, third weekend in July. Wenonga Days in Battle Lake, last weekend in July. Art in the Park in Pelican Rapids, fourth Saturday in July. Vining Watermelon Days, third Saturday in August. Perham Black Powder Shoot, third weekend in August. Lincoln Avenue Fine Arts Festival in Fergus Falls, Labor Day weekend. Lake Region Pioneer Threshermen's Show in Dalton, second weekend in September.

Nightlife. A Center for the Arts in Fergus Falls schedules events most weekends, (218) 736-5453, www.fergusarts.org.

More Information. Call Fergus Falls tourism, (800) 726-8959, www.visitfergusfalls.com, for a visitors guide and map of the scenic byway. Otter Tail Country Tourism also is helpful, (800) 423-4571, www.ottertailcountry.com.

Pioneer Prairie

29. New Ulm: A Pocket of Germany in Minnesota

The founders of New Ulm may have left their homeland, but their homeland never left them.

Members of a German land society came to southern Minnesota in 1854 and chose a hilly site at the confluence of the Minnesota and Cottonwood Rivers. The land nearby was rich and fertile, and the people prospered. They named their village after the southern German town of Ulm, and from the beginning, hung onto Old World traditions fiercely.

During the annual Heritagefest parade, their past rolls before their eyes. There go gymnasts from the Turners, evolved from the health-minded group of German socialists and freethinkers who founded the town. There goes the horse-drawn beer wagon from Schell, New Ulm's last surviving brewery, run by the great-great-grandson of the man who founded it in 1860. There go the cannons of the New Ulm Battery, formed after the fiercest battle of the 1862 Dakota Conflict nearly leveled the young town. There go the *Narren,* or fools, who wear hand-carved wooden masks with long, bulbous noses and chins and are mascots of a culture in which myth and legend run deep.

The *Narren* also come out during Fasching, a Fat Tuesday festival that, like Mardi Gras, mixes ancient pagan rituals with Lenten traditions. There's an evening concert and costume parade at Turner Hall, hosted by the Concord Singers, known as the foremost German-language male chorus in America.

But the real action is at Bock Fest, on the picturesque grounds of Schell Brewery, where hundreds of party-goers search for wooden goat heads hidden by Ted Marti, August Schell's great-great-grandson. *Bock* is the German word for billy goat, as well as the caramel-colored beer traditionally drunk in

New Ulm's *Narren*, or fools, hobnob with onlookers in parades and festivals.

early spring, and prizes are given to those who find the heads. Those who come out of the woods without one kind of bock can quickly get their hands on another, drinking it to the rollicking music of the Bock Fest Boys.

Through its festivals, New Ulm maintains its connection to tradition. Fasching, also called *Karneval,* is celebrated all over Germany. In October, when the beer is flowing in Munich, New Ulm celebrates Oktoberfest.

But the town's biggest celebration is Heritagefest, a Germanic extravaganza of pilsener, polka music, and pork sandwiches smothered with sautéed onions. Musicians from Germany, Austria, and Switzerland fly in for the occasions, performing alongside New Ulm's Concord Singers, which was founded in 1931. Its lighthearted repertoire never fails to get an audience on its feet: If New Ulm had a nickel for every time someone wagged his elbows to the "Little Chicken Dance," it could buy a bratwurst for everyone in Minnesota.

Though many tourists reduce German culture to beer-drinking songs, garden gnomes, and cuckoo clocks, New Ulm takes its heritage seriously. In 1897, while churches and schools still were going up, it erected a monument to the Alemannic warrior Hermann, who routed the Romans from the Teutoburg Forest in 9 A.D. The 32-foot Hermann now brandishes his sword atop a 70-foot columned dome in Hermann Heights Park, and visitors can scale a spiral staircase for a magnificent view of the Minnesota River Valley. Today, Hermann still is the poster boy for the sentimental pride that flourishes in New Ulm.

New Ulm takes its beer seriously, too. In fact, the slogan of Schell Brewing Company is "When your brewery is surrounded by 14,000 thirsty Germans, you'd better make a darn good beer." August Schell was an early arrival in New Ulm and one of its most nostalgic; the brewery's picturesque wooded grounds include three pine trees he brought from his Black Forest hamlet. Deer—a stag is the Schell's trademark—roam around the grounds.

From the brewery, trails lead along the looping Cottonwood River and into adjoining Flandrau State Park. The Dakota hunted and camped on these prairie bluffs until the U.S.–Dakota Conflict of 1862, when hungry young Dakota plundered and burned the young town. The two-year-old brewery, however, whose owners had shared food with their neighbors, was left un-harmed.

Today, this brewery still is a neighborly place; its wooded grounds have been open to the public since they were landscaped in the 1880s. Visitors wander the garden pathways around August Schell's 1885 brick home, visit the deer park, and sit in a gazebo with forest gnomes who play cards. The workingman's boarding house now is a gift shop and the carriage house a museum, from which tours start. According to beer guru Michael Jackson, it's "the prettiest location of any brewery in the USA."

The shops, too, attract crowds. Domeiers draws shoppers by the busload; sometimes, not everyone can fit in the tiny store, where every inch of space is filled with glittering glass ornaments and twittering cuckoo clocks. A former grocery that, in 1963, began to cater to German-born brides brought home by New Ulm servicemen, it's a good place to buy Advent calendars, brandy-filled chocolates, and other imported goods.

Downtown, Lambrecht's and the Christmas Haus are among other shops that sell imported gifts. On Center Street, visitors will notice a fanciful build-ing whose stepped gables and alternating brick and white terra cotta bands make it look like a wedding cake. It's the Brown County Historical Society, where exhibits tell the story of the early settlers and the native Dakota, whose cultures clashed so calamitously.

A block away, the elegant 1887 John Lind House also is open for tours; Lind was Minnesota's fourteenth governor. Young fans of the children's classic *Millions of Cats* can tour the 1894 childhood home of its author and illustra-tor, Wanda Gag, at North Washington and Third. On Minnesota Steet, the town's glockenspiel also is a popular stop. Its carillon bells play twice every afternoon, as three animated polka-band figures twirl year-round except Christmastime, when they're replaced by a Nativity scene.

There's not much in the way of German culture that New Ulm has over-looked. It may not be Munich, but it's definitely the next best thing.

Trip Trips

Accommodations. Deutsche Strasse B&B is in an 1893 brick Victorian near downtown; five rooms, $60–$80, (507) 354-2005. The Holiday Inn at the east edge of town, (507) 359-2941, has a pool and a German restaurant, $69–$139. There's also a Super 8, (507) 359-2400; Budget Holiday, (507) 354-4145; Colonial Inn, (507) 354-3128; and New Ulm Motel, (507) 359-1414. It's a good idea to book rooms early, especially for the summer and fall festivals.

Dining. The Heidelberg at the Holiday Inn serves sauerbraten, Wiener schnitzel, and other German specialties, as does Veigel's Kaiserhoff downtown, known for its delicious, meaty ribs.

Events. Fasching and Bock Fest, weekend before Ash Wednesday. Heritagefest, second and third weekends of July. Oktoberfest, first and second weekends of October.

Flandrau State Park. The park, which lies in a wooded valley on the southern edge of town, has a pool with sand bottom and 8.5 miles of hiking trails, some on a bluff overlooking the Cottonwood River. During World War II, it was the site of a German prisoner of war camp; (507) 233-9800; for campsite reservations, call the Connection at (800) 246-2267.

Hermann Monument. The spiral staircase to the top of the dome is open 10 A.M.–4 P.M. daily in summer and during Oktoberfest, $1. The surrounding park is a good place for a picnic.

Schell Brewery Tours. In summer, tours are at 3 and 4 P.M. Monday–Friday and 1, 2, 3, and 4 P.M. Saturday and Sunday. Tours also are given on Oktoberfest weekends. Cost is $2; (507) 354-5528, www.schellsbrewery.com.

Morgan Creek Vineyards. Run by George Marti, this vineyard 8 miles east of town is open for tours, tastings, and picnics from May through October; (507) 947-3547.

Shopping. Domeiers, 1020 S. Minnesota St., is open daily except Wednesday; (507) 354-4231.

More Information. (888) 463-9856; www.newulm.com.

30. Walnut Grove: Shrine to a Pioneer Girl's Memories

People come from all over the world to a little town on the Minnesota prairie.

There's nothing remarkable about Walnut Grove, population 625. It has a few buildings, a few trees, and flat fields all around. But those who come here have imaginations, and in their imaginations they're seeing much more: a little girl picking wild plums and making necklaces of rushes. A kindly man playing the fiddle. A church bell ringing in a white steeple.

Walnut Grove's annual pageant celebrating Laura Ingalls Wilder draws thousands to the banks of Plum Creek.

The bell is all that's left of Laura Ingalls Wilder's three and a half years in Walnut Grove. They weren't happy years for her family. Her father, while hardworking and generous—he donated the enormous sum of $26.15 toward the bell, as he and his four daughters went without shoes—had a knack for failure.

From Pepin, Wisconsin, he led his family to land in Kansas that was still owned by the Osage; to a dugout in Walnut Grove a year into a grasshopper plague; and to a failing hotel in Burr Oak, Iowa, just as the plague ended and crops flourished. They returned to Walnut Grove, where his daughter Mary became blind during an epidemic of scarlet fever, but soon moved on to De Smet, South Dakota, where the family nearly starved during the bitter winter of 1880–81.

Traveling around Laura Land

Pepin, Wisconsin. Laura was born in 1867 in a cabin above Pepin, just across the Mississippi. Her family moved to Kansas when she was two, but returned to Pepin when she was four and lived there for another three years; it's the setting for Laura's first book, *Little House in the Big Woods.* An unfurnished log house called the Little House Wayside stands 7 miles up County Highway CC and can be visited any time; in Pepin, the Pepin Historical Museum, also known as the Laura Ingalls Wilder Museum, is open from mid-May to mid-September. Laura Ingalls Wilder Days, the third weekend of September, includes a parade, a Laura look-alike contest, and a play based on *Little House in the Big Woods;* (715) 442-3011.

Independence, Kansas. Thirteen miles southwest of town, a furnished log-cabin replica of the Little House on the Prairie sits next to the foundation of the Ingalls house and the well Pa dug. It's open daily from May 15 through Labor Day. Nearby are a post office and schoolhouse from Laura's era; (800) 882-3606.

Burr Oak, Iowa. In tiny Burr Oak, just over the Minnesota border on Highway 52, the Laura Ingalls Wilder Park and Museum is open weekends in May and daily through September; other months by appointment only. This town calls itself "the missing link" because Laura never wrote about it. It was a sad year: An infant brother, Freddie, died on the journey there; the family lived next to a saloon; and they were so poor a doctor's wife tried to adopt Laura; (319) 735-5916 or (800) 463-4692 (Decorah). Burr Oak Mercantile and Country Café is next door.

De Smet, South Dakota. This prairie town, two hours from Walnut Grove, was the end of the line for Pa and Ma and the setting for five of Laura's books. The Wilder Memorial Society gives tours of the Surveyor's House and Ma and

That was the story of Laura's life—except that in the eight books she wrote about her childhood, it didn't sound like failure. It sounded like fun.

Laura did write about deadly blizzards and voracious grasshoppers, but also about sleigh rides and swimming holes and fiddle music by the fire. And those stories are what readers remember, as well as her curiosity and irrepressible spirit, which never flagged from one disaster to another.

Walnut Grove wasn't mentioned by name in *On the Banks of Plum Creek*, and locals didn't know about the connection until 1947, when illustrator Garth Williams arrived in town to sketch sites for the books. It was the hit TV series "Little House on the Prairie" that made the town famous. Walnut Grove was mentioned often in the highly romanticized series, which ran from 1974 to 1983 and was popular all over the world, especially in Japan.

Pa's 1887 home, which holds many of their possessions, daily June–September and Monday–Saturday from April to May and October to December, (800) 880-3383, www.liwms.com. De Smet's annual pageant, based on various books, is held the last weekend in June and the first two weekends in July.

Spring Valley, Minnesota. The parents of Laura's husband Almanzo lived in this southeast Minnesota town, and Laura, Almanzo, and their daughter Rose spent one and a half years with them, recovering from illness and crop failures, before moving, briefly, to Florida. The 1876 Methodist Church, which the family attended, now is a museum and contains Wilder exhibits. Open daily in summer; (507) 346-1015.

Mansfield, Missouri. This town of 1,400 was Laura's home from 1894, when she arrived with her husband, Almanzo, and their daughter, Rose, until 1957, when she died at age 90. All nine books (*Farmer Boy*, about Almanzo's childhood, is set in New York) were written in the house they built room by room between 1896 and 1913; it's preserved as it was in the 1940s and 1950s. There's a trove of family heirlooms and memorabilia in the adjoining museum, including Pa's fiddle. Open daily April through October; (877) 924-7126, www.bestoftheozarks.com/wilderhome.

The "Little House Memories" outdoor musical pageant is held in late August and September, the Laura Ingalls Wilder Festival on the third weekend of September, and Authors Day at Rocky Ridge on the third weekend of October. For a Missouri visitors guide, call (800) 519-1500, ext. 112.

Background Reading. William Anderson's *The Little House Guidebook* ($8.95, HarperTrophy), which includes photos of all the home sites, is very useful to Laura tourists.

When tourists began arriving, townspeople started the museum, and a few craft and antiques shops sprang up.

In 1978, the town began performing the annual "Fragments of a Dream" pageant, a prairie passion play that draws thousands of "Little House" pilgrims every July. The open-air play begins with an adult Laura sitting at her typewriter, musing, "Where should I begin, for a family that spent its whole life beginning?" Then the story unfolds, with exuberant acting and nifty special effects, including a prairie fire created from buried gas lines. Wooden sets are moved by hydraulic lifts, and there's an improbably cute dugout, adorned with window boxes full of geraniums.

Traces of the real Ingalls dugout—which prompted virtually the only complaint Ma made in eight books—"Oh, Charles, we've never had to live in a dugout yet"—can be seen not far north of town. It was scraped out of the steep banks of Plum Creek and had a single greased-paper window; once, one of the family's steers put his foot through the grass-covered roof. The dugout washed away in the 1920s, but the site remains as Laura described it. Wheat grows a few yards above the remaining depression, and the wild plum trees below still shade the creek's muddy waters.

The pageant and accompanying Pioneer Festival, held on two of the three pageant weekends, is held west of town, in Plum Creek County Park. Children splash through the creek, just like Laura, and dress up in borrowed bonnets and britches for old-time photos. There's bluegrass and folk music, a petting zoo, old-time photos, and demonstrations of such pioneer arts as broom making.

But tourists stream into Walnut Grove all year, following the Laura Ingalls Wilder Historic Highway from Mankato to the South Dakota border. At the Wilder Museum in town, the attendance board records visitors from three dozen countries and every state. The museum, a collection of buildings that includes an 1898 depot, an 1880s chapel, and an onion-domed Grandma's House, holds only one item owned by the family, a quilt made by Laura and her daughter, Rose. Other exhibits include letters written to Wilder by schoolchildren around the world, newspaper clippings, and publicity photos of the "Little House" TV stars, who have made much-heralded visits to Walnut Grove over the years. The most interesting exhibit is on grasshoppers, which plagued the area in 1873–77 but also as recently as 1989.

And there's a gift shop, of course; Laura's starry-eyed fans like souvenirs. But it's her memories, passed through her books, that are most cherished.

Trip Tips

Accommodations. A few residents of Walnut Grove rent rooms in their houses; the museum keeps a list. Campsites at Plum Creek Park are first-come, first-served.

Stan McCone's sod house is a tribute to the tenacity of prairie pioneers.

Little Sod House on the Prairie

Sometimes, it comes as a shock to tourists, especially those who grew up watching the TV show "Little House on the Prairie," that life on the frontier wasn't all that fun.

Twenty miles east of Walnut Grove, Stan McCone tells it as it was. A farmer, he'd heard stories about the early sod houses. None remained, so he decided to build one of his own, using an old sod cutter. "There were thirteen sod houses in this neighborhood, and those are just the ones we know about," he says. "But with all those, there's zero recollection of them, and I know why—because of all the buried children alongside them. They had such hardship."

Actually, McCone built two sod houses. The poor man's soddie is small and dark: "I think that's the best exhibit of all," McCone says. "That's how people lived. You walk in and think, oh, man, how did they raise children here?" The rich man's soddie, however, has whitewashed walls, paned-glass windows, and a roof supported by planks and covered with tarpaper under the sod. It would have cost about $50, and the family who built it would have been considered rich.

Stan and Virginia McCone run this soddie as the Sod House Bed and Breakfast, and diehard Laura Ingalls Wilder fans find their way to it from all over the world. There are two comfortable beds with quilts, an armoire, a rocker, and a dining table. Heat comes from corncobs burnt in the woodstove, light

(Continued)

175

(Continued)
from a kerosene lamp, and plumbing—well, bathroom facilities are in another little house outside. Once, Stan cooked breakfast on the soddie's 1886 cast-iron stove—"great, if you know how to cook on 'em"—but now Virginia brings a hot breakfast in a basket.

Near the farmhouse, there's an old camper filled with bonnets, pinafores, shawls, and britches, in case guests want to dress like Laura. And they do. Then they head off, swinging their arms, along paths lined with prairie grasses and wildflowers—dame's rocket and beardtongue, ox-eye daisy, and black-eyed Susan.

The guests, over the years, have added to the McCones' sod-house lore. "We've heard some real interesting stories; some are mind-boggling," says Stan McCone. "We had one woman from Bakersfield, California, tell us about a family who lived in a dugout on Dutch Charley Creek and lost seven children in one winter. They had diphtheria, which blocks the air passages. Then the eighth child, a baby, got it, and a neighbor came over and forced a hot stove iron down her throat—and she was the lone survivor.

"I think that's why so little was written down about that era," he says. "It was something you really didn't want to talk about."

Trip Tips

Getting There: The sod house is 7 miles west of Springfield, just off Highway 14.

Tours: Self-guided tours cost $3.

Accommodations: It's $90 for two and $130–$150 for three to five people, open April through October; (507) 723-5138. Reserve early for summer weekends.

The Sod House on the Prairie B&B near Sanborn is $90–$150, (507) 723-5138. Springfield has campsites at Riverside Park, (507) 723-3517 or (507) 723-5290, and rooms at the Plains Motel, (507) 723-6474.

In Lamberton, 10 miles east, there's the Lamberton Motel, (507) 752-7242. Tracy, 7 miles west, has the Cozy Grove motel, (507) 629-3350, and 1902 Valentine Inn B&B (children over 12), (507) 629-3827; 10 miles south of Tracy, there's camping at Lake Shetek State Park, (800) 246-2267. Marshall, 40 minutes from Walnut Grove, has five larger chain motels and a nice municipal pool and water slide, (507) 537-1865, www.marshall-mn.org.

Dining. Nellie's Café is open daily for breakfast and lunch, and for dinner Monday–Friday and during the pageant, when churches and community groups also put on suppers.

Pageant. It's the first three weekends of July; the Pioneer Festival is held the second and third weekends. Reserved seats are $8, general-admission seats $7; (888) 859-3102.

Museum. The Laura Ingalls Wilder Museum is open daily April through October, (507) 859-2358, www.walnutgrove.org, and other times by appointment. Admission is $3, $1 for ages 6–12.

Ingalls Homestead. It's a mile and a half north of town off County Highway 5 and it's open from May through October. Admission is $3 per car.

Other Fun Stops. New Ulm, about 50 miles east of Walnut Grove, has many attractions. In between, Sleepy Eye has a small beach on Sleepy Eye Lake, and Springfield has a playground, pool, and water slide in pleasant Riverside Park; the Victorian Garden gift and coffee shop offers a "Laura's lunch" to go, (507) 723-6594. On the way to De Smet, South Dakota, from Walnut Grove, Balaton has a roadside beach on Lake Yankton. Tyler, settled by Danes, has a Danish bakery, a gift shop, and the Danebod folk school. Lake Benton has a wayside rest with a dock on the lake and an 1896 opera house.

More Information. Redwood Regional Tourism, (800) 657-7070, sends out a brochure about the towns along Laura Ingalls Wilder Historic Highway.

31. Minnesota River Valley: Land of Beauty and Conflict

By 1862, the Dakota nation of Minnesota had endured more than a century of disruption. The Ojibwe had pushed them out of their hunting grounds in the North Woods. French, British, and American fur traders had introduced disease and liquor. Then the settlers moved in with their plows. They scared away the game, but refused to share with their neighbors when they had nothing to eat.

When the Europeans were just passing through, the Dakota benefited. Traders gave them brass kettles to replace bark pots, soft cloth to supplement hides, needles and glass beads to replace bone awls and porcupine quills. Many admired the Dakota. Cartographer Joseph Nicollet, who traveled along the Minnesota River in 1838, wrote, "Nothing equals the reserve and discretion of these good people. Once they know who you are, what you are doing and that you treat them well, it takes so little to make them your friends. I cannot conceive why so many whites blunder in their dealings with them."

But when the Europeans began taking Dakota land, things got ugly. By 1862, the Dakota were confined by treaty to a 10-mile-wide strip south of the Minnesota River. Crops had failed the previous summer, and the winter was harsh. By June the Dakota were starving, but they put off their annual buffalo hunt in the West to wait for their annuity payment, part of the treaty agreement. But the gold was late, held up in a Washington drained by the Civil War. At the Lower Sioux Agency, an arrogant new agent refused to release all of the food and other provisions due under the treaties until the gold arrived.

The gold, two months late, had nearly reached Fort Ridgely when four young braves, on a dare over the theft of eggs, shot and killed five settlers 40 miles north of the river, in Acton. Despite the prophecies of their eloquent leader, Little Crow—"The white men are like the locusts when they fly so thick that the whole sky is a snowstorm . . . kill one, two, ten, and ten times ten will come to kill you"—the Dakota, already in trouble, decided to try to drive out the settlers.

In the next six weeks, they killed at least 360 settlers. No one knows how many Dakota were killed fighting U.S. soldiers, about 90 of whom died, but the conflict ended that December with the hanging of 38 warriors at Mankato, the cancellation of all treaties and debts, and the banishment of the Dakota from Minnesota.

They were shipped to barren reservations in South Dakota, where many died, but in the 1880s, they began coming back. A century later, they opened Jackpot Junction, a booming casino and resort that now is the largest employer in Redwood Falls. It's just down the road from the post where trader Andrew Myrick, informed that the Dakota were starving, said, "Let them eat grass." He was killed on the first day of the conflict and his mouth stuffed with grass.

The U.S.–Dakota Conflict of 1862 was a defining moment in Minnesota history, and a visit to its sites, preserved by historians, is sobering and thought provoking.

The serpentine Minnesota River was silty even before it became polluted by agricultural runoff; in Dakota, *Minnesota* means "cloud-tinted water." But the valley is lush and beautiful, cutting a broad, deep swath through some of the world's richest farmland.

The first stop is St. Peter, which sprang up around a historic crossing. Just north of town, there's a natural ford over the river, used by Dakota on their way from the northern forests to hunting grounds on the plains and later by explorers and traders. It became an important stop on the southern branch of the Red River Ox Cart Trail. From Winnipeg and Pembina, the métis drivers of these two-wheeled, all-wood carts would screech across the prairie with caravans loaded with furs, meeting traders at this crossing, called Traverse des Sioux.

The first of two 1851 treaties was signed here by the Sioux, or Dakota, giving up 24 million acres. The Treaty Site History Center, near the old crossing, contains fascinating exhibits on the characters of the era, including Nicollet, French Canadian trader Louis Provencalle and Mazasha, or Red Iron, the well-regarded chief of the Dakota village at the site. There are copies of the "trader's papers" that claimed virtually all the money the Dakota received under 1851 and 1858 treaties, and an eye-opening list of the signers: the whites, who became the richest men in the territory—Ramsey, Steele, Goodhue, Faribault—and the Dakota, who gave their names to the white man's towns—Sleepy Eye, Wabasha, Good Thunder—but became impoverished.

The site of the 1862 hanging, the largest mass execution in U.S. history, is marked at Mankato's Reconciliation Park, off Riverfront Drive. Into the 1970s, the Dakota refused to go into Mankato. Now, as part of reconciliation efforts, the Mdewakanton Mah-Kato Powwow is held there every September, in Land of Memories Park.

New Ulm was besieged the second day of the 1862 conflict by young Dakota who wanted to plunder it. The Dakota, who shared freely in times of want as well as plenty, and the Germans, who believed in saving for a rainy day, never understood each other. The citizens kept the Dakota at bay from behind a barricade, but the city burned. A monument in a street median is the only reminder.

The detour to New Ulm probably saved Fort Ridgely, which Chief Big Eagle called "the door to the valley as far as St. Paul." Now a state park and Minnesota Historical Society site, it has an interpretive center in the restored commissary that tells how those inside, without a stockade or even a well, held off the Dakota with artillery.

On the way, stop at the Harkin Store, a historical society site that's frozen in 1870. Once a busy general store catering to steamboat traffic, it faded after the railroad bypassed the river town of West Newton in 1873. Today, cos-

How the Indians Lost Their Land

When French fur traders arrived in the Upper Midwest in the seventeenth century, the land belonged to the Ojibwe and Dakota—except they did not believe land could be owned, or transferred by a piece of paper. This fundamental difference in perception colored agreements between Indians and Europeans for the next two centuries.

In the beginning, when land was plentiful, the newcomers took the high road: The 1787 Northwest Ordinance stated, "The utmost good faith shall always be observed toward Indians; their land and property shall never be taken from them without their consent; and in their property, rights and liberty, they shall never be invaded or disturbed."

But when the Europeans needed land, they took it. In 1830, President Andrew Jackson's Indian Removal Act shoved Indians west of the Mississippi River and out of Missouri, Arkansas, and Louisiana. In 1854, the Indian Appropriations Act gave Congress authority to establish Indian reservations. In 1862, the Homestead Act unleashed a stampede of settlers, who swarmed to Indian lands and increased pressure for treaties.

By 1887, even the land Indians held on reservations seemed like too much, and the Indian Allotment Act eliminated the rights of Indians to hold tribal land in common. Their reservations were taken away and exchanged for allotments of 160 acres per head of household. Many Indians, unable to make a living, sold their land to settlers. The land taken away—90 million acres—also was sold to settlers.

tumed interpreters chat with customers about the goods, 40 percent of which are original to the era.

The most important site is the Lower Sioux Agency, on the other side of the river. This is where the government encouraged the Indians to farm, promising houses in return, and where annuities were paid. The annual gathering of thousands of Dakota was a colorful affair that drew tourists. The 1861 "Grand Excursion" from St. Paul by steamer, attended by Henry David Thoreau, botanist Horace Mann Jr., and Gov. Alexander Ramsey and his wife, Anna, is re-created each June by costumed interpreters. The site also is where the first traders and settlers were killed. Today, the fine interpretive center tells of the events that led to the conflict.

At the Birch Coulee Battlefield, across the river, self-guided trails show where Dakota warriors surprised a burial party sent from Fort Ridgely, in a battle that became the biggest setback for U.S. troops.

Back on the south side of the river, the neon lights of Jackpot Junction bring in tourists from all around the region to gamble, but also to golf and

---

In Minnesota, the Dakota and Ojibwe lost most of their land east of the Mississippi in the treaties of 1837. In 1851, the Dakota, under duress, signed away most of southern Minnesota. Each chief also had to sign a "trader's paper," whose demands nearly equaled the amounts the Dakota were to receive under the treaty.

This plundering was no secret at the time. As Episcopal bishop Henry Whipple, a friend of the Dakota, later noted, "The treaty is usually conceived and executed in fraud. The ostensible parties to the treaty are the government of the United States and the Indians; the real parties are the Indian agents, the traders and politicians."

By 1854, the Ojibwe had been forced to cede most of northern Minnesota, and by 1858, the Dakota were confined to a 10-mile-wide strip south of the Minnesota River. After the War of 1862, they lost even that and were banished from the state.

The Dakota started drifting back in the 1880s, and eventually the U.S. government purchased small reservations for them at Prairie Island, near Red Wing; at Shakopee, just west of the Twin Cities; and at the Upper and Lower Sioux Agencies along the Minnesota River.

The Ojibwe have much larger reservations: White Earth, in the northwest, the largest; Red Lake, north of Bemidji; Leech Lake, around Walker; Nett Lake, or Bois Forte, south of International Falls; Grand Portage, at the far tip of the North Shore; Fond du Lac, west of Duluth; and Mille Lacs.

A stone warehouse was the only building left standing at the Lower Sioux Agency, where the 1862 U.S.–Dakota conflict started.

attend concerts in a 2,411-seat amphitheater. Redwood Falls, just to the west, is named for the red dye the Dakota daubed on trees, to show that blood would run if the Ojibwe dared to hunt there, and for the waterfalls in Alexander Ramsey Park, which is the largest city park in Minnesota and has its own zoo.

In North Redwood, a 22-year-old railroad freight agent named Richard Sears began to parlay an unwanted consignment of watches into the world's largest mail-order business. From North Redwood, County Highway 15 hugs the lush river plain, passing the Schwandt Memorial, commemorating the deaths of a German family on the first day of the war, and the Joseph R. Brown Wayside. Brown was one of the more colorful players in territorial politics, a classic opportunist. Here, shortly after leaving his lucrative post as Lower Sioux Indian agent, he built a 19-room mansion of rose granite; it was burned less than a year later by the Dakota.

Across the river is the Upper Sioux Agency, now a state park. An interpretive center tells about the Dakota farmers who lived here, derisively called "cut-hairs" by Dakota who did not want to abandon their traditional lifestyle. Many of the Upper Sioux Dakota helped whites escape during the war. Two miles south, a granite shaft at Wood Lake marks the battle where the war ended, six weeks after it began.

Dakota land followed the Minnesota River all the way to Ortonville, on the South Dakota border. Today, it's lined by other historic sites, state parks, wildlife refuges, and settlements founded by Norwegians and other immigrants. Granite Falls is the home of Andrew Volstead, whose name is on the bill launching Prohibition but who preferred to be remembered for his bill allowing farms to form cooperatives to bargain for higher prices. His house now is a museum.

Another historical site, on the north side of the river, is worth visiting. It's the 1901 brick home of Olof Swensson, a tyrannical Norwegian farmer and self-styled preacher who built a chapel in his home and, when his followers drifted back to the local Baptist church, preached to feed sacks propped in the pew. He was a candidate for governor, and his proposed 1892 amendment to the U.S. Constitution—forbidding any man to own more than 360 acres, and barring inheritances for illegitimate children (as was one of his)—is posted in the house, next to pleas for support from kings, emperors, and sultans throughout the world.

Montevideo is thoroughly Norwegian, though it celebrates Fiesta Days and has a statute of José Artigas, the nineteenth-century hero of Uruguayan independence, on Main Street. Near Smith Park, Historic Chippewa City, a collection of 23 original and re-created buildings, shows how early settlers lived.

The Minnesota River widens into Lac Qui Parle Lake, which has a state park on its southern shore. It's part of the legacy of Glacial Lake Agassiz, the largest lake that ever existed. As it drained after the last Ice Age, it carved the Minnesota River Valley.

From here, a series of lakes, sloughs, and marshes culminates in the scenic expanses of Big Stone Lake Wildlife Refuge, where birds lounge on sloughs as big as runways and bison roam in a restored tall-grass prairie. Just to the north, Ortonville sits on the southern tip of 26-mile-long Big Stone Lake, to which the railroad brought thousands of tourists until state highways were built and the tourists forsook it.

It's the end—or beginning—of a route that still resonates with the steps of those who first used it.

Trip Tips

Accommodations. Lower Sioux Lodge at Jackpot Junction has 276 rooms and suites, some with fireplace and whirlpool, and an indoor pool and spa, $55–$75 including $15 in coins; (800) 946-2274, www.jackpotjunction.com.

Upper Agency State Park rents two tepees, $20, as well as campsites; call the Connection, (800) 246-2267.

There are many motels along the route: St. Peter, (800) 473-3404, www.tourism.st-peter.mn.us; Mankato, (800) 657-4733, www.Mankato.com; Redwood Falls, (800) 657-7070, www.redwoodfalls.org; Montevideo, (800) 269-5527, www.montechamber.com; and Ortonville, (800) 568-5722, www.bigstonelake.com.

Camping. To reserve sites at Minneopa, west of Mankato; Flandrau adjoining New Ulm; and Fort Ridgely, Upper Sioux, and Lac Qui Parle state parks, call the Connection at (800) 246-2267; www.dnr.state.mn.us/parks.

Jackpot Junction. The big casino resort also has dining, at Café Dacotah and the State Fair-themed Carousel Buffet; free weekend entertainment and concerts by national performers; and golf at the 18-hole Dacotah Ridge; (800) 946-2274, www.jackpotjunction.com.

Treaty Site History Center. It's just north of St. Peter, off Highway 169, and is open 10 A.M. to 4 P.M. Mondays–Saturdays from April through September, and 1–4 P.M. October through March. Admission is $3 for those over 12; (507) 934-2160.

Historic Sites. All offer many special events in summer, www.mnhs.org. High season is May through October; call for exact hours. Harkin Store, (507) 354-2016; Fort Ridgely, (507) 426-7888; Lower Sioux Agency and Birch Coulee Battlefield, (507) 697-6321; Upper Sioux Agency, (320) 564-4777, www.mnhs.org.

Events. Big Stone Bird Festival, early May. Fiesta Days in Montevideo, mid-June. Lower Sioux Pow Wow in Morton, mid-June. Upper Sioux Wacipi at Upper Sioux Agency State Park, first weekend in August. Corn Fest in Ortonville, third weekend in August. Rock Bend Folk Festival in St. Peter, weekend after Labor Day. Mdewakanton Pow Wow in Mankato, second or third weekend in September.

Big Stone Lake Cruises. From Ortonville, Judy Drewicke gives very interesting narrated cruises on her pontoon boat, the *Eahtonka II.* They're held mid-May to mid-September, $8.50; (800) 519-7075.

Background Reading. *The Sioux Uprising of 1862,* by Kenneth Carley, and *Through Dakota Eyes,* edited by Gary Clayton Anderson and Alan R. Woolworth, are available from the Minnesota Historical Society, (800) 647-7827.

More Information. For maps of the scenic byway that include historic sites, call Redwood Falls at (800) 657-7070. Prairie Waters is a consortium of towns along the river, (800) 269-5527, www.prairiewaters.com. For finding Dakota Conflict sites, a DeLorme *Atlas & Gazetteer* also is helpful.

32. Pipestone: For Centuries, a Sacred Spot

It's easy to see why the Plains Indians saw the Great Spirit at work in a far corner of Minnesota.

Amid an ocean of tall grass, a fractured pile of hard red rock suddenly erupts from the sod. This is Sioux quartzite, once sand at the edge of a red ocean, cooked and pressed into marble-like stone over a billion years. Beneath the quartzite is a thin seam of a softer stone, a red, hardened clay that's barely harder than a fingernail.

This is pipestone, mined for centuries by people of many tribes, who carved it into effigies and pipes called calumets, whose smoke carried messages to the Great Spirit. Artist George Catlin, the first European to see the

A trail through an island of jagged red quartzite leads to Winnewissa Falls.

quarry, recorded a Dakota account of its origin: the Great Spirit, in the form of a large bird, called all the tribes together and, forming a pipe from the stone, smoked it and told all his children its stone was their flesh, and the grounds from which it came sacred.

Some tribes believed the quarry was where the Great Spirit created man, and others that he sent a flood to cleanse the Earth, and that the pipestone is the blood that remains. Some believed it was uncovered by the hooves of a white bison; others by the great spirit of thunder.

Catlin's accounts of the rare stone engaged the imaginations of others, too, far beyond Minnesota's borders. In 1855, Henry Wadsworth Longfellow penned the popular poem "Song of Hiawatha," mixing Iroquois and Ojibwe legends with Victorian romanticism and setting it to the meter of a Finnish epic poem. It began, "On the mountains of the prairie/On the great red pipestone quarry/Gitche Manito, the mighty/He the master of life, descending/On the red crags of the quarry/Stood erect, and called the nations/Called the tribes of men together." The 23-part poem put Pipestone on the map, drawing a stream of tourists that has never stopped.

Today, the quarries are protected as part of Pipestone National Monument and are worked only by enrolled members of tribes, in the traditional way—by hand, after a prayer. Still, there are those who treat pipestone as if it were no more sacred than gravel. As visitors turn into the monument drive, past the souvenir shop Fort Pipestone, they see a sign—$3 a pound for pipestone that's hacked out of a private lot with a backhoe.

All around Pipestone, Indian culture exists cheek-by-jowl with European culture. Across from the monument entrance, three granite boulders sit, fragments of a 50-foot boulder carried down from Canada by a glacier. These Three Maidens are considered the dwelling place of spirits who guard the quarries, and Indians who visit often tuck offerings of tobacco or sage into their crevices.

Just a few yards away, brightly colored bleachers and concession stands surround a small pond, part of an old quartzite quarry. The "Song of Hiawatha" pageant, staged by townsfolk in fringed buckskin and braided wigs, annually brings 10,000 spectators to Pipestone over three summer weekends. Before the townsfolk started putting it on in 1949, it was performed by the eighth-grade graduating class of the Pipestone Indian Training School, one of the boarding schools to which children were sent to "unlearn" Indian language and customs. The school closed in 1953, and now is Southwestern Technical College.

Just down Hiawatha Avenue, a giant peace pipe sits outside the 1890 cream-brick Rock Island Depot. This is the home of Rock Island Espresso & Art Gallery, run by the Keepers of the Sacred Tradition of Pipemakers, who promote American Indian traditions and public awareness of them.

Some feel pipestone should be used only for sacred purposes, by Indians. But others, like the Keepers, feel pipestone objects are invested with sacred

Bison are permanent residents of Blue Mounds State Park.

Blue Mounds: A Lovely Patch of Prairie

In the southwest corner of Minnesota, the prairie rises gradually atop a dome of hard quartzite, the uplifted floor of an ancient sea. This prairie coteau, known locally as Buffalo Ridge, juts into northwest Iowa on one edge and North Dakota on the other, rising to more than 750 feet above the surrounding plain. Waters flowing off its eastern flank go into the Mississippi River; off the west, into the Missouri.

Its bedrock pops out of the earth at the famous quarries of Pipestone and at the Jeffers Petroglyphs. And near Luverne, 6 miles north of I-90, it's exposed in a spectacular cliff line, 90 feet high and 1.5 mile long. In the far-off haze, this red quartzite escarpment looked blue to approaching settlers, who called it Blue Mounds. The land around it was too rocky to farm, and today it's preserved as Blue Mounds State Park.

When it became a state park in 1961, three bison were brought in from Nebraska. The park's herd now numbers about 50 and can be observed from platforms near the park's north entrance and from Mound Trail, which follows the fence of their summer pasture.

Blue Mounds also is one of the best places in the state to drink in the beauty of the prairie. Its interpretive center is the former home of author Frederick Manfred, a six-sided aerie he called a "tipi." From there, 13 miles of paths, broken by clumps of blood red rock, wind through restored prairie. In the late spring, the filmy pink strands of prairie smoke wave in the breeze, and in June and July, yellow blooms burst from prickly pear cactus. The prairie landscape is most striking in late summer, when it becomes a sea of tall grass and big bluestem.

(Continued)

meaning only when they have been blessed for ceremonial uses, and that exposure to the traditions helps white people understand and respect Indian culture. Among those the group honors is Joe Taylor, a Santee Dakota who made his living carving pipes in front of the railroad depot and selling them up and down the aisles of trains that passed through.

All paths lead eventually to Pipestone National Monument, established in 1937. There's an eight-minute slide show in the interpretive center, and tribal artisans often demonstrate carving techniques. From there, the mile-long Circle Trail leads past small operating pits and stands of sumac, whose pithy wood is hollowed out and used as pipe stems. Then stacks of quartzite begin to push through the earth. One lone column is called Leaping Rock, from which young men proved their valor by jumping six feet to another ledge.

On one mound are initials from the first official visitors, members of the 1838 Nicollet Expedition, which produced the first accurate map of the Upper Mississippi region. "This admirable hill awaits the poet and the painter, who should visit it when the last rays of the setting sun are falling upon it," cartographer Joseph Nicollet said of the quarry area. Nearby, Inscription Rock still bears the names of pioneers who visited a half-century later. The trail continues through an arched stairway and above Winnewissa

(Continued)

It's a tableau best seen early in the morning, when wildflowers emerge from haze and the cliff line gleams red in the morning sun, or late, when the slow-moving bison are silhouetted against the horizon. These also are the best times to hear the calls of grassland birds.

To see portraits of Blue Mounds in every season, stop by the Brandenburg Gallery in Luverne, the hometown of *National Geographic* photographer Jim Brandenburg. On the gallery's walls hang photos so beautiful it's as if God arranged all the elements just for him—lightning bolts snaking toward Earth, Indian grass glowing in the fierce orange of the setting sun, clouds sitting plump and rosy in endless sky.

To the Indians, this was God's canvas, the spiritual backdrop for their culture. "We did not think of the great open plains, the beautiful rolling hills, and winding streams with tangled growth, as wild," said Lakota chief Luther Standing Bear. "Only to the white man was nature a wilderness, and only to him was the land infested with wild animals and savage people. To us, it was tame. Earth was bountiful, and we were surrounded with the blessing of the Great Mystery."

Trip Tips

Getting There. Interesting stops along Interstate 90 include Fairmont, built

Falls, Winnewissa being the Dakota word for "jealous maiden." From the other side, there's a view of a rugged profile jutting from the quartzite—the Oracle, whom tribal shamans believed could talk.

This red and pink rock, as hard and grainy as the pipestone is soft and smooth, has given the town of Pipestone a handsome downtown, with 20 quartzite buildings on the National Register of Historic Places. The 1888 Historic Calumet Inn, the town meeting place since frontier boom days, is made of it. So is the 1896 Leon Moore Building, whose namesake not only owned a quarry but could sculpt its stone—the façade includes a dozen sandstone gargoyles, including an ogre blowing a raspberry and a jester wrinkling his nose.

An 1897 stone building next door houses the Pipestone Performing Arts Center, and around the corner is one of the most ornate buildings, its 1896 quartzite facade topped by stepped gables. Once City Hall, it's now the home of the Pipestone County Museum, whose galleries include the accouterments of white settlers and local tribes, including items used in the movie *Dances with Wolves* and by Civil War soldiers from the area.

Upon quartzite, the pioneer culture was built, and upon pipestone, the Indian culture.

---

around a chain of five lakes, and Worthington, built around 785-acre Lake Okabena.

Accommodations. There are several motels in Luverne, including a Super 8, (507) 283-9541, and a Comfort Inn, (507) 283-9488.

Dining. On Main Street, the Coffey Haus is a pleasant place for lunch.

Events. Buffalo Days in Luverne, first weekend in June.

Blue Mounds State Park. It holds an open house the first Sunday in June, with free bison burgers served at a picnic, (507) 283-1307, www.dnr.state.mn.us/parks/bluemounds/. For campsite reservations, call the Connection at (800) 246-2267.

Brandenburg Gallery. It's on Main Street and open daily in the summer, Monday–Saturday the rest of the year; (507) 283-1884.

More Information. (888) 283-4061, www.luvernemn.com.

Trip Tips

Accommodations. The Historic Calumet Inn on Main Street has attractive rooms, some furnished with antiques and some modern rooms, $65–$80, and some with whirlpools, $100–$130; (800) 535-7610, www.calumetinn.com. There's also a Super 8, (507) 825-4217.

The Pipestone RV Campground, across from the national monument, rents tepees as well as RV and tent sites and has a heated swimming pool. Open from May through October, (507) 825-2455, www.pipestonervcamp ground.com.

Dining. The Calumet's dining room is a nice place for dinner. At the edge of downtown, Lange's Café is a good place for breakfast, or a meal any time— it's open 24 hours a day, seven days a week.

Pipestone National Monument. It's open daily. For quiet strolls, arrive early or late; it's open till 8 P.M. on summer weekends. Admission is $2 per person or $4 for families; free for American Indians and children 16 and under; (507) 825-5464, www.nps.gov/pipe.

Jeffers Petroglyphs. These ancient characters—including serpents, buffalo, stick figures, handprints—carved into red Sioux quartzite tell the story of an ancient people. Guides lead visitors along trails and help them see the carvings. From Highway 71 north of Windom, take County Highway 10 east for 3 miles, then County Highway 2 for 1 mile to the site. It's open daily from Memorial Day to Labor Day, and Friday–Sunday in May and September. Admission is $3, $1.50 children 6–15. In summer, the site holds programs on prairie flora and fauna, as well as ancient and modern Indian customs, (507) 628-5591, www.mnhs.org.

Events. Water Tower Festival, last weekend in June. Song of Hiawatha Pageant, last two weekends in July and first weekend of August. Civil War Festival, third weekend in August in even-numbered years. Pow Wow and Blessing of Quarries, last weekend in August.

Nightlife. Pipestone Performing Arts Center on Main Street hosts theater performances by the Calumet Players as well as concerts and other events, (877) 722-2787.

Recreation. The Family Aquatic Center has slides, one a 126-foot body flume slide, and geysers.

More Information. (800) 336-6125, www.pipestoneminnesota.com.

Section VI

Bluff Country

33. Northfield: The Town That Foiled Jesse James

As the James-Younger Gang found out, there's more to Northfield than meets the eye.

This town, so amply endowed with sugar maples, ivy-covered stone buildings, and people in tweed, looks placid today. It was pretty quiet in 1876, too—but that year, it was violence that made the town's name go down in history.

In 1876, Northfield had two young colleges—Carleton and St. Olaf—and a thriving grain mill on the Cannon River. Its townspeople were going about their business on the afternoon of September 7, when three men in long white dusters strode into Northfield's First National Bank. Another two men, Cole Younger and Clell Miller, slowly rode toward the bank, and Miller took up guard at its door. But a nosy local man named Joseph Allen tried to get inside; instead of pulling him in, Miller shoved him away, whereupon Allen cried, "Get your guns, boys, they're robbing the bank."

A former Union sharpshooter and an expert hunter were nearby; they grabbed rifles and, in a few minutes, Miller was dead. So was William Stiles, part of a rear guard that included Jesse James and Jim Younger. Bob Younger, Cole Younger, and Charlie Pitts were wounded. Frank and Jesse James escaped, but Pitts was killed by a posse from the town of Madelia, and the Younger brothers were captured and served terms at the state prison in Stillwater.

No one knows for sure why the James-Younger Gang ventured into Minnesota to rob Northfield's First National Bank. But the mill owner may have known. Adelbert Ames, a Union commander during the war, had just been impeached as governor of Mississippi and had returned to his family's mill business in Northfield. He was a director in the bank, and his father-in-law, General Benjamin Butler, was a major investor.

Butler also was one of the most hated men in the South. He was infamous for filching Confederate silver—his nickname was "Spoons"—and for his occupation of New Orleans in 1862, when his Woman Order decreed that any local woman who insulted a Union soldier would be treated as a prostitute. Around the South, his face was often featured on the bottom of chamber pots.

The bank continued operating and today is part of the Northfield Historical Society Museum, with displays that include the original gilt vault door, desk, clock, and plank floor, plus guns used in the raid by Charlie Pitts and Cole Younger. The Ames Mill is part of Northfield's Malt-O-Meal plant. Carleton and St. Olaf built national reputations as fine liberal arts colleges.

And the people of Northfield, which became known as "The Little Town That Defeated the Jesse James Gang," continued the maverick tradition. The St. Olaf Class of 1924 created the nation's first listener-supported radio station, WCAL. Economist Thorstein Veblen, who grew up nearby, coined the term "conspicuous consumption." Paul Wellstone was a Carleton professor before Minnesota voters voted him into the U.S. Senate, where he became a thorn in the side of many well-entrenched legislators.

But Northfield hasn't foiled any desperadoes since 1876. Today, it lives by the motto "Home of Cows, Colleges and Contentment."

Less than an hour from the Twin Cities, it's one of Minnesota's best weekend destinations, and perhaps *the* best for travelers on a budget. The Archer House, a mansard-roofed hotel opened the year after the bank raid, is now a historic landmark with 36 individually decorated rooms, many of them inexpensive. In the Tavern, the cozy, stone-walled restaurant that's been downstairs since 1877, it's hard to spend more than $20.

And the entertainment—sometimes world-class—almost always is free. On the handsome hilltop campus of St. Olaf, there are concerts and recitals nearly every night, given by faculty, students, and, sometimes, nationally known musicians. The college, founded by Norwegian immigrants in 1874, is known worldwide for its choirs, orchestras, and bands, and its annual Christmas Festival usually is broadcast by PBS.

Carleton also puts on concerts and theater performances, and its free Friday-morning Convocation lectures, featuring national speakers on issues of the day, can be packed and raucous. Carleton students are known for independent thinking; the college is considered one of the best liberal arts colleges in the nation.

It also supplies one of the best places to reflect and rejuvenate. In Carleton's 400-acre Arboretum, or Arb, trails wind along the Cannon River past a restored oak savanna. In May, the hiking trails of Nerstrand Big Woods

The mansard-roofed Archer House is a landmark on Northfield's Division Street.

State Park, 15 miles to the south, are lined with delicate wildflowers that draw crowds, and in the fall, the park's maple-basswood forest glows with color.

The streets of Northfield, population 15,200, also are worth walking. Between downtown and the Carleton campus, they're lined with handsome old houses—Queen Anne, Craftsman, Tudor Revival—many of them rich in architectural detail and lovingly restored. The stately campus of St. Olaf is on a hilltop on the west edge of town, and Division Street lies between the two campuses, dominated by the red-brick Archer House, with its arched dormer windows and long portico, which passes the little shops that flank the hotel lobby. It's also worth exploring the gift shops, used-book stores, cafés, and coffeehouses sprinkled elsewhere along Division.

The Cannon River—misnamed from the French *La Riviere aux canots,* or canoes, given because Indians and traders often hid their canoes around the river's mouth—flows right behind Division Street. There's a walkway following its placid waters, which the mill dam turns into furious white water. Right off the falls is picturesque Bridge Square, the heart of the town.

The Northfield Historical Society Museum is next to the square. No one should miss its gripping video of the annual bank-raid re-enactment, which includes the action inside the bank, when cashier Joseph Lee Heywood, who had refused to open the vault, was shot and killed, reportedly by Frank James. Volunteers also discuss some of the mysteries of the raid, including smuggled cadavers, a mystery skeleton, and the bizarre fates of the gang members who survived the raid.

Every September, Northfield stages a vivid reenactment of the famous 1876 bank raid.

But anyone who can should come to Northfield the weekend after Labor Day, when townspeople re-enact the famous raid. At the appointed time, as spectators watch from the sidelines, women and men in 1870s garb begin to walk up and down Division Street. "Who could have suspected," the announcer asks, "that violence lurked just a moment away?" Then three men in long white dusters enter the bank, and soon the street is filled with the thundering of hooves and din of gunfire. Horses wheel and rear, and at the end, three men lie still in the street—one representing a recent immigrant from Sweden who didn't understand English.

The re-enactment, performed several times a day during the festival, is a crowd pleaser, and the saga fascinates new visitors every year. But, luckily for Northfield, the long-ago notoriety isn't the only reason to visit.

Trip Tips

Accommodations. The Archer House has 36 individually decorated rooms that range from $40 to $140, most with country floral décor but some with themes. Ten of the rooms have double whirlpools. The next-to-smallest rooms are the best value. Of the more expensive rooms, the Manor House is especially charming; (800) 247-2235, www.archerhouse.com.

In peaceful Dundas, just 2 miles away, the 1869 Martin Oaks B&B has three attractive rooms, $75–$85; (507) 645-4644.

Dining. The Tavern, in the lower level of the Archer House, serves an inexpensive array of interesting dishes. Chapati, also in the Archer House, serves the cuisine of India (closed Sundays). The Contented Cow, on Division Street, is a nonsmoking pub that specializes in such British fare as shepherd's pie, ploughman's lunches, and treacle tart. The Reub 'n' Stein is a longtime student hangout with happy hours, drink specials, and a menu of lasagna, reubens, burgers, and other basics.

At the foot of Manitou Heights, in an 1889 frame house, the Ole Store has been a grocery and cafe for Oles—St. Olaf students—since 1909. It's a good place to have pie or an Ole Roll, a pecan caramel bun that's so famous it has its own song, sung to the tune of "O Tannenbaum."

Events. Thursday evenings on Bridge Square, summer concerts, ice-cream socials, and variety shows. Defeat of Jesse James Days, four-day weekend after Labor Day, including the Jesse James Bike Tour on Saturday. Tour of Homes, October.

Historical Society Museum. It's open 10 A.M. to 4 P.M. Tuesday through Sunday, $2; (507) 645-9268.

Nightlife. Call St. Olaf for a calendar of concerts. Downtown, the Contented Cow schedules music Thursdays–Saturdays during the school year, (507) 663-1351, www.contentedcow.com.

St. Olaf. For a music calendar, call (507) 646-3179. For theater, call (507) 646-3240, www.stolaf.edu.

Carleton. For a list of Friday-morning lectures and other events, call (507) 646-4183, www.Carleton.edu.

Carleton Arboretum. There are 10 miles of hiking and skiing trails in Carleton's Arboretum, just northeast of downtown along the Cannon River.

Nerstrand Big Woods State Park. It has 13 miles of hiking trails and 8 miles of cross-country ski trails. From downtown Northfield, take Division Street (Highway 246) south for approximately 11 miles to County Highway 40 and into the park. There's a loose-leaf wildflower guide in the park office; (507) 334-8848, www.dnr.state.mn.us/parks.

More Information. Northfield visitors bureau, (800) 658-2548, www.northfieldchamber.com.

34. Lanesboro: Renaissance on the Root River

In an isolated bluff-country valley, reached only by small, winding roads, lies one of Minnesota's favorite weekend getaways.

There are no resorts here, no chic boutiques, no—heaven forbid—national franchises. The aroma of manure hangs over downtown on Fridays, when the weekly livestock auction is held. Only 860 people live here, and they can't afford to advertise much, so most visitors come via word of mouth.

Even so, Lanesboro is the town every other small community in Minnesota wishes it could be. Located 40 miles southeast of Rochester and about a two-hour drive from the Twin Cities, Lanesboro is right on the proverbial

Lanesboro's downtown hums with activity in summer and fall.

196

street paved with gold. The beautiful Root River State Trail goes through town, following the looping river and crossing it on dozens of wooden bridges. A professional theater company stages plays 11 months a year. Dozens of artists work here; many sell their art at a cooperative gallery. B&Bs occupy lovely Victorian houses, and shops fill the century-old brick storefronts.

Lanesboro, hemmed in on three sides by tall limestone bluffs, always has been picturesque. In the late 1860s, its four-story Phoenix Hotel was the largest hotel west of the Mississippi, thanks to land speculators who envisioned a spa on the site. But the hotel burned, and the town turned to agriculture.

By the 1970s, Lanesboro had fallen asleep. The last train had gone through, and the movie theater had closed. Downtown storefronts were used as grain silos. Lanesboro, with no county seat and no major highway, was the center of nothing.

Then, a miracle happened. During the 1980s, the paved trail was created along the old rail bed, and throngs of bicyclists began to show up. Native son Eric Lorentz Bunge moved back from Denver in 1989 and opened the Commonweal Theatre in the old St. Mane movie house. The Cornucopia artists' collective took over an 1879 general store, covering its high walls with art and placing sculptures on its sturdy floors.

Now, Lanesboro is the recreational and cultural capital of southeast Minnesota. During the summer, Commonweal puts on six shows a week, and on Sunday evenings, the live radio show "Over the Back Fence" takes over the St. Mane. Cornucopia puts on eight or nine shows every year. Both are running out of room, and in 2000, the Legislature allotted $1 million for a new arts center that will house them both.

But the theater and gallery don't have a lock on culture. Touring folk, blues, and jazz musicians perform in the 250-seat auditorium at Eagle Bluff Environmental Learning Center, four miles west of town. Back in Lanesboro, there's often live music and dancing at the Sons of Norway hall, a homey nook next to Sylvan Park. Next to the trail, the Lanesboro History Museum holds a trove of town memorabilia.

Parkway Avenue is the hub of activity. Along with the shops, there's Scenic Valley Winery, where visitors can sample fruit wines, and Das Wurst Haus, a German deli that makes its own mustards and root beer. On the other side of Parkway, bicyclists mob the Ford Soda Fountain, once a Model T dealership, and River Trail Coffee, which sells smoothies.

In 1998, Lanesboro won a Great American Main Street award from the National Trust for Historical Preservation. And there's no question that downtown Lanesboro is a very nice place to be.

But, as busy as its streets are, most people take themselves elsewhere, for Lanesboro is just ground zero for explorers. From it, bicyclists head east to

Houston, a 31-mile stretch, or west to Fountain, an 11-mile uphill stretch. But another trail begins 4.5 miles into the Fountain stretch. At Isinours Junction, cyclists can turn south onto the Harmony-Preston Valley State Trail, riding 5.5 miles into Preston; this shaded stretch, along the South Branch of the Root River, is the prettiest of the whole system. From Preston, it's 12 miles up an 8 percent grade to Harmony; the last half is through farm fields.

Canoeists also frequent the Root River, and trout fishermen cast their lines from the shady banks of the many creeks. The hills are the domain of turkey hunters and, in early May, of those who stalk the marvelous morel mushroom, which hides amid the roots of dying elms. Also, picnickers head for Inspiration Point on County Highway 16, which has a beautiful view of Lanesboro.

The ultimate view is reserved for daredevils. At Eagle Bluff Learning Center, on a ridge high above the North Arm of the Root River, a series of 30-foot-high cables stretch between towers. This is the Treetops High Ropes Course, and if you can get yourself to walk sideways on a narrow cable, pulling yourself from one short, knotted rope to another, you'll be rewarded by a stupendous view.

During the week, schoolchildren come to Eagle Bluff to learn about life in the forest. But weekends are devoted to groups and families, and the public can drop by for Saturday-night concerts and Sunday brunch, along with a naturalist program or a cruise along the ropes course.

Today, people from all over the nation and world visit Lanesboro, a fact that still amazes the townsfolk. It's said that some of the old-timers are a little peeved they no longer get "their" parking space when they go downtown. But for everyone else, it's a sacrifice they're willing to bear.

Trip Tips

Accommodations. See "Lodging in Lanesboro," pages 199–201.

Dining. In downtown Lanesboro, Old Village Hall has a very pleasant patio and serves good pastas and grilled meat and fish; (507) 467-2962. Also downtown, Nick's Ribs is friendly, informal, and serves good food. Mrs. B's serves a fine five-course, $26 menu Wednesday–Sunday by reservation, (507) 467-2154. The Victorian House serves rich French cuisine Tuesday–Saturday, (507) 467-3457.

Events. Candlelight skiing, January in Preston and February in Whalan. Norske Vinter Fest, Presidents' Day weekend. Sykkle Tur, festivities in all trail towns, third weekend in May. Art in the Park, Father's Day. Buffalo Bill Days, first weekend in August. Oktoberfest, first Saturday in October.

In the bucolic hills outside Lanesboro, Berwood Hill Inn is the fanciest of the area's many bed and breakfasts.

Lodging in Lanesboro

Twenty years ago, the only places to stay in Lanesboro were some small hunters' cabins near the city park. That was before there was anything to do in the isolated village besides hunt and fish. Now, with visitors pouring in, Lanesboro has become the bed-and-breakfast capital of the state, with more B&Bs than any other town, plus several inns.

And they're still not enough for everyone who wants to visit on prime weekends in summer and fall.

But if you make your reservation early enough, you'll find lots of choices, from the romantic Berwood Hill, an inn Martha Stewart could love, to the cozy Knotty Pine cabins, a nice place for families. From May through October, especially on weekends, rooms are hard to get; reserve early.

Anna V's B&B is a 1908 Queen Anne with three attractive rooms, one with two-person Jacuzzi and two with small fridges, $95–$130. Mike and Gail Eckerman, (507) 467-2686.

Berwood Hill Inn, a renovated 1870s farmhouse, sits on a ridge 4 miles outside Lanesboro and has a lovely view of the countryside from its landscaped grounds. The interior looks like a magazine spread; four very attractive rooms are $150–$200; (800) 803-6748, www.berwood.com.

Brewster's Red Hotel is on the second level of an 1870s building, right off

(Continued)

Nightlife. Commonweal Theatre performs Tuesday–Sunday afternoon in summer; Thursday–Sunday in May and September to December; and Friday–Sunday from February to April. Tickets are $15 adults, $7 children; (800) 657-7025, www.commonwealtheatre.org. On Sunday evenings in summer, the live radio show "Over the Back Fence" is presented, $3. Touring musicians also perform at the St. Mane.

Bicycle Rental. Little River General Store on Parkway Avenue rents bikes and canoes and also offers a shuttle service, (507) 467-2943, (800) 994-2943 (summer only), www.lrgeneralstore.com.

(Continued)

the trail downtown. Six pleasant rooms with TV are $45–$75, but there are no common rooms or breakfast. Mark Brewster, (507) 467-2999.

Cady Hayes House B&B is a classic 1890 Queen Anne with three attractive rooms, one with fold-out sofa, $80–$115. The Norwegian and Garden rooms are particularly nice, and proprietor Peggy Hanson knows everything going on around town, (507) 467-2621.

Carrollton Country Inn, an 1880 and 1900 farmhouse 2.5 miles from town, is just off the trail. Four attractive rooms, two with shared bath, are $65–$100. The Carrollton Room, with its balcony view, is especially nice. Proprietors Gloria and Charles Ruen, who live nearby, leave breakfast in the kitchen; (507) 467-2257.

Coffee Street Inn is a hotel in a newly renovated building downtown. Four nice rooms have a private bath and coffeemaker; three other rooms share a bath, kitchenette, and living room, $40–$75. Deb Danielson, (507) 467-2674.

Cottage House Inn, a modern inn across from the Commonweal Theatre, is always a good bet, especially in the off season. Fourteen simple but attractive rooms, seven with two beds, are $60–$70, $30–$45 between November to April. A large, hot breakfast is $6. Two-bedroom duplex apartments around the corner rent for $80–$120. Proprietors Waldo and Marilyn Bunge are friendly and down-to-earth; (800) 944-0099.

Galligan House B&B, a homey turn-of-the-century Victorian, has three attractive rooms, $70–$100; the simple white Vista Room is especially nice. Longtime resident Doris Dybing is the personable proprietor, (800) 430-7557.

Green Gables Inn, a newer motel with a sunken stone patio and backyard that goes to the river, is a nice place to stay with children. Twelve attractive rooms, one with kitchen, go for $55–$80. Two-night minimum weekends; (800) 818-4225.

Habberstad House B&B is an 1890 Queen Anne with four attractive, window-lined rooms, one with two-person whirlpool, $95–$125; (507) 467-3560.

Eagle Bluff. The center offers inexpensive Family Getaway Weekends that include three excellent meals daily, activities, a concert, and accommodations in carpeted dormitory rooms, each with a private bath; (888) 800-9558, www.eagle-bluff.org.

More Information. (800) 944-2670, www.lanesboro.com, www.bluff-country.com.

Hillcrest Gäst Hus is a renovated house with a panoramic view of the bluffs; two attractive rooms go for $50–$65. Paul and Carole Fry, (507) 467-3079.

Historic Scanlan House B&B is a classic 1889 Victorian with an over-the-top décor that B&B aficionados may enjoy. Six lavishly decorated rooms, four with two-person whirlpool, $70–$135, and three new luxury suites, $185–$260. Kirsten, Mary, and Gene Mensing are the enthusiastic proprietors, (800) 944-2158, www.scanlanhouse.com.

Knotty Pine Cabins is a good place to stay with children; the three clean, cozy cabins have a yard and playground. They're $35 and $45. Dean and Elaine Hove, (507) 467-3779 or, in the off-season, (651) 436-5046.

Mrs. B's B&B, an 1870 stone commercial building right on the river, has 10 small but attractive rooms, one with twin beds, $50–$95. Breakfast is served at small tables, for those who like early morning privacy; (507) 467-2154.

O'Leary's B&B is a 1910 Victorian with Arts and Crafts interior accents. Five simple but attractive rooms, one with twin beds and one with a king, are $75–$95, and there's a $30 loft room children love. Breakfast is a continental buffet. Open weekends only. Proprietor Bonnie Handmacher is a triathlete and dispenses advice on running and bicycling routes, (507) 467-3737.

Sleepy Nisse (in Norwegian, elves; pronounced NI-seh) B&B, is an 1892 Queen Anne with a Norwegian theme. Four nice rooms, two with private bath, $75–$115. Proprietors are Jerry and Elaine Johnson, (507) 467-2268.

Thompson House B&B is an 1872 Italianate house next to the river, with airy common rooms decorated with antiques and folk art. Four old-fashioned but attractive rooms, $75–$125. The Maid's Room, with its view of the dam waterfall, is especially nice. Kathy and Robert Culbertson, (507) 467-2253.

If camping is more your style, sites at Lanesboro's Sylvan Park, on the river, are first-come, first-served. Tent sites are $10 and camper sites $17. Old Barn Resort is right off the trail, at Isinours Junction, and has a heated pool, restaurant, and golf course. Tent sites are $12 for two people and camper sites $20–$23.50. Hostel beds are $11–$35; (800) 552-2512.

Bicycle Trails: Minnesota's Paved Favorites

In 1977, one of the first paved bicycle trails in the nation opened in northern Minnesota. The 27-mile Heartland State Trail, which linked the lake resort towns of Park Rapids and Walker, was appreciated, but it didn't bring a flood of tourists. Other trails followed, built on abandoned rail corridors. But it wasn't until the late 1980s, when the Root River State Trail was developed through picturesque bluff country, that the miraculous fruits of bicycle tourism began to be felt.

Lanesboro, a quaint but virtually abandoned backwater along the trail, blossomed into a tourist favorite. The Lanesboro effect has galvanized towns throughout Minnesota, and they're not waiting around for state money to develop trails. As a result, Minnesota is one of the best states in the nation to ride bicycles. In total miles of rail corridors converted to trails, it's usually second only to Wisconsin, with Michigan, Pennsylvania, and Iowa rounding out the top five.

Most of the trails in those states, however, are crushed limestone. Minnesota's are asphalt, which holds up better in bad weather, is easier for cyclists pulling child carts, and can be used by in-line skaters. More important, tourists love them. Now, the secret is out, and Minnesota's trails are attracting weekenders from many other states. Sometimes, the most popular trails are a little crowded—but more miles are being added all the time.

Trip Tips

More Information. The annual *Minnesota Bike Trails & Rides* guide is a handy list of bicycle tours and trails, with maps and highlights. It's available May 15, free along the trails or $4 from Minnesota Bike Trails & Rides, P.O. Box 28, Nevis, MN 56467, (218) 652-3475, www.mnbiketrails.com. To get free individual maps of the state trails and the Cannon Valley Trail, call the Department of Natural Resources (DNR) at (651) 296-6157, (888) 646-6367 from outside Minnesota, www.dnr.state.mn.us.

Trails

Cannon Valley. This 20-mile trail between Cannon Falls and Red Wing is one of the most popular in the state. It's a beautiful, shady ride above the Cannon River with a picnic area and ice cream store in Welch, its midpoint. The trail can be crowded on weekends. In Red Wing, catch the trail off Bench Street, near Pottery Place, or 1.5 mile north, off Highway 61. Maintained by a trail association; daily fee is $2; (507) 263-0508, www.cannonvalleytrail.com.

Douglas. This is a pleasant, 12.5-mile ride through rolling farmland between Pine Island's city park and the outskirts of Rochester. There's a snack stop in Douglas; (507) 285-7176.

(Continued)

Gateway. It's 18 miles from Cayuga Avenue in St. Paul, just east of Interstate 35E, to Pine Point Park in Stillwater Township. Many people park in a lot near Highway 36 and Hadley Avenue in Oakdale, where the trail parallels Highway 36 before it heads into the country.

Glacial Lakes. This scenic trail through the Little Crow Lakes region starts from the Civic Center at the northeast edge of Willmar and winds 12 miles to New London, passing the big beach on Green Lake in Spicer. From Spicer, it follows Highway 23 but is shielded by trees. Another 6 miles of compacted granite continue from New London to Hawick; (800) 845-8747, www.kandi yohi.com.

Harmony-Preston Valley. From Isinours Junction, 4.5 miles west of Lanesboro on the Root River State Trail, this 18-mile trail goes through Preston and up to the farm town of Harmony. The 5.5 miles to Preston, which follow the South Branch of the Root River, are the most bucolic of the whole system. The last third of the trail, up to Harmony, is up an 8 percent grade; (800) 247-6466, www.bluffcountry.com.

Heartland. There are lots of towns to explore on this 27-mile ride between Park Rapids and Walker. Dorset, an odd little oasis that has as many restaurants as houses, is a frequent destination. Nevis has shops, cafés, and a city beach on Lake Belle Taine. Akeley is the home of the state's biggest Paul Bunyan, on whose outstretched hand people pose for pictures. The 9-mile stretch from Akeley to Walker is the most scenic. An 18-mile extension from Walker to Cass Lake is scheduled for 2001. Park Rapids, (800) 247-0054, www.parkrapids.com; Walker, (800) 833-1118, www.leech-lake.com.

Lake Wobegon. This 28-mile trail passes a series of picturesque old churches in towns that inspired the stories of Garrison Keillor, who lived near Freeport while working at Minnesota Public Radio's first station, in nearby Collegeville. Charlie's Café in Freeport, in fact, is supposed to be the model for Wobegon's Chatterbox Café. The trail ends in Sauk Centre, the home of Sinclair Lewis, who also chronicled the foibles of middle America. The eastern trailhead is a block from Avon's city beach, on Middlespunk Lake; (320) 255-6172.

Mesabi. The 132-mile, paved Mesabi Trail will connect Grand Rapids and Ely when completed. The longest section is the 50-mile stretch from Nashwauk to Eveleth, passing the Hull-Rust mine, Ironworld, and Mineview in the Sky. There's also a 15-mile stretch between Grand Rapids and Taconite. A Wheel Pass, $10 yearly, $5 weekly, can be bought from local businesses and visitor centers. Check for updates at (877) 637-2241, www.mesabitrail.com. Iron Trail tourism, (800) 777-8497, www.irontrail.org.

Paul Bunyan. This trail winds 48 paved miles through lake country from

(Continued)

(Continued)

Brainerd to Hackensack, and on to Bemidji for a total of 100 miles. It starts justeast of the Paul Bunyan Amusement Center, off Highway 371 at Excelsior Road. The 15 miles to Nisswa is the trail's quietest stretch. After Nisswa, the trail follows 371, separated by trees, until 3 miles north of Pequot Lakes, where it loses its tree cover until Backus. The 7 miles from Backus to Hackensack are the most scenic. There are also 5 miles paved from the northern trailhead in Lake Bemidji State Park. Another 18 miles from Hackensack to Walker and beyond may be paved in 2001. Check for updates at www.paulbunyantrail.com, or call Brainerd tourism, (800) 450-2838, www.brainerd.com.

Root River. This 42-mile trail, in lovely bluff country between Fountain and Houston, is Minnesota's pride and joy. Crossing dozens of bridges, it follows the Root River while passing the burgs of Lanesboro, Whalan, Peterson, and Rushford. It also connects to the 18-mile Harmony-Preston Valley Trail. Lanesboro tourism, (800) 944-2670, www.Lanesboro.com.

Sakatah. This low-profile, 39-mile trail between Faribault and Mankato has a mixture of scenery. Between Faribault and Waterville, it skirts lakes along a shady corridor. From there, it plunges into cool woods, passing Sakatah Lake State Park (*Sakatah* is Ojibwe for "singing hills"; it's pronounced sah-KAH-tah) and Elysian, where flocks of pelicans hang out on Lake Elysian. West of Madison Lake, the trail is away from the highway but on open fields. In Faribault, start off County Highway 21, on the south side of the Cannon River, or along Highway 60 just west of I-35. In Mankato, the trailhead is on Highway 22, near its junction with U.S. 14. The lakes are pretty but shallow; in late summer, they are generally full of algae, making swimming unpleasant. (800) 507-7787, www.mnlakesregion.com.

Soo Line. The 11-mile Soo Line Trail cuts through countryside on Mille Lacs' south shore, between the old depot behind Onamia's Main Street to the playing field in Isle. From Onamia, it's a 6-mile ride on County Highway 26 to Mille Lacs–Kathio State Park; in Isle, Father Hennepin State Park adjoins the town; (888) 350-2692, www.millelacs.com.

Sunrise Prairie. North of the Twin Cities, 23 miles of open trail wind from Hugo, just off U.S. Highway 61, to North Branch. The 7-mile stretch from Hugo to Forest Lake is known as the Hardwood Creek Trail; it follows the highway but is shielded by trees. The 16-mile stretch from Forest Lake is near the highway until, south of Stacy, it veers away. Traffic is heavy in Forest Lake; other towns make better starting spots. Chisago County Parks, (651) 674-2345, www.ccbiketrail.org.

Willard Munger. This 70-mile trail between Hinckley and Duluth is the nation's longest paved trail. The 55.5 miles from Hinckley to Carlton is known as the Fire Trail, as it passes through countryside scorched by the cataclysmic

Bicyclists head toward the town of Fountain on a picturesque stretch of the Root River State Trail.

Hinckley Fire of 1894 and the Cloquet and Moose Lake Fire of 1918, each of which killed more than 400 people. The trail starts in Hinckley near the green-frame Fire Museum, which holds fascinating exhibits about the cyclonic 1894 fire, and continues to Willow along a rail corridor that was the scene of a dramatic rescue. From Barnum, the trail follows Highway 61 into Carlton. The next 14.5 miles, through gorgeous Jay Cooke State Park, along the St. Louis River and downhill to Duluth, is the most scenic stretch of trail in the state; (888) 263-0586, www.munger-trail.com. For tourism information, call Hinckley at (800) 996-4566, www.hinckleymn.com, or Moose Lake at (800) 635-3680.

Day Tours

For a more complete list of day tours, consult Minnesota Bike Trails & Rides. Most cost $15–$25, with a discount for preregistration. Here are some of the most popular.

Minnesota Ironman. The last Sunday of April, benefiting Youth Hostelling International. There are rides of various lengths, including a century; (612) 378-3773, www.ironmanbikeride.org.

MS 60/30. One of the first Saturdays in May, benefiting the Minnesota chapter of the Multiple Sclerosis Society. It's 30 or 60 miles from Maplewood

(Continued)

(Continued)
along the Gateway Trail; (612) 335-7900 or (800) 582-5296, www.mssixty30.com.

Tour de Lake Minnetonka. Third Sunday in May, benefiting the Lake Minnetonka Association. It's 25 or 45 miles. Call (612) 378-5714, www.pro-events.com.

Moonlight River Ramble. The first Saturday in June, benefiting the Minnesota Coalition of Bicyclists. It's 12 or 20 miles from Fort Snelling. Call (612) 378-5714, www.pro-events.com.

Tour of Saints. The fourth Sunday in June. It's 35 or 50 miles out of Cold Spring, near St. Cloud, (800) 651-8687, www.tourofsaints.com.

Jesse James Bike Tour. The Saturday after Labor Day, benefiting the Mill Towns Trail. It's 10, 30, 60, or 100 miles out of Northfield; (800) 658-2548, www.northfieldchamber.com.

St. Paul Classic. The Sunday after Labor Day, on city streets, many closed to motorized traffic. There are 15- and 31-mile routes, with lots of music, food, and festivities; (952) 882-3180, www.spnec.org.

Stillwater Bicycle Classic. The third Sunday in September, benefiting the Gateway Trail Association. It's 20, 35, or 60 miles. Call (612) 378-5714, www.pro-events.com.

Headwaters 100. The fourth Saturday in September. It's 62.5 miles (a metric century) or 100 miles from Park Rapids to Itasca State Park and back; (800) 247-0054, www.parkrapids.com.

The Ride Across Minnesota (TRAM). This ride heads from the western border of the state to the east during the last week of July. The route changes every year but generally is around 300 miles. Sponsored by the MS Society since 1990, it's a very well-organized, well-supported ride through some of Minnesota's most scenic countryside and most interesting towns. Most of the 1,500 or so riders camp, though lodgings in motels and private homes are available. Host towns provide free entertainment and a variety of food to buy, from lasagna dinners and breakfasts in churches to state fair–style food from booths. Riders range in age from 5-year-olds on tandems to 80-year-olds.

Don't miss it—it's a blast. Registration is $55–$65 and includes camping, baggage hauling, and plentiful food at rest stops. The minimum pledge is $200; (612) 335-7900 or (800) 582-5296, www.mnms.org.

The MS Society also sponsors the very popular MS 150 on the second weekend of June, from Duluth to Anoka, with an overnight in Hinckley. Registration is $30–$35, with a $200 minimum pledge; (612) 335-7900 or (800) 582-5296, www.mnms.org.

35. Harmony: A Window on Amish Ways

In a state whose culture has been enriched by a melting pot of immigrants, there is still one group that remains resolutely unassimilated.

In 1974, families of Old Order Amish from Ohio began moving to the hilly countryside around Harmony, near the Iowa border. Locals watched, amazed, as they bought farmhouses only to rip out electricity and plumbing, setting bathtubs in yards to water calves. They put up windmills and fitted windows with smaller panes, to minimize reflections. They drove into town in horse-drawn buggies, with steel-rimmed wheels that clattered on the pavement.

A farmstead near Harmony includes a big, sturdy barn, the central feature of Amish farms.

They spoke a Low German dialect used four hundred years ago and led a lifestyle dictated by a strict interpretation of the Bible, refusing to be photographed (Deuteronomy 5:8), wearing only plain, dark colors (Peter 3:3-4), and covering their hair (Corinthians 11:5).

The Amish were different, all right. But they also were good neighbors to the nearby "English," as they called them. When locals helped out the Amish—providing rides to medical appointments in other towns, for example—they found their favors returned threefold.

Eventually, Harmony folk became friends with their Amish neighbors, who raised extra money by selling baskets, jams, baked goods, and vegetables along roadsides. The townsfolk started leading groups of curious tourists to visit their friends, so the Amish could make money right on their farms and the tourists could learn more about why the Amish live as they do.

The Amish are direct descendants of the Anabaptists, a Swiss group that believed Martin Luther and other leaders of the Reformation didn't go far enough in returning the church to Scripture. Around 1720, they arrived in America, where they continued to reject vanity and materialism, according to John 2:15: "Do not love the world or the things in the world; if anyone loves the world, love for the Father is not in him."

But tourists who visit Amish farms find that the Amish, though disciplined, are not stern and, in fact, often show gentle senses of humor. They'll explain how they wrest a living out of the often-rocky land around Harmony, cobbling together various jobs and putting everyone in the family to work. A 16-year-old girl may work as a schoolteacher in the one-room schoolhouses dotting the countryside; a teen boy will help on the farm and may also learn carpentry, making birdhouses to sell on the Village Green in Harmony, alongside a mother selling pickles and eggs.

Often, work is turned into a social event, such as a barn raising, also called a frolic. Young Amish are bused in from settlements around Oelwein, Iowa, and Cashton, Wisconsin, not only to build the new barn, but to socialize with each other and, perhaps, to marry outside their communities. Because of generations of intermarriages, genetic disorders are a serious problem, and visitors on tours may meet family members who have Down's syndrome.

In many ways, the Amish seem wonderfully exotic—the apple-cheeked youngsters in bonnets and straw hats, the jolly women selling jams and turnovers, the men who labor in the field, pausing to wave at an English passerby. But tour guides are careful to point out the liabilities of the Amish lifestyle. Because they do not accept health insurance—not to mention farm subsidies or Social Security—the Amish are vulnerable to catastrophic illness. Their many cottage industries are one way they put something aside for a rainy day.

Visitors may be embarrassed by the almost irresistible temptation to stare. The Amish, say guides, are used to that, and welcome tourists. After all, they've got lots to sell—sublime cashew crunch and berry jam; potholders and quilts, in bright colors or the blues and blacks they themselves use; and exquisite handcrafted furniture, for which there's usually a waiting list.

Visitors who spend an afternoon with the Amish will be deeply impressed by their resourcefulness, warmth, and dedication to family. Nevertheless, they probably won't want to give up their washer and dryer any time soon.

Trip Tips

Accommodations. The 1910 Selvig House has solicitous proprietors and four attractive rooms, three with private bath, $80. Carol and Ralph Beastrom, (888) 887-2922, www.selvighouse.com. The Country Lodge is a friendly little motel with 24 rooms, three with whirlpools, including buffet breakfast, $43–$85; (800) 870-1710.

In Preston, the JailHouse Inn B&B, (507) 765-2181, is an 1869 Italianate building that was the former county jail; one of the rooms retains a cell block. Twelve attractive rooms, four with fireplaces, three with whirlpools, $55–$159, (507) 765-2181, www.jailhouseinn.com. The Country Hearth Inn has 40 rooms and suites, some with whirlpool, and an indoor pool, $70–$135 in summer and fall, including breakfast buffet; (888) 378-2896, www.countryhearth.com.

Dining. The Harmony House downtown serves a traditional menu, (507) 886-4612.

Amish Tours. Michel's Amish Tours and Amish Country Tours give two- to three-hour tours Mondays-Saturdays all year. They're $25 per car with a ride-along guide and include stops at Amish farms as well as other attractions, such as Austin's angora goat farm and the 1865 stone Lenora church. Michel's, (800) 752-6474; Amish Country, (507) 886-2303.

Events. Fall Foliage Fest, fourth weekend in September.

Bicycling. The Harmony-Preston Valley State Trail descends from the Village Green 12 miles from Harmony to Preston, from which the 5.5-mile Isinours stretch goes on to connect to the Root River State Trail.

More Information. (800) 247-6466, www.harmony.mn.us, www.bluffcoun try.com.

36. Cave Country: Two Limestone Labyrinths

Beneath the placid farmland of southeastern Minnesota between Harmony and Preston, another world awaits visitors.

Underlying the cornstalks is karst country, an area of porous limestone cut through by underground streams and linked to the surface by sinkholes. A million years ago, rain, gases, and acid began to eat cavities in this limestone, once the silty muck on the bottom of an inland sea. The underground streams carved twisting labyrinths, picking up minerals that colored the walls—manganese for purple and black, iron oxide for shades of red, calcite for white.

Over eons, mineral-laden rivulets dripped into the cavities, creating drapery-like flowstone along the walls, glistening stalactites on the roofs, and nubby stalagmites from the floor. Chalk-white soda straws, baby stalactites, growing at the rate of an inch a century, line ceilings.

One of these caverns was discovered in 1924, when three pigs disappeared from a farm near Harmony. The farmer, looking for his missing pigs, found a sinkhole and sent some neighbor boys down by rope. Seventy-five feet later, they found the pigs—still alive—and a huge labyrinth of underground canyons.

Tours began at Niagara Cave in 1934; the pigs' landing spot is called the Reception Room. Today, the cave draws visitors from around the world to see its 60-foot waterfall and fantastical formations, including the Elephant Head, with a draped gray ear and wrinkled trunk; the three-layer Wedding Cake, with icing dripping over its top; the Mighty Mo, with the jutting prow of the battleship *Missouri*, and the Liberty Bell, complete with crack.

And of course, there are the formations of the imagination: Like clouds, flowstone often takes on the aspect of something, often spooky. Ribbon stalactites look just like skeletal fingers. Holes in rock, drilled by pebbles bouncing in long-ago streams, look like the sunken eye sockets of a skull. Yet many people find the look romantic. Niagara Cave also has a wedding chapel, with a "steeple" and "fireplace," and it's been used for hundreds of weddings.

Another cave was discovered on a frigid day in 1937, by a man walking along the South Branch of the Root River. Because the air inside the cave is 48 degrees Fahrenheit year-round, it had melted the snow on the ground around a sinkhole, and steam was rising from it. He found a whole system of caverns, and tours of Mystery Cave started 10 years later.

The Minnesota Department of Natural Resources bought the cave in 1988, and today it's part of Forestville State Park, west of Preston. Naturalists lead tours of parts of the 12 miles of passages, using the red pinpoint of a laser to point out interesting formations and fossils, such as the 15- to 20-foot-long cephalopods that were the forerunners of today's octopus and squid.

Four species of bats live in the cave, coming and going through a window cut above its vaultlike door, and naturalists discuss how female bats catch newborns in a pouch; how sleeping bats, if disturbed, need half an hour to raise their metabolism enough to fly; how bats can eat a third of their body weight in mosquitoes every night.

And without fanfare, groups come upon perfect Turquoise Lake, shimmering blue and serene 130 feet below the surface.

The two tours are conducted very differently, Niagara's in the grand tradition of kitsch and Mystery's with a scientific slant. But anyone who takes both will end up knowing quite a bit about the mysteries of caves.

Trip Tips

Niagara Cave. It's open daily from May through September, weekends in April and October and otherwise by appointment. Admission is $7.50, $7 for those 13–17 and $4.25 for those 4–12. To get there, drive 2.5 miles south of Harmony on Highway 139, then 2 miles west on County Highway 30; (800) 837-6606, www.niagaracave.com.

Mystery Cave. Hour-long tours of Mystery Cave are handicapped-accessible and are given weekends from mid-April to Memorial Day, daily until Labor Day, then weekends through October. On summer weekends, two-hour afternoon tours are given of another section of the caves, known as Minnesota Caverns, where visitors carry hand-held lanterns. Visitors caravan from Mystery Cave to the entrance. The entrance is 5 miles west of Forestville State Park, between Harmony and Preston. Call for directions. Cost for each tour is $7 for adults, $4 children 5–12, and a $4 state park sticker is also required. Call (507) 937-3251.

Forestville. Within Forestville State Park, across from a little steel bridge, is a pocket of 1899, transported intact into the twenty-first century. Founded in 1853, the historic village of Forestville once was a place where farmers came to trade produce for goods and services at Meighen's store. The village began to fade after it was bypassed by the railroad in 1868, and Thomas Meighen eventually bought all the buildings and surrounding land. But in 1902, rural delivery was started, and neighboring farmers no longer had to go to the store to pick up mail. Meighen closed the store in 1910.

At historic Forestville, interpreters play the part of people who once lived in the rural town.

But his daughter Margaret sold it to the state, complete with inventory. Now, the store, along with Meighen's brick home, a wagon barn, granary, and animal barn, is a living-history site operated by the Minnesota Historical Society. Costumed interpreters play real people, including Meighen's wife, Mary, and laborers Charles Ball and Charlie Martin.

It's open from Memorial Day through Labor Day, daily except Mondays. Special events include an 1899 Fourth of July celebration and typical "evenings of leisure" as held in 1899. It's free with a state park sticker; (507) 765-2785, www.mnhs.org.

Section VII

Twin Cities and Environs

37. Minneapolis: It Started with a Waterfall

The Falls of St. Anthony weren't very tall. But the waterfall was broad and thundering, and the only major drop on the Mississippi.

More importantly, it got good PR from two best-selling travel guides, Father Louis Hennepin's 1683 *Description de la Louisiane* and Jonathan Carver's 1778 *Travels through the Interior Parts of North-America*, both of which exaggerated its height. Other explorers came, and in the 1820s ordinary tourists followed the first steamboats up the Mississippi, where they admired the falls, gawked at the Dakota living in nearby tepees and dined on such Wild West delicacies as buffalo, elk, and sturgeon.

But even then, early entrepreneurs were laying plans to harness the power of the falls. By the 1870s, stone mills crowded the falls. In 1880, Minneapolis took the flour-milling crown away from St. Louis; its Washburn "A" mill alone could produce half a million pounds of flour a day. In 1883, railroad tycoon J. J. Hill built the gracefully curving Stone Arch Bridge, which brought wheat from the Red River Valley right to the doors of the flour mills.

The industry began to decline after World War I, when Minneapolis was supplanted as the nation's largest producer of flour by Buffalo, New York. By the 1960s, the riverbanks and Nicollet Island were shabby and neglected. Minneapolis was more enthralled by its new pedestrian-friendly Nicollet Mall, which stretched away from the river, and then by the new buildings along it: the blue-glass IDS tower, which became the city's tallest building in

Downtown and Nicollet Mall

Since it opened in 1967, this pedestrian thoroughfare has been the center of downtown Minneapolis.

It's no longer quite as happening as it was in the 1970s, when Mary Tyler Moore shot her famous hat-tossing scene on the corner of Nicollet and Seventh Street, and it's not as hip as the Warehouse District, three blocks to the west.

But it's still the place to be. Conventioneers roam up and down it year-round, seeking—and finding—good dining spots and sidewalk cafes. Marshall Field's—which appeared at Nicollet and Seventh as Dayton's in 1902—is a shopping anchor, and Saks Fifth Avenue, Neiman Marcus, and the other shops of Gaviidae Common draw upscale browsers.

At the south end of Nicollet Mall, the ugly but acoustically superb Orchestra Hall is the home of the Minnesota Orchestra and also hosts touring musicians. Two restored vaudeville houses on Hennepin Avenue, the 1920 State and the 1921 Orpheum, provide a jewel-box venue for traveling productions, and the concrete behemoth Target Center in the Warehouse District hosts the biggest rock acts and the Timberwolves' basketball games. All venues are within eight blocks of each other, and nights when each is holding an event can get pretty busy.

Summer always is beautiful in Minneapolis, with free outdoor concerts performed around downtown, but the holidays are an especially fine time to visit, when the jolly, illuminated Holidazzle Parade draws thousands of spectators to Nicollet Mall between Thanksgiving and Christmas. Marshall Field's puts on an annual animated extravaganza based on a children's story, and Peavey Plaza, outside Orchestra Hall, is turned into an ice rink. The Minnesota Orchestra performs Handel's *Messiah,* and the Guthrie Theater puts on *A Christmas Carol.*

The Guthrie, the pride of Minneapolis since it opened in 1963, is a 15-minute walk west of Orchestra Hall, through pretty Loring Park. Walker Art Center, built around the collection of lumber baron T. B. Walker, is housed in the same building. And at its feet spreads the delightful Minneapolis Sculpture Garden, whose whimsical *Spoonbridge and Cherry,* framed by the downtown skyline and the Basilica of St. Mary, has become the city's unofficial symbol.

Trip Tips

Accommodations. Among the many hotels, DoubleTree Guest Suites is especially well-located, a block from Orchestra Hall. Rooms start at $119; (612) 332-6800 or (800) 222-TREE, www.doubletreehotels.com. Holiday Inn Express is near the Convention Center and a little cheaper, $79–$139; (612) 341-3300, (800) 465-4329, www.hiexpress.com/msp-downtown.

Events. Holidazzle, from the day after Thanksgiving to the day after Christmas. Aquatennial, the 10 days around the third week of July, starts off with the Block

Party, with free concerts that draw tens of thousands, and parades through downtown; (612) 331-8371, www.aquatennial.org.

Dining. Across from Orchestra Hall, Brit's Pub is an atmospheric place to have some fish and chips, and seats at its sidewalk café are always in demand; (612) 332-3908. Aquavit is a Scandinavian temple of gastronomy and perhaps the hippest restaurant in the Twin Cities, (612) 343-3333, along with the posh Goodfellows, (612) 332-4800. Zelo is a hip but more casual restaurant, (612) 333-7000, and Oceanaire, in the Hyatt Regency, is known for fresh, but expensive, seafood, (612) 333-2277.

In the Warehouse district, around Target Center, Café Brenda is a venerable vegetarian venue, (612) 342-9230, and the New French Café is a longtime favorite, (612) 338-3790. D'Amico Cucina, in Butler Square, serves nouvelle Italian, (612) 338-2401, and Palomino serves elegant European bistro fare, (612) 339-3800.

At the edge of Loring Park, the Loring Bar and Café is a hip spot; its alley dining is especially popular in summer, (612) 332-1617. Across Hennepin Avenue at Walker Art Center, the rooftop Gallery 8 serves excellent, inexpensive lunches with a spectacular view, Tuesday–Sunday.

Nightlife. The Minnesota Orchestra performs in Orchestra Hall, and free concerts often are held outside, on Peavey Plaza, (800) 292-4141 or (612) 371-5656, www.mnorch.org. A mile to the west, through Loring Park, the Guthrie Theater is the most prestigious of the many theaters in the Twin Cities, which often is said to have more theaters per capita than any U.S. city outside New York, (612) 377-2224, www.guthrietheater.org.

In the Warehouse District, the Target Center is the venue for the biggest touring acts, (612) 673-0900, www.targetcenter.com. TC Tix in City Center, on Nicollet Mall between Sixth and Seventh streets, sells half-price tickets to theater performances, concerts, and sports events, (612) 288-2060, www.tctix.com. Patrons must buy tickets in person on the day of the event.

Art. Walker Art Center, which specializes in contemporary art, shares a building with the Guthrie, (612) 375-7600, www.walkerart.org. The Minneapolis Institute of Arts, a half mile down Third Avenue from the Minneapolis Convention Center, is a wonderful, world-renowned repository of all kinds of art; it's also free, (612) 870-6323, www.artsmia.org.

Professional Sports. The Timberwolves of the National Basketball Association play at the Target Center in the Warehouse District, www.timberwolves.com. The Vikings play their National Football Leagues games at the Metrodome, www.Vikings.com. For tickets for both teams, call Ticketmaster at (612) 371-2000, www.ticketmaster.com.

More Information. (888) 676-6757, www.minneapolis.org.

James J. Hill's Stone Arch Bridge is a pedestrian favorite.

1973, and Orchestra Hall, its orange and red interior studded by acoustic "ice cubes," opened in 1974 at the mall's far end.

But the riverbanks began to come back in the 1980s. Now even the mill ruins are coming back; the Washburn "A" mill is being restored into a heritage center by the Minnesota Historical Society, complete with an eight-story ride called the Flour Tower. Along the river, vintage illuminated signs celebrate the industrial era: Pillsbury's Best Flour, North Star Blankets, Milwaukee Road, Grain Belt Beer.

Nicollet Island, a peaceful oasis right between downtown and the dining-entertainment district on northeast Hennepin Avenue, is a great base for exploring this newly lively area. The limestone Nicollet Island Inn, built in 1893 as the Island Door and Sash Company, was handsomely refurbished and opened in 1982 with a glass-lined restaurant and bar. On the 48-acre island, guests can listen to free concerts, at an amphitheater in a wooded glade or in a cavernous pavilion, once an 1893 steam plant. On the other end of the island, a slum just a few decades ago, houses have been restored into colorful showplaces, from an 1886 purple Queen Anne with teal trim to a yellow 1867 Greek Revival and the 1875 limestone Grove Street Flats, now condos.

Downtown and the Warehouse District is a short walk across a fancy new suspension bridge where, in 1855, the first-ever bridge over the Mississippi was built. But it's more fun to walk across an 1887 trestle bridge to cobblestoned Main Street, shaded by cottonwoods planted by a pioneer entrepreneur.

The restored brick storefronts of St. Anthony Main led the river renaissance in the 1980s, and, though most of the shops have disappeared, its cinema and shops still are a magnet. Red RiverCity trolleys trundle by on their rounds, and fireworks and festivities are held on New Year's Eve and the Fourth of July.

The Stone Arch Bridge, once slated for demolition, now is one of the most beloved spots in the city. Open only to pedestrians, bicyclists, and trolleys, it provides an unparalleled view of the falls and both sides of the river, and plaques explain milling history. From here, bicyclists and skaters can race up the west side of the river all the way to the Plymouth Avenue bridge and across to Boom Island Park, from which the sidewheeler *Anson Northrup* takes excursionists upriver. From Boom Island, a tiny trestle bridge crosses the channel back to Nicollet Island.

The most up-and-coming neighborhood in Minneapolis is just across the channel. Beyond the 1857 Lady of Lourdes Church, whose steeple is a Minneapolis landmark, cafés, coffeehouses, and nightclubs line northeast Hennepin. Once a tired-looking neighborhood of Eastern European émigrés, many of whom had moved on by the 1980s, it's now the home of affluent empty-nesters, drawn from the suburbs to new riverside condos and townhouses, and of artists, drawn to cheap studios. But its heritage lives on at Kramarczuk's, where stout matrons dish up borscht and pierogies, and whose aromatic sausage counter has been supplying homesick émigrés since 1954. Baltic Imports, next door, is one of the Twin Cities' best sources of Ukrainian etched eggs. Nye's Polonaise Room, famous for its polka bands and piano chanteuse, is such a 1950s time capsule it's become popular with the Gen-X set.

The more sophisticated of them dine at Bobino, a hip wine bar with imaginative cuisine, and a somewhat older set at the slickly art-deco Sophia, where couples dance cheek to cheek to bluesy jazz standards sung by a sequined diva. The swanky Times Bar and Café also offers jazz, sometimes to big bands, and Ground Zero plays really loud techno.

From any sidewalk, the skyscrapers of downtown Minneapolis can be seen, pointing to the sterile fate this little neighborhood escaped. Today, this east-side stretch is called the Mississippi Mile. But it may as well be called the miracle mile.

Trip Tips

Accommodations. Nicollet Island Inn has 24 individually decorated rooms, all with views and some with whirlpool, $135–$170; ask about packages. (612) 331-1800, www.nicolletislandinn.com.

The Hyatt Whitney Hotel is a small, European-style hotel in a renovated 1879 flour mill on the west side of the river; it's often the choice of visiting celebrities. Rates for its rooms and suites begin at $169; (612) 339-9300, (800) 233-1234, www.hyatt.com.

The 1896 Queen Anne–style LeBlanc House, in the northeast Hennepin neighborhood, has two rooms, $85–$115; (612) 379-2570, www.leblanc house.com.

Dining. Reservations are wise at Bobino, (612) 623-3301; Sophia, (612) 379-1111; and the Nicollet Island Inn. If you're really hungry, Kramarczuk's is a good place for lunch. The wine and cheese shop at Surdyk's is a very good place to buy pâté, cheese, and baguettes for a picnic on Nicollet Island.

Mall of America

Twin Citians can boast all they want about their quality of life, their lakes, their squeaky-clean politics, their urban civility. But all most people in other states and countries really want to know about is . . . the megamall, and the fact that Minnesota has no tax on clothing.

Opened in 1992, the Mall of America was an instant hit, attracting eager shoppers from all over the world. It's the No. 1 attraction in Minnesota—those ten thousand lakes aren't even in the running—drawing 42.5 million people to its 4.2 million square feet of stores, restaurants, and amusement parks. In addition to more than 520 stores, it holds the seven-acre Knott's Camp Snoopy Theme Park, Jillian's Hi-Life bowling lanes, and Underwater Adventures, which includes a 1.2 million-gallon aquarium, a pirate-ship playground, and a virtual submarine ride.

There's even the 75-seat Chapel of Love, which averages three weddings a day. Many celebrities and politicians make appearances in the rotunda of the three-story mall, also the stage for many other spectacles and public events. In many ways, the mall is the Twin Cities' town square.

Trip Tips

Getting There. It's in the southern suburb of Bloomington, just southwest of the airport, at the southeast corner of Highway 77, or Cedar Avenue, and I-494/Highway 5. Northwest Airlines often offers low-priced weekend packages, (800) 225-2525, www.nwa.com.

Accommodations. The Bloomington Convention and Visitors Bureau has a

Concerts. In summer, free concerts along Main Street are held on weekends and nearly every evening on Nicollet Island; call (612) 661-4875 or the Mississippi Mile hot line, (612) 673-5123, www.mississippimile.org.

Events. Mississippi Mile Fireworks Extravaganza, New Year's Eve and July 4. Stone Arch Festival of the Arts, third weekend of June. Aquatennial, the 10 days around the third week of July, including water-ski shows and a fireworks show that is one of the largest in the nation; (612) 331-8371, www.aquatennial.org.

River Cruises. From Boom Island, one-and-a-half-hour cruises on the *Anson Northrup* and *Betsey Northrup* are given May–September, $12, $6 children 5–12. Check for dinner and brunch cruises; (651) 227-1100, www.padelfordboats.com.

discounts program at the many nearby hotels, (800) 346-4289, ext. 34, www.Bloomington-mn.org. or www.bloomingtonmn.org.

Knott's Camp Snoopy. An all-day wristband for admission to more than 25 rides is $22; birthday-party packages reduce prices significantly for groups; (952) 883-8600, www.campsnoopy.com.

Underwater Adventures. Summer admission is $14 adults, $11 ages 13–17, and $8 children 3–12; in winter, rates are $12, $10, and $7; (888) 348-3846, www.underwateradventures.cc.

Nearby attractions. The Minnesota Zoo, 12 miles south in Apple Valley, is one of the best in the nation and includes the Discovery Bay aquarium and an IMAX theater. Admission is $10, $5 for children 3–12; with an IMAX show, it's $16 and $10, and monorail rides are $3 for ages 3 and older; (952) 431-9200, www.mnzoo.com. Valleyfair amusement park is southwest of the Twin Cities in Shakopee; it has 75 rides, a water park, and an IMAX theater. It's open daily Memorial Day–Labor Day and weekends in May and September. All-day admission is $29, $9 for those 60 years and older and those 4 years and older and also less than 4 feet tall. Parking is $7; (952) 445-7600, www.valleyfair.com.

Mystic Lake Casino, southwest of the Twin Cities in Prior Lake, is the largest casino in Minnesota and its second-biggest attraction; (800) 813-7349, www.mysticlake.com. The horse-racing track Canterbury Park is nearby, (952) 445-7223, www.canterburypark.com.

More Information. (952) 883-8800, www.mallofamerica.com.

The Chain of Lakes

Every big city has skyscrapers. Every big city has museums and monuments. But no other city has the beautiful lakes and parks Minneapolis does.

Early in the city's history, when its lakes were swampy boondocks, city fathers decided to make their shores public property. Today, the most expensive homes in the city face the lakes, but the public—in-line skaters, bicyclists, dog walkers—owns the shorelines.

In the summer, everyone who isn't working flocks to the lakes to canoe, sail, skate, swim, and picnic. Concerts are held nearly every evening at the lovely Lake Harriet bandshell, and neighborhood festivals and theater performances are held in lakeside parks. During Aquatennial in July, the lakes become the setting for dozens of events, including sand-castle competitions, milk-carton boat races, and regattas.

Paved paths—one for walking, one for bicycling and skating—link the lakes in south Minneapolis, looping around Lake of the Isles, Calhoun, Harriet, and Nokomis and extending across the city and up along both sides of the Mississippi River. They're hugely popular with runners and walkers, who can be found on them year-round.

These paths now are part of the Grand Rounds National Scenic Byway, which extends into north Minneapolis for a total of 53 miles. To make a shorter loop, however, bicyclists can connect the lakes with the river by riding through downtown. The 19-mile stretch from the Metrodome, around the lakes and up the river to the Franklin Avenue bridge, also is the first part of the Twin Cities Marathon, called the most beautiful urban marathon in America.

Lake of the Isles can be found just beyond the Guthrie, bordering the west end of Franklin Avenue. The most baronial houses are found here, along with the most geese and other wildlife; there are no beaches, but two islands serve as wildlife refuges, and there's an ice rink in winter. Canoeists can put in on Lake of the Isles and navigate a shady little canal to Cedar Lake, which has an official beach on the west side and an unofficial beach on the east. It's three blocks from the big Victorian known as the Mary Tyler Moore house, on the southwest corner of Kenwood Parkway and West 21st Street.

Lake Street passes between Lake of the Isles and Lake Calhoun and heralds the Uptown neighborhood, just to the east. Skates and bikes can be rented here, and every kind of snack found—smoothies, ice cream, cappuccino. It's also a shopping and restaurant center, especially for young people, and is the liveliest neighborhood in the city both day and night.

Lake Calhoun has three beaches and the most open expanses; it's often used for windsurfing and sailing. It connects to Lake Harriet, the prettiest and most family-oriented lake; a vintage streetcar also connects the two lakes. On the northeast corner of Lake Harriet, the Rose Garden is a favorite spot, as well as the two beaches, the bandshell, and playground nearby.

For a pleasant detour, venture two blocks from the western side of Lake Harriet to the little shops and cafés of the Linden Hills neighborhood, at the corner of Upton Avenue and West 43rd Street. Then continue around Lake Harriet to Minnehaha Creek, which the path follows to Lake Nokomis. This lake has a big, broad beach, with an up-close view of planes going to and from Minneapolis–St. Paul International Airport. Lake Hiawatha, across the parkway, has a smaller beach.

It's not far to Minnehaha Park, whose thundering falls have been a tourist attraction since the city's birth. Footpaths wind through the gorge at the foot of the falls, following the creek to its meeting with the Mississippi. The path continues up the river, as it flows upstream to the Falls of St. Anthony. The campus of the University of Minnesota straddles the river north of the Franklin Bridge; the Weisman Art Museum, a fractured silver pile on the east side of the river, is worth a stop.

From there, it's not far to J. J. Hill's Stone Arch Bridge, where everything started.

Trip Tips
Grand Rounds Scenic Byway. For a map of this great area route, call (612) 661-4875, www.byways.org. Bicycling is best on weekdays, when it's less crowded, but on Sundays, when there's little traffic downtown, cyclists can make a loop by riding down from Lake of the Isles, through downtown, and onto the river paths.

Dining. In Uptown, Giorgio's on Lake is a pleasant Italian bistro, (612) 822-7071. Campiello is hipper and noisier, (612) 825-2222. Figlio has great people watching from sidewalk tables, (612) 822-1688. Chino Latino is the noisiest and most eye-popping of all, with a "south of the equator" menu. Lucia's, on 31st Street, is the spot for a more romantic dinner, (612) 825-1572.

In Linden Hills, Zumbro Café, at West 43rd Street and Sheridan, is a good spot for breakfast and lunch.

Sports Rentals. For bike and in-line skate rentals, there are three places between Lake Calhoun and Hennepin: Calhoun Cycle, (612) 827-8231; Cal Surf & Sport, (612) 822-6840; Studio A Skates, (612) 825-3077. Paths on lakes Calhoun and Harriet have the best surfaces for skating. Canoe rentals are available at the refectory on Lake Calhoun, (612) 370-4964.

(Continued)

(Continued)

Concerts. Free concerts are given nearly every summer evening at the Lake Harriet bandshell, usually at 7:30 P.M.

Train and Trolley Rides. The Como-Harriet Streetcar takes 15-minute runs from Lake Harriet, near the bandshell at Queen Avenue and West 42nd Street, to Lake Calhoun daily in summer, 6:30 P.M. to dusk, and 12:30 P.M. to dusk weekends and holidays from May–October. Fare is $1.50; (651) 228-0263, www.mtmuseum.org. The RiverCity Trolley Tours gives a Chain of Lakes Tour in summer; (612) 204-0000, www.Minneapolis.org.

Events. Aquatennial, the 10 days around the third week of July, (612) 331-8371, www.aquatennial.org. Uptown Art Fair, first weekend in August, (612) 823-4581, www.uptownartfair.com. Twin Cities Marathon, first Sunday in October, (952) 925-3500, www.twincitiesmarathon.org.

Nightlife. At Uptown and Hennepin, Famous Dave's BBQ and Blues features blues nightly, (612) 822-9900.

More Information. Minneapolis Parks and Recreation, (612) 661-4800, www.minneapolisparks.org.

Trolley Tours. RiverCity Trolley Tours run every half hour and begin at St. Anthony Main, Walker Art Center, and the Convention Center. The narrated tours last 65 minutes and are given daily from May–October; (612) 204-0000, www.Minneapolis.org.

St. Anthony Falls Visitors Center. Minnesota Historical Society staff talk about local history and give out brochures for self-guided tours, Wednesdays–Sundays from Memorial Day to Labor Day at the center, 125 Main St. S.E., (612) 627-5433, www.mnhs.org.

More Information. Be sure to get the handy Mississippi Mile guide, (612) 673-5123, www.mississippimile.org.

38. St. Paul: Founded by a Man Named Pig's Eye

It's ironic, considering its past, that St. Paul is such a wholesome destination.

Liquor brought the first white resident to Minnesota's capital. He was Pierre Parrant, a swinish, one-eyed former voyageur known as Pig's Eye. He set up his first tavern near Fort Snelling, but was rousted in 1837 by officers who were tired of the trouble it caused.

The hovel he built in a cave downriver was St. Paul's first building, and the area around the tavern he built later, in the future downtown, was known briefly as Pig's Eye. But missionaries were close on the heels of sin, and one of them, a French-speaking priest, was able to rename the little settlement St. Paul.

The town grew as a transportation center, at first faster than its flour-milling rival across the river, and was made the state capital. In the 1920s and 1930s, it became known as a haven for gangsters—John Dillinger, Alvin "Creepy" Karpis, Ma Barker, Baby Face Nelson—many of whom were tried at the castlelike Federal Courts Building downtown.

Today, St. Paul is known as the friendlier, less glamorous of the Twin Cities, perhaps because of its strong neighborhoods and quieter downtown. For tourists, especially those with children, it's a good base for explorations.

Many of St. Paul's prime attractions are within a few blocks of each other. The spanking-new building of the Science Museum of Minnesota, at the top of the bluff, overlooks the Padelford Packet Boat landing, from which paddlewheelers cruise up and down the Mississippi, and the picnic areas and playgrounds of Harriet Island. Two blocks away, on Rice Park, the turreted stone courts building where FBI agents once stood with machine guns now is the Landmark Center, home of the SteppingStone youth theater, the Minnesota Museum of American Art, and many other arts organizations. Free concerts are often held at noon on weekdays and Sunday afternoons, and the Landmark Center also hosts many city festivals.

Rice Park is an intimate, European-style square, ringed by impressive buildings: the elegant, contemporary Ordway Center for the Performing

The castlelike Landmark Center is the backdrop for the annual Winter Carnival ice-carving competition.

Arts; the 1916 Beaux Arts central library; and the stately 1910 hotel the Saint Paul. A bronze statue of F. Scott Fitzgerald stands there, coat over arm, as well as a pigtailed girl in a fountain. Ice sculptures fill the park during Winter Carnival, a huge city celebration started in 1886 in response to a New York City reporter's gibe that St. Paul was "the Siberia of North America."

On the other side of the Ordway, home of the St. Paul Chamber Orchestra and the host of touring Broadway shows, are three venues that bring thousands to downtown: the Roy Wilkins Auditorium, a mid-size concert hall; RiverCentre, a convention center that hosts many crafts and hobby shows; and the brand-new, glass-walled Xcel Energy Center, a state-of-the-art concert arena and home of the Minnesota Wild hockey team.

At the other end of downtown, Garrison Keillor and his cadre of down-home musicians and wry comedians hold forth on Saturday nights at the Fitzgerald Theater. The Great American History Center stages original plays a block to the west, and the new purple-and-red building of the Children's Museum occupies a block nearby.

There still are saloons in St. Paul, where, in 1882, Mark Twain observed that whiskey is "the earliest pioneer of civilization." But St. Paul, especially for families, has come a long way since then.

Trip Tips

Accommodations. The St. Paul Hotel is steps from the Ordway and River-Centre; rooms start at $145, (800) 292-9292, www.stpaulhotel.com. The Radisson Riverfront is three blocks away but faces the river and has a pool; rooms start at $129, but Weekend Getaway deals may lower it to $99, (800) 333-3333 or (651) 292-1900, www.Radisson.com. The Holiday Inn River-Centre is right across from Xcel arena, (800) 465-4329, www.holiday-inn.com.

Dining. Four fine restaurants are within a block of the Ordway and River-front Centre: Pazzaluna, a fun Italian spot, (651) 223-7000; Kincaid's, a steak and chop house with windows facing Rice Park, (651) 602-900; the St. Paul Grill, a clubby classic in the St. Paul Hotel, (651) 224-7455; and Sakura, a good place for sushi, (651) 224-0185. Ruam Mit Thai, at St. Peter and Seventh Street, has plain décor but fine Thai dishes, (651) 290-0067; and Mickey's Dining Car, on Seventh near the Children's Museum, serves a good breakfast and is on the National Register of Historic Places, to boot. On the other side of the Xcel Energy Center, on West Seventh Street, Vine Park Brewing Company serves quite good food with its brews, (651) 228-1358.

Nightlife. Ordway Center for the Performing Arts is the home of St. Paul Chamber Orchestra and hosts national touring musicals and musicians; (651) 224-4222, www.Ordway.org. Nearby, on West Seventh Place, Park Square Theatre puts on fine plays, (651) 291-7005, as does the Great American History Theater, (651) 292-4323.

The intimate Fitzgerald Theater hosts many concerts, and *A Prairie Home Companion* is broadcast here on many Saturdays at 4:45 P.M., $17–$27; (651) 290-1221, www.fitzgeraldtheater.org.

Just across the river, the Wabasha Caves, a former gangster hangout, hosts various events, including Thursday swing dances, (651) 292-1220, www.wabashastreetcaves.com. The Landmark Center hosts many events, www.landmarkcenter.org.

Events. Winter Carnival, last week of January and first week of February around St. Paul, (651) 223-4710, (800) 488-4023, www.winter-carnival.com. Festival of Nations, first weekend in May at RiverCentre, (651) 647-0191, www.festivalofnations.com. Taste of Minnesota on the grounds of the state capitol, week of Fourth of July. Minnesota State Fair, 12 days before Labor Day, at the fairgrounds off Snelling and Como avenues, (651) 642-2200, www.mnstatefair.org. Capital New Year's downtown, New Year's Eve, (952) 920-5875, www.capnewyear.org.

Summit and Grand Avenues: Remnants of a Gilded Age

Even tourists from the great European capitals are impressed by Summit Avenue. It's not just one mansion, but one after another, all the way from the Mississippi River to the imposing stone Cathedral of St. Paul, overlooking downtown and the state capitol.

This five-mile stretch is one of the most splendid, best-preserved Victorian streets in America. The oldest are at the east end, on the lip of the bluff overlooking downtown and the Mississippi River gorge. The richest man in Minnesota built his home here, a 36,000-square-foot Richardsonian Romanesque mansion of red sandstone, with 13 bathrooms and 22 fireplaces. Today, the James J. Hill House is owned by the Minnesota Historical Society, which holds tours year-round as well as parlor concerts, art exhibits, lectures, and such seasonal programs as Victorian ghost stories and holiday vignettes by costumed "servants."

In the summer, guides lead Summit Avenue walking tours from the Hill House, and the Summit Hill Association opens nearly two dozen public and private homes during its September tour. The five blocks between the Hill House and the 1912 University Club are lined with an astonishing cavalcade of houses, with turrets, towers, columns, and such embellishments as carved-stone medallions, nudes, and cherubs.

The University Club, at the brow of Ramsey Hill, was a haunt of F. Scott Fitzgerald, who attended its dances. During the summer of 1919, he lived in a townhouse at 599 Summit, where he wrote *This Side of Paradise*, his first published novel. Fitzgerald, however, was not fond of Summit, which he called "a museum of American architectural failures." The previous year, another writer, Sinclair Lewis, had lived down the street at 516 Summit. The novel Lewis was working on, about the recently deceased J. J. Hill, was never completed.

The houses west of Dale Street include Georgian Revivals, Queen Annes, and Italianesque manors that are only a little smaller than their neighbors to the north. At 1006 Summit, a Tudor built in 1911 now is the governor's residence. William Mitchell College of Law is across the street, and farther down, Summit splits into a boulevard, passing the campuses of Macalester College and the University of St. Thomas. A few blocks later, it meets the river.

Summit still is the city's most prestigious address; those who live there, it's assumed, have arrived.

But only one block to the south, Grand Avenue is a popular residence for those who have just arrived, period. Lined with classic old brownstone apartment houses as well as middle-class Victorians, Grand Avenue is the home of many students and young professionals as well as the premier shopping, eating, and strolling street of St. Paul. From Grand and Dale to the Macalester campus, around Snelling, the street is lined with interesting spots. Victoria Crossing, at Grand's junction with Victoria, is one of the shopping and dining hubs, with small complexes on all four corners. Around Lexington, another cluster of innovative shops draws a steady stream of visitors, and many of the houses in between also hold one-of-a-kind businesses.

This is shopping for people who hate malls—though that doesn't preclude crowds: In June, the street festival Grand Old Day draws 250,000 or more people.

Trip Tips

J. J. Hill House. Open Wednesday–Saturday year-round, $6, $4 for children 6–15. For special events and reservations, call (651) 297-2555, www.mnhs.org.

Summit Avenue Tours. Ninety-minute walking tours start at the Hill House and are given at 11 A.M. and 2 P.M. Saturdays, May–September, $6, $4 children 6–12. The Summit Hill Association Neighborhood Homes Tour is the third Sunday in September, (651) 222-1222.

Dining. On Grand Avenue, Dixie's is a sports-bar-style Southern restaurant; the Barbary Fig has a patio facing the avenue and serves fine Mediterranean food. At Victoria Crossing, Café Latte, a nouveau cafeteria with a wine and pizza bar, is famous for its desserts, and Ciatti's is popular among those who like American-style Italian food. Sidney's has a front patio and well-priced pasta and pizza, as does the even more inexpensive D'Amico and Son, a hip but very good place to take children. The venerable Lexington is a good place to take parents or grandparents, (651) 222-5878.

On Selby Avenue, in the Cathedral Hill neighborhood, W. A. Frost is one of the most romantic places in town, with a tree-shaded stone patio out back, (651) 224-5715. Zander Café is a popular bistro, (651) 222-5224, and the Vintage is a fun place to sample wines, (651) 222-7000.

Red Fish Blue, a fun "ocean diner," is very popular; call (651)699-6595 for reservations.

Events. Grand Old Day on Grand Avenue, first Sunday in June, (651) 699-0029, www.grandave.com.

Professional Hockey. The Minnesota Wild, one of the National Hockey League's newest teams, play at Xcel Energy Center; (651) 222-9453, www.wild.com.

Museums. Built into the bluff overlooking the river, the Science Museum is stuffed with exhibits and hands-on activities; $7, $5 children 4–12; $11 and $8 including IMAX shows; (651) 221-9444, www.smm.org. The Minnesota Children's Museum is a colorful new structure, with many special exhibits. It is geared to children ages 6 months to 10 years, $6, $4 ages 1–2; (651) 225-6000, www.mcm.org.

Minnesota History Center. This free center between the capitol and cathedral has lots of exhibits and activities geared to children, (651) 296-6126, www.mnhs.org.

River Cruises. From Harriet Island, hour-and-a-half cruises on the *Jonathan Padelford* and *Harriet Bishop* are given May–September, $12, $6 children 5–12. Check for dinner and brunch cruises; (651) 227-1100, www.padelford boats.com.

Gangster Tours. Two-hour motorcoach tours are given at noon Saturdays from the Wabasha Street Caves and include kidnapping sites, speakeasies, and the apartment building where John Dillinger and police traded machine-gun fire. A costumed gangster character acts as guide, $18; (651) 292-1220, www.wabashastreetcaves.com.

More Information. (800) 627-6101, www.stpaulcvb.org, www.ilovestpaul.com.

39. Excelsior: Historic Resort Town on the Lake

Until 1822, only the Dakota knew about Lake Minnetonka, the big lake west of the Twin Cities. Then a 14-year-old son of a colonel and a runaway drummer boy paddled a canoe up Minnehaha Creek from Fort Snelling, right into Gray's Bay. The tourists have been coming ever since.

Stagecoaches began to run from St. Anthony Falls in 1855 and were met by the first ferry boats. Trains reached the lake in 1867; one left St. Paul at 4:30 A.M., carrying sportsmen who wanted to hunt and fish "in the wilds of Minneapolis." In the late 1870s, vacationing flour millers and businessmen whose names remain today on Minneapolis buildings and parks—Pillsbury, Northrup, Bell, Loring, Peavey—began to build summer cottages on the lake. J. J. Hill built a grand hotel in 1882 and ran his railroad to its door. Wealthy Southerners flocked to the lake to escape the summer heat, settling into big resort hotels.

By the turn of the century, the rich had begun to vacation elsewhere. Day-trippers, however, had begun to come by the thousands on the St. Paul & Minneapolis Suburban Electric Railway, whose western terminus was Excelsior. The cars came right up to the lake, from which passengers could board fleets of steamboats that ferried them all around the lake. They could gamble in the casino, dance in the pavilion, or play in the Commons, where children chased greased pigs or rode water toboggans into the lake.

After 1925, they came to ride the roller coaster at the new Excelsior Amusement Park. In the 1940s and 1950s, thousands went there to see Miss Minnesota pageants, and in 1962, the Beach Boys drew huge crowds. In 1964, the Rolling Stones made their Minnesota debut in the park's Danceland ballroom, though they drew only 283 people. Then, in 1973, the amusement park and the streetcar line closed, and sprawling suburbia began to surround Excelsior.

The Victorian age, however, is not over on Lake Minnetonka. The bright-yellow 1906 streetcar steamboat *Minnehaha* still sails to Wayzata, after being rescued from the bottom of the lake and returned to service in 1996 by Minnesota Transportation Museum volunteers. Now, the volunteers chat with excursionists when they're not working the finicky boiler, pointing out such sites as the Big Island, where an amusement park operated from 1907 to 1911, and big houses built by famous people, among them railroad baron J. J. Hill.

Hill, who built the biggest house in St. Paul as well as the biggest hotel on Lake Minnetonka, had a love-hate relationship with Wayzata, which wanted the right-of-way to the lake. During a 15-year feud, he moved the rail depot outside village limits, saying, "Let them walk a mile for the next twenty years." The townspeople had their own saying: "Twixt hill and hell, there's just one letter; were Hill in Hell, we'd feel much better."

But in 1906, Hill built a better depot downtown, and every September, the town celebrates J. J. Hill Days. The *Minnehaha* docks in front of the depot, from which passengers can walk to the shops of Wayzata, Excelsior's one-time rival. Railroad tracks still separate the town from the water, but the shoppers along Lake Street have a beautiful view of the lake and passing sailboats.

Pleasant as Wayzata is, however, it still feels like a suburb. Only Excelsior, somehow, has retained the feel of a small town. On Water Street, there's a pet store, a bakery, a barbershop, a bookstore, and a cinema, in addition to gift and antiques shops, most inhabiting old brick storefronts. The restored 1896 Excelsior Streetcar runs up and down the street on weekends, giving passengers a small taste of the old days.

And Excelsior still is a tourist destination. Weekenders can stay in an 1858 rooming house, now a handsome B&B. The Old Log Theater, founded in 1940 and the nation's oldest continuously operating professional theater, puts on seven shows a week at its log complex near downtown. Known for screwball comedy, it's been overseen since 1941 by Don Stolz, who's still directing and has been joined by four sons. Alumni include Nick Nolte and Loni Anderson, whose photos adorn the lobby walls.

Mick Jagger also makes a cameo in town history. According to local lore, one of the Rolling Stones' most famous songs was conceived in Excelsior in 1964. Jagger was at the soda fountain of Bacon Drugstore, the story goes, and couldn't get a drink made the way he wanted; local character Jimmy Hutmaker, known as Mr. Jimmy, was next to him and said, "You know, you can't always get what you want."

In summer, visitors can easily spend a whole day riding the *Minnehaha* and hanging out on Excelsior Commons, which has a nice sand beach, tennis courts, baseball diamond, and bandshell. The 15.5-mile north corridor of the Southwest Regional LRT Trail goes right through town and connects to the trails of Carver Park Reserve, 6 miles to the west. Nearly everyone stops for ice cream at Licks, at the end of Water Street.

Excelsior may be surrounded by suburbia. But it hasn't lost its character.

Some Day Trips for Kids

Life at a Fur Post. Just west of Pine City, the modern world fades away. Over a fire, Ojibwe women stir hominy seasoned with bear grease. Children try to pull each other off stumps in the game of cat and mouse. A birchbark lodge is out-fitted with all the comforts of life—in 1804.

The palisaded North West Company Fur Post, where costumed voyageurs, clerks, and Ojibwe women tell children about their roles in the fur trade, is a treasure. It's free, too. Run by the Minnesota Historical Society, it's a re-cre-ation of a post that once stood on the site, next to the Snake River. Many spe-cial events are held, including maple sugaring, monthly Family Fun Days, and wild ricing. The biggest event of the year is Fall Gathering in mid-September, when voyageurs and other fur trade re-enactors gather to dance, sing, tell sto-ries, and demonstrate skills of the era. It's open May through Labor Day, Tuesday–Sunday; (320) 629-6356, www.mnhs.org. One hour north of the Twin Cities.

If the kids like that, and they will, don't miss the Big Island Rendezvous, the first weekend of October in Albert Lea, an hour and a half south of the Twin Cities. It's one of the best in the Midwest, with 1,000 re-enactors providing plenty of entertainment; (800) 345-8414, www.albertlea.org.

Trains from the Past. Every summer, Minnesota Transportation Museum vol-unteers show children what travel used to be like: noisy, smelly, but lots of fun. From the 1916 brick depot in Osceola, Wisconsin, just across the St. Croix River and south of Taylors Falls, volunteers run steam and diesel passenger trains to Dresser and across the river to Marine on St. Croix. The 10-mile Dresser trips take 50 minutes, $10 adults, $5 for children 5–15. The 20-mile trips to Marine on St. Croix take an hour and a half, $13 adults, $7 children 5–15. Caboose rides are available some days, $20–$15 and $10–$7. They're held weekends from Memorial Day to mid-October. Bring a jacket on cool days, because the trains are unheated; (651) 228-0263, www.mtmuseum.org. Osceola is one hour north of the Twin Cities.

Wowed by Powwows. Every Minnesota child, especially those who know Indians only from Disney's *Pocahontas* or *Davy Crockett*, needs to go to a pow-wow, or *wacipi*.

For the Dakota and Ojibwe of Minnesota, a powwow is a time to greet old friends, show off achievements, and replenish a sense of cultural identity. For the public—and the powwow's tradition of welcoming outsiders is an old one—it's a window into a culture rich with nature-based spirituality and sym-bolic meaning.

(Continued)

(Continued)

Don't miss the Grand Entry, after which the dancing begins: men's traditional, with older dancers wearing turkey-feather bustles and using a controlled step. Fancy dancing, with leaping and spinning, and grass dancing, where streamers fly. Women step to and fro in jingle dresses, their silver ornaments fashioned, traditionally, from the lids of snuff cans.

It's a swirl of activity that may be hard to digest at first. Some powwows have educational tents, where visitors can learn more about the culture. Three powwows are held within an hour of the Twin Cities: the Grand Celebration Powwow at Grand Casino Hinckley, last weekend of July, (800) 472-6321; Mdewakanton Powwow near Mystic Lake Casino in Shakopee, around the third weekend in August, (952) 445-8900; and Mdewakanton Mah-Kato Powwow in Mankato, usually the third weekend of September, (800) 657-4733.

Cave Exploring. In 1881, a boy chasing a squirrel near Spring Valley, Wisconsin, discovered Crystal Cave. When it disappeared into the ground, he poked around with a stick and found a hole. The next day, his parents lowered him and his brother into it, along what now is called "the slide."

The cave still is thrilling kids today, with its bats, fossils, and formations. Daily tours are $8 adults, $4.50 children 4–12; (715) 778-4414 or (800) 236-2283, www.cavern.com/crystalcave/. From the Twin Cities, take the Ellsworth exit from I-94 and follow the signs; one hour east of the Twin Cities.

For a scenic side trip, follow the Eau Galle River southeast of Spring Valley, along County Highway B and Highway 128 through Elmwood, then take Highway 72 east into Downsville, the halfway point on the 14.5-mile Red Cedar State Trail, a popular bike path. The Creamery restaurant has lovely perennial gardens and a back patio; for the lavish Sunday brunch, children are charged only 75 cents per year, up to age 12 (715) 664-8354, www.creameryrestaurant-inn.com.

Trip Tips

Getting There. From the Twin Cities, take Highway 7 to Oak Street, then turn right onto Water Street.

Accommodations. The James Clark House on Water Street has four attractive rooms, one with double whirlpool, $109–$159. The Garden Room, with painted ivy and a gas fireplace, is a particular favorite, $129. Skip and Betty Welke, (952) 474-0196, www.bbonline.com/mn/jamesclark.

Fancy dancers swirl by the crowd at the Mdewakanton Mah-kato Powwow in Mankato.

Dining. Yumi's Sushi Bar, downtown, is open for dinner. No reservations; (952) 474-1720. Maynard's, a sports-oriented restaurant and bar on Excelsior Bay, is a popular spot; (952) 470-1800.

Events. Art on the Lake, second Saturday in June. Fourth of July on Excelsior Commons (it's a lot of fun, but don't get caught in the traffic jam after the fireworks). Apple Days, first Saturday following Labor Day. Holiday Home Tour, second weekend in December.

Old Log Theatre. The season runs year-round and includes December and summer children's plays. Shows and dinners are Wednesdays–Sundays, $15–$24; (952) 474-5951, www.oldlog.com.

Nightlife. The cozy Excelsior Bean & Wine Café on Water Street often brings in musicians on weekends.

Boat Cruises. The *Minnehaha* sails on weekends from mid-May to mid-October. There are two 2 1/2-hour round-trip cruises to Wayzata each day, $10 adults and $6 children under 16, as well as 1 1/2-hour morning and afternoon cruises around the Big Island, $7 and $5; for times, call (952) 474-4801 or (800) 711-2591, www.mtmuseum.org.

Streetcar Rides. The Minnesota Transportation Museum gives rides up and down Water Street on the restored 1896 Excelsior Streetcar, weekends from Memorial Day to early October, $1.

Bicycling. The 15.5-mile north corridor of the crushed-limestone Southwest Regional LRT Trail runs through Excelsior. From the trailhead in Hopkins (just north of Mainstreet, off Eighth Avenue), it's 9.5 miles to Excelsior, and from there 5.5 miles to Victoria, passing Carver Park Reserve, which has 8.5 miles of paved trails. Area Wide Cycle on Water Street rents bikes, (952) 474-3229.

Skiing. Carver Park Reserve has 21 kilometers of cross-country ski trails, 6 of them groomed for skating. The warming house rents skis, $7.50 adults, $5 children, and Lowry Nature Center rents snowshoes, $4.50, and sleds, $2; (952) 472-4911. There's a $5 per-car entry fee.

More Information. (952) 474-6461.

40. Stillwater: Darling of Day-Trippers

After 150 years, this Minnesota river town's unrefined early days are history.

Once, legions of unkempt lumberjacks mobbed the streets of Stillwater, spending their wages at saloons and bordellos. Now, mobs of weekend tourists roam through town, sipping cappuccinos, sampling wine, and shopping for antiques and rare books.

Stillwater has come a long way since the days when King Pine ruled. Reminders of the era are everywhere, however, in mills that now house antiques malls and splendid houses in a dizzyingly ornate variety of styles. Many of the lumber barons' houses now are bed and breakfasts and still carry their names—Bean, Mulvey, Sauntry, Staples. But a walk along any Stillwater street will yield a bumper crop of painted ladies, complete with turrets, cupolas, gables, and wraparound porches.

On Main Street, old brick storefronts now showcase antiques shops and antiquarian booksellers. Hundreds of dealers operate out of Stillwater's antiques stores, but the town is just as well known for its many booksellers, who prevailed upon legendary Welsh bookseller Richard Booth in 1994 to make Stillwater the first "Book Town" in the United States. (Booth's own town of Hay-on-Wye in Wales became the world's first Book Town in 1977.)

With its high-level shopping and high-level lodgings—most of the rooms in the town's B&Bs are lavishly appointed, with such romantic features as fireplaces and double whirlpools—Stillwater over the years has become a popular destination for couples.

But people of all kinds enjoy a ride on the motorized red trolleys that chug up and down Stillwater's hills, with narrators explaining the colorful history of the town, and why Stillwater calls itself Minnesota's birthplace: not because it was the first town, but because it hosted the 1848 convention that made Minnesota a territory.

Older people make return visits to the venerable Lowell Inn, the scene of many honeymoons, anniversaries, and birthdays over the last 70 years. Stillwater still is a popular place to stage important occasions. In addition to the inns, the refurbished train Minnesota Zephyr, which takes passengers on romantic dinner excursions into the countryside, also serves as a place to celebrate.

Twenty-somethings patronize the bars, stroll along the riverfront on warm evenings, and churn up the St. Croix on paddle-wheeler party boats, which look much like excursion steamers of a century ago.

Even children like Stillwater. Up on Second Street, they can play at Pioneer Park, a tiny square with a vast view of the St. Croix River Valley. On Main Street, they can stop at sunny Darla's for a malt and a burger and go into the Lower River Visitor Center, where National Park Service rangers show nature movies and let them handle turtle shells and beaver tails. The rangers also give advice to canoeists planning trips on the 252 miles of the St. Croix National Scenic Riverway, which includes the Namekagon River.

And everybody will enjoy the air of festivity on Stillwater streets—one more thing that hasn't changed since lumberjack days.

Trip Tips

Accommodations. Be sure to reserve early for weekends all year, especially for summer, fall, and Valentine's Day. Stillwater is well-supplied with B&Bs in historic Victorians, all with luxuries that include double whirlpools and fireplaces: the 1878 Ann Bean Mansion, $109–$199, (651) 430-0355, www.annbeanmansion.com; the 1892 Aurora Staples Inn, $115–$180, (651) (351) 1187, www.aurorastaplesinn.com; the 1883 Elephant Walk, $129–$269, (888) 430-0359, www.elephantwalkbb.com; the 1878 James A. Mulvey Residence Inn, $99–$209, (800) 820-8008, www.jamesmulveyinn.com; the 1895 Lady Goodwood, $79–$189, (651) 439-3771, www.ladygoodwood.com; the 1859 Laurel Street Inn, $99–$199, (888) 351-0031, www.laurelstreetinn.com; the Rivertown Inn, $150–$250, (651) 430-2955, www.rivertowninn.com; and the William Sauntry Mansion, $119–$199, (800) 828-2653, www.saun trymansion.com.

Just off Main Street, the Lumber Baron's Inn faces the St. Croix River and has 41 rooms, all with double whirlpool and most with fireplace, $129–$199; (651) 439-6000, www.lumberbarons.com. There are many less-expensive lodgings up on Highway 36, including a Country Inn and Suites, (651) 430-2699, and Super 8, (651) 430-3990.

Dining. On a beautiful summer's day, the Dock Café on the river is irresistible, (651) 430-3770, as is the deck of the Freighthouse, (651) 439-5718. On Main Street, Savories Bistro serves elegant breakfasts and lunches, as well as dinners, (651) 430-0702, and Darla's is a good place to have lunch with kids.

Also on Main Street, La Belle Vie serves an imaginative (and expensive) French-Mediterranean menu, (651) 430-3545. Queen Victoria's at the Lum-

One-Stop Weekends: Good Spots for Romance and Relaxation

Sometimes, on a raw, bone-chilling winter weekend, or a relentlessly rainy day in spring, it's nice to go to a cozy inn and burrow in for a few days.

Guests at these inns—all with fine restaurants under the same roof and, sometimes, shops or a theater—don't have to venture out once they check in. That's especially nice if the weather's bad—or if romance is the object.

Most of these inns can be rather expensive, but going to them midweek and in the off-season brings down costs substantially. Always ask for specials or packages, and reserve early for weekends year-round.

Archer House, Northfield. This 1877 landmark on Northfield's Division Street has 36 individually decorated rooms, $40–$140, and includes a half-dozen shops, a coffeehouse, and two inexpensive restaurants under its roof. This is a great budget destination—a weekend, including a free concert up at St. Olaf, need cost no more than $100 per couple; (800) 247-2235, www.archerhouse.com.

Fitgers Inn, Duluth. This hotel is the anchor of the renovated 1881 Fitger's Brewery Complex on Lake Superior and has 60 rooms and suites, many with double whirlpools, lake views, and exposed brick walls, $80–$250, (888) 348-4377, www.fitgers.com. The sprawling complex includes the tony restaurant Bennett's on the Lake, which puts on dinner theater four times a year, (218) 722-2829, www.bennettsonthelake.com, as well as the Tap Room and Brewhouse Brewery and Grille, which have live music. There's also a day spa and many excellent shops.

Lumber Baron's Hotel, Stillwater. This renovated downtown hotel faces the St. Croix River and has 36 rooms, all with double whirlpool and most with fireplace, $129–$199. Queen Victoria's Restaurant is downstairs, and shops line the streets; (651) 439-6000, www.lumberbarons.com.

Nicollet Island Inn, Minneapolis. This 1893 limestone inn has a wonderful location and 24 rooms, all with views and some with whirlpool, $135–$170; for a treat, ask for a corner room. There's a fine restaurant downstairs, and the nightlife and dining of the historic St. Anthony Main and northeast Hennepin areas are a short walk across a trestle bridge; (612) 331-1800, www.nicolletis landinn.com.

Outing Lodge at Pine Point, Stillwater Township. This 1923 brick building in the country, along the Gateway Trail, has 14 rooms, one with fireplace and

(Continued)

ber Baron's Hotel is a romantic spot, (651) 439-6000. At the Lowell Inn on North Second Street, a new chef has revived the reputation of this sentimental favorite. It's known for the four-course fondue dinner in the Matterhorn Room, $60 with wine, and serves classic continental cuisine in the elegantly old-fashioned George Washington Room and the Garden Room, which has a trout pond; (651) 439-1100, www.lowellinn.com.

Events. Rivertown Art Festival, third weekend in May. Taste of Stillwater, third weekend in June. Wednesday evening concerts in Lowell Park, June–July. Lumberjack Days, last weekend of July. Rivertown Restoration Home Tour, third Saturday in September. Fall Colors Fine Art and Jazz Festival, first weekend of October. Christmas at the Courthouse, weekend before Thanksgiving.

Antiques. Main Street is lined with shops. The Mill Antiques, at the north end in the old Staples lumber mill, includes 75 dealers on three levels, and

---

(Continued)
some with whirlpool, $110–$240 in the main lodge and $110–$140 in the Gardener's Cottage; dinner guests get a reduced rate, $90–$150 in the lodge and $90 in the cottage. It's best known for its lavish "culinary outings," which include a seven-course blowout Babette's Feast, Russian New Year's, and Mardi Gras; (651) 439-9747, www.outinglodge.com.

St. James Hotel, Red Wing. This 1875 hotel has 61 rooms, $89–$215. There are two restaurants and two pubs, including the elegant, fifth-floor Jimmy's, and an inside court lined with small shops; (800) 252-1875, www.st-james-hotel.com.

Schumachers' Historic European Hotel, New Prague. This renovated 1898 hotel on Main Street in this Czech town, an hour south of the Twin Cities, has 16 rooms, many with fireplace and double whirlpool, $98–$250, as well as an atmospheric little bar and a fine (though expensive) restaurant. Packages that include dinner and breakfast for two are $245–$345, available Sunday–Friday; (800) 283-2049, www.schumachershotel.com.

Thayer's Historic B&B, Annandale. This renovated 1895 inn, an hour west of the Twin Cities, has 11 rooms, $125–$245, including four-course champagne breakfast, and hosts regular murder-mystery dinners as well as swing, jazz, and

Mulberry Point Antiques has 65 dealers on four levels. Mid-Town Antiques, downtown, includes 80 dealers, and More Antiques has another 65 next door. Stillwater Antiques has 60 dealers, and there are also many individual shops.

Spa Services. Just for Me on Greeley Street offers massages, facials, and other services, (651) 439-4662, www.justformespa.com.

Train and Trolley Tours. The Minnesota Zephyr goes more than seven miles into the countryside on three-and-a-half-hour excursions, including a five-course dinner, $65; (651) 430-3000, (800) 992-6100, www.minneso tazephyr.com.

Stillwater Trolley Company offers 45-minute narrated tours daily from May through October and weekends in April and November, $10 adults, $6 children 16 and under. Tours leave from behind the Freighthouse Restaurant; (651) 430-0352.

---

blues shows. There's a sauna and a large outdoor hot tub. Proprietor Sharon Gammell also gives psychic readings; (800) 944-6595, www.thayers.net.

There are also three good inns in western Wisconsin.

Canoe Bay, Chetek. This ultra-luxurious resort on a private lake has 19 rooms in nine buildings, many designed in Frank Lloyd Wright's Prairie style. Rates are $195–$470, including breakfast brought to the door. A cottage is also available at $600–$750, with a two-night minimum on weekends. Five-course dinners are $55 per person; (800) 568-1995, www.canoebay.com. Two hours from the Twin Cities.

The Creamery, Downsville. This renovated rural creamery south of Menomonie has 12 rooms, 10 with double whirlpools, $115–$160, including breakfast and an appetizer; it also houses a fine restaurant. The scenic 14.5-mile Red Cedar Trail, used for bicycling in summer and skiing in winter, is nearby; (715) 664-8354, www.creameryrestaurant-inn.com. An hour-and-a half trip from the Twin Cities.

Fanny Hill Inn and Dinner Theatre, Eau Claire. This Victorian-style country inn overlooking the Chippewa River has 11 rooms, nine with whirlpools and fireplaces, two with especially panoramic views, $94–$194, including breakfast. A fine restaurant and a theater are under the same roof; (800) 292-8026, www.fannyhill.com. One and a half hours from Minneapolis/St. Paul.

The river, shops, and historic neighborhoods draw day-trippers to Stillwater.

Walking Tours. Valley Tours at the Historic Courthouse, (651) 439-6110.

Boat Tours. The *Andiamo* paddleboat gives public excursions, (651) 430-1236, www.andiamo-ent.com.

Wine Tour. Northern Vineyards on Main Street gives tours on Saturdays and daily tastings, (651) 430-1032.

More Information. (651) 439-4001, www.ilovestillwater.com, www.stillwater guide.com.

41. Taylors Falls: Pothole Capital of the World

There's only one place in the Midwest where potholes are a tourist attraction instead of a nuisance.

Standing at the bottom of the 35-foot-deep Bake Oven, touching walls as smooth as vinyl, it's easy to imagine the scene ten thousand years ago, when sheets of water from a melting glacier roared past Taylors Falls, into what now is the St. Croix River Valley. They came with such fury that whirlpools laced with sand and gravel drilled cylindrical holes into solid rock—potholes, the world's deepest.

On the Minnesota side of the river, that fury must have been of apocalyptic proportions. Behind Angle Rock, where the river takes a hard right, there's an otherworldly place of giant slabs and cavities. Here, so many potholes formed that they merged into what is now called the Devil's Parlor. The Bake Oven, where one pothole bored into another, is nearby, along with the Lily Pond, the Hourglass, and the 67-foot Bottomless Pit.

Along the river, the waters tore away everything but the hardest volcanic rock. Its vagaries nudged relentlessly at softer rock, leaving formations that have long fascinated tourists, especially the craggy Old Man of the Dalles.

Named Dalles of the St. Croix—*dalle* is French for rocky slab—this gorge is a first cousin of the Wisconsin Dells, where meltwater sculpted riverside formations out of softer sandstone. The St. Croix Dalles occupy a shorter stretch of river, but the captains of the paddlewheelers who have been showing it to tourists since 1904 have plenty to point out: the Devil's Chair, the Lion's Head, the Elephant's Head, the Turk, and the Holy Cross, for which French fur traders named the river. From a different angle, the Holy Cross turns into a face that the loggers called the Old Egyptian.

Minnesota's Interstate State Park preserves the western shore, and Wisconsin's Interstate State Park preserves it on the east; together, they're called "Gift of the Glaciers." Everyone comes here: Hikers, to walk along the high bluffs. Rock climbers, to rappel down the hairline of the Old Man. Children, to gambol like mountain goats among the fantastic formations. Canoeists, to

Paddlewheelers give passengers a good view of the famous Dalles of the St. Croix

paddle down river. And sightseers, to look at fall colors and browse in the shops of Taylors Falls' tiny downtown.

There's always been plenty of traffic around Taylors Falls. In the 1840s, lumbermen from Maine streamed into the St. Croix Valley to launch the nation's next timber boom. It arrived with a vengeance. In 1886, three miles of logs, enough to build 20,000 three-bedroom houses, created the world's largest logjam around Angle Rock; it took 200 loggers six weeks to clear.

Settlers followed in the 1850s, among them groups of Swedes who walked from Taylors Falls' steamboat landing into Chisago County, giving it the largest concentration of Swedes outside Sweden. Swedes still are coming to Taylors Falls, now as tourists: The area was featured in *The Emigrants* and three other historical novels written by Swedish author Vilhelm Moberg, who spent the summer of 1948 in Chisago City while researching pioneer letters and diaries.

It was the Yankees, however, who first got a foothold in Taylors Falls. W. H. C. Folsom came to Prairie du Chien in 1836 at age 19, having spent $200 to buy independence from his father in Maine. He worked his way up to Taylors Falls, prospered in the lumber and mercantile businesses, and, in 1855, built a Greek Revival house on the hill overlooking the town and valley. It and its furnishings stayed in the family until it was bought, restored, and opened for tours by the Minnesota Historical Society.

The Folsom House is the largest of a collection of Federal and Greek Revival homes, all white with green shutters, that sit in a parklike setting that

St. Croix Valley

In the last half of the nineteenth century, the St. Croix River hummed with frontier entrepreneurs seeking fortunes and steamboats full of immigrants, seeking a new life.

Today, the shores of the St. Croix Valley still buzz with activity, especially on lovely summer and fall weekends, when day-trippers turn out to take Sunday drives, visit antiques shops, and explore the valley's many attractions.

Taylors Falls, with its craggy dalles and paddleboat excursions, has been a tourist destination for a century. Across the river, St. Croix Falls is the starting point for two trails: the 1,000-mile Ice Age Trail, whose first 7 miles start at the Ice Age Interpretive Center in Wisconsin's Interstate Park and wind through town to Lions Park, along the river; and the 48-mile Gandy Dancer State Trail, a crushed-limestone bike path that goes through nine villages on its way to Danbury. On Washington Street, a 1917 vaudeville house is the home of the St. Croix Festival Theatre, which specializes in "lost" Broadway hits from the first part of the twentieth century.

Five miles south, skiers glide down wooded slopes at Trollhaugen. In Osceola, Main Street is a good place to browse for antiques and have a coffee, and a trail leads down through a shadowy glen to Cascade Falls, around which the town was built in 1844. In summer, vintage trains leave Osceola's 1916 depot for excursions to Dresser and to Marine on St. Croix, across the river.

At Marine, Minnesota's first sawmill was built in 1839; its remnants can still be seen in a wooded ravine behind the white clapboard Village Hall. The picturesque village is a favorite ice cream and coffee stop for bicyclists, hikers, and skiers going to and from William O'Brien State Park, just up Highway 95. The metro area's best swimming beach, on clear Square Lake, is just to the west, up County Highway 7 and south on Paul Avenue. The eastern trailhead of the Gateway State Trail is nearby, in Pine Point Park, though paved trail extends to Square Lake Trail.

The stretch of Highway 95 from Marine to Stillwater is one of the prettiest, especially in fall, and turns into Stillwater's Main Street, which is often clogged on weekends. Across the 1931 Lift Bridge and south on Wisconsin 35, Hudson is a quieter village, also with a beautiful riverfront park, antiques shops, and ornate Victorians, including the 1855 Octagon House, now a museum.

Back on the Minnesota side of the river, Highway 95 continues south, through Bayport and Lakeland to the village of Afton. This was the site of Minnesota's first flour mill, but, like Marine, it's now a refuge for city folks and a destination for day-trippers, who stop for ice cream at Selma's and to look at the perennials and gifts at Squire House Gardens. Afton State Park is down the

(Continued)

immigrant workers sarcastically dubbed "Angel Hill." Visitors can still see the dent in the plank floor from Mary Jane Folsom's heel where she worked the pedal of the piano Bill shipped in from St. Louis. They see a favorite cabinet, finished with buttermilk and blueberry juice, and one of Mary Jane's hoop skirts, worn by a mannequin. It's a vestige of a steamboat era that hardly seems gone in Taylors Falls.

Trip Tips

Accommodations. Old Jail B&B, in an 1869 saloon and an 1884 jail on a hill at the edge of downtown, is best located and has three apartment-style suites, the Overlook, Original Jail Cottage, and Cave Suite, $99–$130. Prudence Johnson and Gary Rue, (651) 465-3112, www.oldjail.com.

The Cottage B&B is an English country-manor house above town, with one suite with private entrance, $95–$115. Larry and Eleanore Collins, (651) 465-3595, (651) 257-3669, www.The-Cottage.com.

(Continued)

road, with hiking and ski trails along more than two miles of riverfront. The bluff above is lined with the steep ski runs of Afton Alps, which transforms into a golf course in the summer.

The rolling countryside south of Afton is lined with orchards. St. Croix Trail leads to Carpenter Nature Center and the river town of Hastings, which has a collection of interesting buildings that includes the 1865 Gothic Revival Le Duc-Simmons Mansion. Here, the St. Croix flows into the Mississippi.

Trip Tips

Accommodations. In Marine on St. Croix, the 1856 Asa Parker House, three rooms and a suite, $99–$179; (888) 857-9969, www.asaparkerbb.com.

In Afton, the contemporary Mulberry Pond on River Road B&B has two rooms with double whirlpool and gas fireplace, $99; (651) 436-8086. In Hastings, the Thorwood Historic Inns have 14 handsome rooms, many with double whirlpools and/or wood-burning fireplaces, and breakfasts are brought to your door or served in the formal dining room, $97–$257; the Mississippi Suite is a particular treat; (888) 846-7966, www.thorwoodinn.com.

Hudson, Wisconsin, just across the river, has several fine B&Bs; call (800) 657-6775 or check www.wbba.org. For details on other inns, call (651) 998-0185, www.innsofthevalley.com.

Dining. Downtown Hudson has some interesting places to eat, including Café Roma, the Winzer Stube, the San Pedro Café, and Barker's Bar & Grill. For a

There are two motels: the Springs Inn, overlooking downtown, (800) 851-4243; and Pines Motel, just down Bench Street, (651) 465-3422.

Wild River State Park, 10 miles north, rents a two-bedroom guest house with wood-burning fireplace, VCR, and fully equipped kitchen, $75. Guests must bring bedding and towels. Soap, some condiments, and firewood are provided. Guests are expected to clean the house before leaving. The park also has two heated camper cabins, $30, with bunks and table but no running water. Reserve up to a year in advance by calling the Connection, (800) 246-2267.

Paddlewheeler Cruises. In summer and on weekends from May to mid-October, 7-mile narrated trips leave daily at 11:30 A.M., 1:30 P.M., and 3:30 P.M., $10 adults, $5.50 children 3–12, and 3-mile trips at 5:30 P.M., $7 and $4.50. The 1:30 P.M. trip is given throughout the season; (651) 257-3550, (800) 447-4958, www.wildmountain.com.

special occasion, try the Bayport Cookery in Bayport, which serves multi-course, fixed-price menus of seasonal delicacies, (651) 430-1066. In an 1867 hotel building, the Afton House Inn is a good place for dine on such dishes as steak Diane and bananas Foster, (651) 436-8883.

State Parks. William O'Brien, (651) 433-0500; Afton, (651) 436-5391.

Swimming. Parking at Square Lake Park is $4, (651) 430-8368. The long, shady park also is a good place for a picnic. There's also a nice beach in William O'Brien State Park, on Lake Alice.

Skiing. Trollhaugen has 22 runs and 3 lifts, (800) 826-7166, www.trollhaugen.com. Afton Alps has 40 runs and 18 lifts, (800) 328-1328, www.aftonalps.com.

Train Rides. The 10-mile trips from Osceola to Dresser take 50 minutes, $10 adults, $5 for children 5–15. The 20-mile trips to Marine on St. Croix take an hour and a half, $13 adults, $7 children 5–15. They're held weekends from Memorial Day to mid-October; (651) 228-0263, www.mtmuseum.org.

Nightlife. The St. Croix Festival Theatre's season extends from mid-summer to the holidays, (715) 294-2991. In Hudson, plays and concerts are held at the Phipps Center for the Arts, (715) 386-8409.

More Information. Hudson, (800) 657-6775, www.hudsonwi.org.

Folsom House. Guided tours are given from May to mid-October, $3 adults, $1 schoolchildren; (651) 465-3125.

Minnesota Interstate Park. Part of its Pothole Trail is disabled-accessible. Daily parking is $4, free with state parks sticker; (651) 465-5711, www.dnr. state.mn.us/parks.

Wisconsin Interstate Park. This park's trails have the best view of the river valley, and the Ice Age Interpretive Center is worth a visit. Entrance is free weekdays to those who have a Minnesota state parks sticker; on weekends, $5 for Wisconsin residents, $7 for non-residents; (715) 483-3747.

Franconia Sculpture Park. It's fun to wander around this collection of outdoor sculptures, on U.S. 8 just outside Taylors Falls.

Wild River State Park. The park is a favorite of cross-country skiers, with 35 miles of groomed trails. A candlelight ski and snowshoe hikes are held annually; (651) 583-2925. Cross-country skis can be rented at the Trail Center, which has a fireplace and snack bar, (800) 996-4448.

Wild Mountain Ski Area. It has 23 runs and quad lifts and usually is the first alpine area in Minnesota to open for the winter. Lift tickets are $22–$29.50 adults, $17–$20 children 6-12; (651) 257-3550, (800) 447-4958, www.wildmountain.com.

More Information. (800) 447-4958.

Index

MORE GREAT TITLES FROM TRAILS BOOKS

Activity Guides

Paddling Southern Wisconsin: 82 Great Trips by Canoe and Kayak, *Mike Svob*

Paddling Northern Wisconsin: 82 Great Trips by Canoe and Kayak, *Mike Svob*

Paddling Illinois: 64 Great Trips by Canoe and Kayak, *Mike Svob*

Wisconsin Golf Getaways: A Guide to More Than 200 Great Courses and Fun
Things to Do, *Jeff Mayers and Jerry Poling*

Wisconsin Underground: A Guide to Caves, Mines, and Tunnels in and around
the Badger State, *Doris Green*

Great Wisconsin Walks: 45 Strolls, Rambles, Hikes, and Treks, *Wm. Chad McGrath*

Great Minnesota Walks: 49 Strolls, Rambles, Hikes, and Treks, *Wm. Chad McGrath*

Best Wisconsin Bike Trips, *Phil Van Valkenberg*

Travel Guides

Tastes of Minnesota: A Food Lover's Tour, *Donna Tabbert Long*

Great Indiana Weekend Adventures, *Sally McKinney*

Historical Wisconsin Getaways: Touring the Badger State's Past, *Sharyn Alden*

The Great Wisconsin Touring Book: 30 Spectacular Auto Tours, *Gary Knowles*

Wisconsin Family Weekends: 20 Fun Trips for You and the Kids,
Susan Lampert Smith

County Parks of Wisconsin, Revised Edition, *Jeannette and Chet Bell*

Up North Wisconsin: A Region for All Seasons, *Sharyn Alden*

The Spirit of Door County: A Photographic Essay, *Darryl R. Beers*

Great Wisconsin Taverns: 101 Distinctive Badger Bars, *Dennis Boyer*

Great Wisconsin Restaurants, *Dennis Getto*

Great Weekend Adventures, the *Editors of Wisconsin Trails*

The Wisconsin Traveler's Companion: A Guide to Country Sights,
Jerry Apps and Julie Sutter-Blair

Home and Garden

Creating a Perennial Garden in the Midwest, *Joan Severa*

Bountiful Wisconsin: 110 Favorite Recipes, *Terese Allen*

Foods That Made Wisconsin Famous, *Richard J. Baumann*